FIRST WITH THE NEWS

MICHAEL EVANS

First published 2016
by Rowanvale Books Ltd
Imperial House
Trade Street Lane
Cardiff
CF10 5DT
www.rowanvalebooks.com

A CIP catalogue record for this book is available from the British Library.
ISBN: 978-1-911240-98-3

I dedicate this book to all my fellow reporters and photographers who have risked their lives covering wars; and to my family for putting up with my frequent disappearances to dangerous places.

REVIEW COMMENTS FOR *FIRST WITH THE NEWS*

"A genuine tour de force, I cannot recommend this highly readable book strongly enough. An exciting autobiography and insightful modern history in one volume, it's beautifully and modestly recounted as is Mike Evans' hallmark."

Lord Richards of Herstmonceux, Chief of the Defence Staff, 2010-2013

"Michael Evans's closet secret is out. To paraphrase from Dr Johnson, I believe he thinks a little meanly of himself for never having been a soldier. He would have made a good and brave one too – despite the self-deprecating way he so often analyses his feelings in this excellent book. It chronicles his particular angle on most of the major British military and political events of our time. Written simply with insightful candour and utter decency this is a story of our time as much as the author's personal recollections. In short, this is a great read."

Colonel Bob Stewart, Tory MP and commanding officer of 1st Battalion Cheshire Regiment in Bosnia

"In two decades of war reporting I only ever encountered one true gentleman of Fleet Street: Michael Evans. This is the tale of his life and times, and it is as fine a read as you could hope for, complete with a fabulous cast of spooks, war lords, gangsters and whores. Most memorable of all though, is Evans' own modesty and tireless professionalism, qualities which run through this dark and exciting world as a

golden thread, drawing the reader effortlessly onward in the footsteps of the author's graceful integrity."

Anthony Loyd, war correspondent for *The Times*

"In a profession tarnished by hackers and liars, Mike Evans is one of the good guys who does in his book what he did all his career – tells it as he sees it. Straight."

Alastair Campbell, Tony Blair's chief press secretary, then director of communications and strategy, 1997-2003

CONTENTS

PREFACE

There is no greater vanity than to believe that other people, apart from family, will want to read about your life. But I have been privileged to work for two great newspapers: the *Daily Express,* in its prime, and *The Times*. I have travelled all over the world, covered six wars and met a vast array of fascinating, sometimes famous, individuals. Above all, I have spent long periods with men and women serving in the armed forces, often in dangerous situations. Such experiences have transformed my life. I have also been lucky to befriend many wonderful fellow journalists, and I am forever grateful for their generosity, courage and companionship.

ACKNOWLEDGMENTS

I would like to thank Jeremy Lewis, author, friend and next-door neighbour, for his invaluable advice on editing my original over-long text and for suggesting the title.

INTRODUCTION
BAPTISM OF FIRE

The young Croatian mother stood at the side of the road with a baby in her arms. The man with her looked in my direction and seemed to mutter something to her. She nodded her head. In the distance, not that far away, was the sound of machine gun fire; sporadic bursts of anger that served as a permanent reminder that this was a warzone. Bosnia-Herzegovina in the 1990s was a small, mountainous and beautiful country, inflamed by centuries-old hatred and bitter memories of past atrocities.

I was with a group of other journalists from national newspapers, and that morning several of us were to make the dangerous journey out of Bosnia-Herzegovina through the mountains and into the safe embrace of Split, in neighbouring Croatia. All of us were feeling tense and ready to swap the unpredictable and life-threatening existence in Bosnia, gripped by ethnic war, for the relative comforts of the Croatian resort. It always seemed strange that a few hours' drive away from this hell hole one could lead a normal life, eat in decent restaurants and walk the streets without the fear of a sniper targeting you or armed, wild-eyed brigands ambushing you. In Croatia, you could roam freely without worrying that there may be mines scattered across the road.

This was my second assignment in Bosnia as defence correspondent of *The Times*. The brutal ethnic-cleansing conflict that erupted there in 1992, stirring up a complex web of murderous rivalry and revenge between Muslims, Croats and Serbs, had been my baptism as a war reporter. I had covered the war in the Falklands in 1982 for the *Daily Express* but I anchored the coverage from the safety of London. The war in Bosnia, one of the countries that emerged as an independent nation after the death of President Tito and the splitting up of Yugoslavia, was my first experience of battlefield reporting. I had been sent to cover the deployment of British troops into the country. Their role was not to end the war or even to intervene in the daily massacres but to provide armed escort for humanitarian aid. The soldiers had the right to defend themselves but not to launch any kind of aggressive action.

For the politicians, it may have looked like an inspired gesture of good will for the thousands of civilians whose lives were at risk because of ethnic divisions going back 300 years. The different ethnic communities had learned to be neighbours and friends and had even intermarried when Yugoslavia held them all together under the autocratic eye and fist of President Tito. But once the nation had broken up into separate independent countries, the three factions had rediscovered their historic hatred for each other and had taken up arms against the people they had lived with amicably for so long.

The British troops, arriving in late 1992 under

a United Nations mandate in the midst of the first European war since the Second World War, were unprepared for what lay ahead. Likewise, we journalists, especially the newly-minted war reporters like me, had no real concept of what life was going to be like. It was exciting but the unknown filled each of us with apprehension. There was no embedding with troops in that war – the common practice that developed in the wars in Iraq and Afghanistan. We, as representatives of the media, were on our own, unprotected and, as it turned out, vulnerable to attack by all three factions in the civil war who cared nothing for freedom of the press.

Snipers, hidden in the hills overlooking the main roads, pulled the trigger in an arbitrary fashion, aiming their sights at individuals, passing vehicles, British troops – anyone who happened to be in the wrong place. Journalists with media stamped on their flak jackets and on the doors of their vehicles were fair game. Many reporters, photographers and cameramen were killed trying to do their job. Every day was dangerous, adventurous and scary – a perfect combination of sensations that either forced you to become a proper war correspondent, learning when to take risks and always to make sure your daily story was filed on time, or to make you realise that you were not cut out for this type of journalism. Some reporters had truly bad experiences and never returned to Bosnia. For some reason I find difficult to explain, I found the experience exhilarating, inspiring and obsessional. I returned to Bosnia again and again, staying for three or four weeks each time. The stories flowed.

Leaving the war behind on each occasion involved a mix of emotions: relief that I had survived and could return to my family and my colleagues, and regret that I was handing responsibility over to the next reporter from *The Times*. There was a small rota of reporters prepared to risk their life for the glory of the Bosnia dateline. They included the indefatigable Richard Beeston, who went on to become an eminent foreign editor on *The Times* and who tragically died of cancer in 2013 at only the age of fifty; Bill Frost, a fine former BBC reporter who was also to die prematurely in tragic circumstances; and Tom Rhodes, an ever-cheerful correspondent whose name was linked to the illustrious Cecil Rhodes, colonialist and founder of Rhodesia.

On this particular day, leaving Bosnia had other complications. A notoriously ruthless Bosnian Muslim band of brigands known as the Fishtank Gang was operating in the hills north of Vitez, where many of the British journalists were based. They were named the Fishtank Gang because there was an old fish farm along the route out of Bosnia heading for the Croatian border. There was only one way out of that end of Bosnia, and that meant driving through the wooded area where the Fishtank Gang was holed up.

That morning, as we prepared to leave, each of us had one thing on our minds: the nightmare ride ahead of us. The Fishtank Gang was led by a wild, bandana-wearing Bosnian Muslim rebel who had switched from fighting Croats and Serbs to running a large group of bandits. These outlaws had decided to take advantage of the anarchy that had overtaken their country by robbing, murdering and spreading terror. Journalists entering or leaving Bosnia with expensive computers, satellite equipment and dollars were considered easy targets. There had been many stories of hijacks and ambushes. A Dutch television cameraman had been stopped en route to Vitez and was forced to his knees as everything was taken – his vehicle, money, computer, satellite phone and body armour. A gun was put to his head, execution-style, but he was allowed to live. He walked to Vitez with a story that frightened all of us.

Those of us leaving Vitez that day resolved to travel in convoy and to accelerate as fast as possible along the track that ran through the Fishtank Gang's wooded territory. The most dangerous section was reckoned to be just a few miles, perhaps fifteen minutes of driving. The prospect of driving for my life, relying on my Lada Niva, flak jacket and helmet to see me safely through an ambush, was daunting. All of us were scared, but it was time to leave and we had no other choice.

The young man across the road left the woman with the baby and approached me. In faltering English, he asked whether I was leaving for Croatia. I said I was, knowing what was coming next.

'Would you please take my wife and baby

with you?' the young Croat asked. He pleaded with me to save his wife and child. Bosnia was too dangerous for them, he said. I was their only hope. They had relatives in Croatia.

The other reporters were urging me to get into my car to start the journey. I knew that if I was to take the woman and her baby with me, I would be facing even greater risks. If we were stopped by a Muslim checkpoint, never mind the Fishtank Gang, and I was discovered harbouring a Croat woman and child, the repercussions could be fatal – not just for me but also for my passengers. The risks were too great. After a desperate few minutes of indecision, I shook my head and said I was really sorry but it would be too dangerous. His shoulders slumped. He turned his head towards his wife and child and slowly moved it from side to side. 'I understand,' he said, 'I understand.' He then walked away.

It was a decision that would haunt me forever.

Soon after, we all climbed into our cars and headed off towards the wooded area where the Fishtank Gang resided. I was at the back of the convoy. When the road became a track it dipped down towards the trees and in two minutes we were in ambush territory. The track twisted precariously through the wood and as soon as the lead car started to accelerate, a dust cloud formed ahead, reducing visibility. Driving fast was the only way to cope with the build-up of fear in the stomach, but the faster we drove the more we were showered with dust. All of us expected at any moment to see Kalashnikov-armed brigands bursting through the trees. I had spent three weeks dodging sniper and mortar fire and talking my way past unpredictable checkpoint guards, but the fifteen minutes it took to drive to safety beyond the Fishtank Gang ambush section was more frightening than anything I had yet faced.

However, we survived. The Muslim brigands did not make an appearance, and when we reached a safer area, the convoy stopped and we all congratulated each other. But all I could think of was the woman and her baby. I had failed them. I had abandoned them to the dangers of life in Bosnia. Above all, I had not been sufficiently courageous to risk my own life to help them escape. As the other journalists laughed with relief and looked forward to visiting their favourite restaurant in Split later that evening, I felt tears forming in my eyes. Would the woman and her baby survive the war? I never found out. I never even knew her name.

I had become a journalist almost by chance after leaving university, switching career ideas from teaching to reporting, mostly as a consequence of advice from my father and partly because of a phone call from a college friend who had joined a local newspaper and was having fun. My subsequent career as a journalist developed through a period of extraordinary change. The whole industry was turned upside down. The gods of Fleet Street, the overpaid and underworked printers, were driven to extinction, new technology took over and national newspapers vanished from one of the most famous streets in London, scattering to different parts of the city. Reporters dependent on typewriters, pens and notebooks metamorphosed into multimedia communicators, skilled exponents of the high-tech age with laptops, satellite phones, video gadgets and mobiles.

Before all that happened, my first taste of journalism was a shock to the system. As a cub reporter on a local newspaper, there was nothing glamorous about the job. I nearly gave up, but I knew that one day I had to get to Fleet Street. That was my goal. But I never imagined that I would end up as a reporter covering wars.

CHAPTER 1
FLOWER SHOWS, DEATHS AND FLEET STREET

David Messer, editor of the *Express and Independent*, a local newspaper based in Leytonstone, East London, was a stern-looking man with thinning hair. He asked me four questions:

'Can you type?'

'No.'

'Can you do shorthand?'

'No.'

'Do you know anything about local government?'

'No.'

'Have you ever written anything?'

I was on firmer ground with that question. I told him I wrote poetry and had written the odd article for the college magazine.

'Mr Evans,' he said. 'I see absolutely no reason why I should give you a job on this newspaper.'

I looked glum. My father had advised me to try journalism and to reject my first choice for a career in teaching. I had taught for two years at the same preparatory school in Sussex where he was deputy headmaster before going to university. I told my father I wanted, above all, to write, and imagined that I could pursue that ambition in the long school holidays. He disabused me of this somewhat naïve dream, saying that I would spend much of the holidays coaching pupils or taking on other part-time jobs to boost the poor teaching salary. He also said I would learn more about the world as a journalist than as a teacher. By then I had also met Nicola Coles, the girl I would eventually marry. We met at a party in a house overlooking the sea at Seaford, where I had grown up and spent two years teaching. She told me she had been born in Karachi, where her father was running a news agency after serving in the Indian Army in the Second World War. So, journalism was already in the family, as it were.

But now, confronted by an unimpressed David Messer, I began to think that perhaps I should be a teacher after all.

'However,' Mr Messer continued after a pause, 'I'll take you on for six months to see how you go.'

I was astonished, relieved and nervous all at the same time. I had spent three years writing lofty essays to try to answer the questions, 'Who was the real King Lear?' 'Did Bottom matter in *A Midsummer Night's Dream*?' and 'Was DH Lawrence obsessed with his mother?' It seemed I would have to throw all that away and conform to a writing style totally alien to an English Literature graduate. Mr Messer offered me twenty pounds a week. A quick calculation and I realised that I would be earning more than 1,000 pounds a year. I had had a friend at Christ's Hospital, the public school where I spent seven years, who disclosed that his only ambition in life was to get a job that would pay him 1,000 pounds a year. I had been paid very little as a preparatory school teacher, so Mr Messer's offer was staggering. I accepted without too much enthusiasm, in case he lowered the salary, and walked out of his office, exhilarated that I was to become a reporter – at least for six months, anyway.

I soon discovered that being a cub reporter on a local newspaper meant covering endless flower shows. What could one possibly write about flower shows? I knew nothing about flowers but it didn't take me long to realise that it was the people who took part in such shows who produced stories, not the flowers themselves. I progressed from flower shows to unexpected deaths. The paper was keen on deaths of local dignitaries and personalities, and I discovered that grieving families liked to talk, once they were prodded gently. I became a good gentle prodder. One woman I interviewed about the death of her husband told me that I would be a good racing driver. I asked why. She said I was very calm and relaxed.

For all the time I spent talking to families of dead people, I had little success in getting stories of any substance into the paper. I was always tucked away, often without a byline. Having your name in the paper is the ultimate ego trip. It's what newspaper journalism is all about. The byline, especially with an unusual dateline, makes all the work and stress worthwhile. The worst remark that can possibly be made by anyone, friend or otherwise, is the following: 'I haven't seen anything by you in the paper in the last few weeks.' It's bad enough if it's true, but much worse if the paper has been filled with my bylines and they just haven't noticed.

When I joined the *Express and Independent* in 1968, I had to learn the very basics of reporting, and after three months of flower shows and deaths I started to wonder whether the newspaper business was for me after all. But, despite his better judgment, the news editor sent me off to cover a burglary. The police had charged a man, and my job was to gather all the facts and write a piece that was intended to be a page lead. I spoke to the police, wrote down the charges and returned to the office to pen my first crime story. My intro was straightforward: 'A man has been charged with burglary after a break in at the home of blaa blaa blaa.' There followed a number of statements from the police and some additional colour about the area where the burglary had taken place. My final sentence went like this: 'The man arrested was also charged with rape.'

When I showed my piece to the news editor, he smiled, as if confirming that he had made a mistake by sending me off to cover a real story.

'Don't you think,' he said cuttingly, 'that your final paragraph should be your intro? The woman was raped, for God's sake.'

I shrivelled visibly. It was obvious when he put it that way but my mind had been set on writing about the burglary and, to me, the rape was not a relevant part of the story. I had a lot to learn.

Learning the journalism trade is like learning

a language. Some have a natural talent for it, some take time to grasp the art, and some never stop believing that their mission in life is to be a 'writer' rather than a reporter. But you don't work for a local newspaper and expect to be launched into a literary career. Stories about rubbish-collection or planning committee meetings do not require mellifluous phrases, let alone verbiage plucked from the Latin dictionary. Very few journalists can get away with quoting Latin in their articles. The late Bernard Levin, also a pupil of Christ's Hospital and a wonderfully acerbic and knowledgeable columnist for *The Times* for so many years, was one of a few who could be forgiven for peppering his beautifully crafted sentences with the odd Latin phrase or saying. But then again, it came naturally to him; he was not trying to show off his classical expertise. But even Mr Levin, if he ever worked on a local newspaper, would not have dared to present his news editor with anything remotely Latin in appearance. Local paper news editors, certainly in my time, did not appreciate having graduates on their staff, let alone college types with a classical education. I had been a classicist at Christ's Hospital.

I learnt from an early stage in my career as a reporter to be humble before the news editor. He or she always knew better – whether this was true or not didn't matter. Although there were exceptions. Mr Messer for some reason recruited a former *Daily Mirror* reporter to be the news editor on the *Express and Independent*, and he arrived all striped-suited and brash, full of ideas about turning the community paper into a Fleet Street tabloid. It was a disaster, both for us and, fortunately, for him. Mr Messer should have asked: why is this man from the Big Street lowering himself to news edit an East London minnow paper? Was this seriously his life's ambition, or had he been fired by the *Daily Mirror*? He lasted only a few months before he took his pinstripes back to where he belonged. Had he been the news editor when I wrote my 'he was also charged with rape' story, I have no doubt I would have been sacked, possibly bringing my journalism career to a premature end.

As it was, he was shown the door and I moved on to greater things. I became news editor and reporter at the branch office in Loughton, Essex, a bit of a backwater compared with crime-rich East London, but challenging because of the extra responsibility that went with the job. My new remit also included covering cases at Epping Magistrates' Court.

Reporting on the Essex criminal fraternity provided a unique insight into a lower form of life. Epping, and in particular Epping Forest, attracted not just the local drug dealers but also the desperate and depressed who sought out the darkness of the wood to end their lives. For a public schoolboy, brought up to treasure life's challenges, the death by hanging of someone from the same generation never failed to be a shock. It was not only my first experience of death, but it was also the first time I had seen a dead body.

When I was a young boy, I had come close to death but was unaware of it. We lived in a former stables next to the main building at Sutton Place School in Seaford. Stable Cottage and the school grounds were a perfect environment for a child. The grounds included a large wood with endless potential for making camps and playing hide-and-seek. During the Second World War, Sutton Place was requisitioned as a training base for Canadian troops. This meant nothing to me until I found an interesting egg-shaped, metal object buried beneath the thick grass in the wood. I extracted it and held it in my hand, wondering what it was. As a boy of seven, it struck me that this was something I needed to keep because I had never seen anything like it before. I carried it to my room at Stable Cottage, put it in a cardboard box and hid it under my bed. I used to check it was still there every time I was sent off to bed.

It lay there for several weeks until for some reason I mentioned my discovery to my father. He immediately looked worried and walked quickly to my room. He drew out the cardboard box and looked inside. His face changed colour like he had discovered a body under my bed. The object I had found and hidden away as my own piece of treasure was a live grenade.

My father, Major William Henry Reginald Evans, always known as Reg, had served with the Royal Engineers in the Second World War and had twice won the Mention in Despatches bravery award. On his way with his men to France, his ship had been torpedoed by a German submarine. He led by example by jumping first into the English Channel and struggled to save the men under his command as they came under machine gun fire. He was to take his unit all the way to Berlin. He rarely spoke of his wartime experience, and tears would always come to his eyes when he recalled the men he had lost.

Faced with an unexploded grenade, he took over calmly and efficiently, and after a phone call, two men in army uniform arrived and took my treasure away. My father turned to me and said, 'Never, *never* do that again.'

After covering relatively mundane stories on the *Express and Independent*, Epping Magistrates' Court provided an insight into a more exciting form of journalism. Learning to be a court reporter, I used to experience the rush of adrenalin that became so familiar when I moved up in the world to work for national newspapers and was sent on foreign assignments. While most of the cases at Epping Magistrates' Court were unglamorous, ranging from traffic offences to exposure of genitalia in public places, there were also more dramatic instances of criminality that had to be sent on to the Crown Court. By now, I had become a more competent reporter, capable of understanding the legal complexities of a courtroom and knowing which elements could be reported and which were not for public consumption.

Mr Messer, it seemed, no longer regarded me as a risky recruit. Indeed, he tried his best to persuade me to sign on for another two years and to enter me for the school of journalism course at Harlow in Essex. I had other ideas. I thought I had been a local reporter for long enough and aimed my sights at Fleet Street. I wrote letters to several national newspapers, including the *Daily Sketch*, the *Daily Mirror* and the *Daily Express*. I couldn't imagine applying to such august newspapers as *The Times* or the *Daily Telegraph*. I was offered an interview with the *Daily Sketch* and the *Daily Express*. I travelled to Fleet Street like an excited schoolboy, apprehensive but hopeful of breaking into the big time. I was doomed to failure.

The man I saw at the *Daily Express* was a gentleman with a huge waistline who was the paper's night editor. John Young was charming and attentive but strongly advised me to spend at least eight years in the provinces, working for a paper in Manchester or Birmingham or Leeds, before trying again to join a national newspaper. In those days, graduates were not given priority. They were treated the same as reporters who left school at sixteen and had spent many years in local papers. The advice from the *Daily Sketch* ran along the same lines. The key to Fleet Street, it seemed, was to gain all-round experience in far-off cities. Even then, the competition for jobs in Fleet Street was so intense that luck was going to play as big a role as talent or experience. I knew no one in what famously became labelled in *Private Eye* as the Street of Shame, so there was no one to phone to put in a good word for me.

Under daily pressure to sign up for the two additional years at the *Express and Independent*, I turned in desperation to news agencies in London. Fleet Street News Agency, one of the main story-providers operating throughout London, offered me a job, and I accepted. After two happy years at the *Express and Independent*, I resigned and informed Mr Messer that I was heading up to Fleet Street. He looked suitably impressed and started to explain how working on his newspaper had helped to groom me for greater things, until I told him that it was Fleet Street News Agency that was about to employ me, not one of the nationals. He then warned me that I would spend my time rushing around from one story to another without anyone appreciating me because my name would never appear in any paper. I had to admit I was worried I might have made the wrong move.

The stroke of luck that I knew would be required if I was ever to make it to the real Fleet Street happened out of the blue and just at the right moment. I was due to start work at Fleet Street News Agency in the summer of 1970 when I received a letter from Mr Young, the kindly giant at the *Daily Express*. He wrote to say that a new department had been set up at the paper, run by Robert Millar, who was keen to employ a graduate as a reporter. If I was interested, I should contact Mr Millar and arrange an interview. The letter implied that I had been recommended to Mr Millar and that the job was mine if I wanted it. I rang Fleet Street News Agency and told them that I would not be coming to work there after all.

The *Daily Express* was a highly successful broadsheet owned by Sir Max Aitken, from the legendary Beaverbrook family. Robert

'Bob' Millar, one of many Scotsmen working for the paper, was a rare beast in the Fleet Street popular newspaper jungle. An Oxbridge graduate, he was in charge of Action Line, a consumer advice column which was created to solve readers' problems and uncover stories that could be published in the paper. It was a new idea, developed well before the successful *That's Life* television programme run by Esther Rantzen.

Bob Millar was a thoughtful, charming Scot, whose daughter, Fiona, later joined the *Daily Express* as a reporter and went on to become press secretary to Cherie Blair. Her partner was Alastair Campbell, Tony Blair's chief spokesman and communications strategist. I was never a political or lobby correspondent but later, when I became a specialist reporter, there were times when it was invaluable to be able to ring up Alastair at Number 10. He always knew what was going on and, when I needed it, he generally steered me in the right direction.

Bob Millar's team consisted of John Whelan, a softly-spoken journalist with a twinkle in his eye, and George Auffret, more of a hard-bitten type. He would always end his phone calls to people he contacted to help with readers' queries in exactly the same way. 'My name is Auffret – that's A for apple, U for uncle, F for Freddie twice, R for Robert, E for Edith, T for Tommy.'

I was offered a salary that doubled my annual income. My job was to find stories that would liven up the Action Line column and, if possible, uncover scandals or unusual legal situations which might find a spot elsewhere in the paper on the news or features pages. The editor at that time was Derek Marks, a large man with a serious, somewhat lugubrious, face who used to be a political correspondent. He was the only editor of about a dozen I worked for over the years who used to give a daily bulletin listing what he judged to be the best stories, features and op-ed pieces in the paper. My greatest triumph as a reporter on Action Line was to appear high up on the editor's bulletin, praising me for writing a comment piece about the dangers of a new trend that was developing in the housing market: gazumping. This was where a new bidder would come in at the last moment and produce a higher offer for a house even after an agreement had been reached between the vendor and another would-be purchaser.

After two years with Action Line, I switched to general reporting. The *Daily Express* was then a great popular newspaper, employing some of Fleet Street's legends, such as Harry Chapman Pincher, the veteran defence correspondent who had worked as a weapons scientist during the Second World War. He had a contacts book filled with his old wartime mates who went into MI5 and MI6 after 1945. Then there was Percy Hoskins, a superlative crime correspondent who was the spitting image of Alfred Hitchcock. I was just a relatively green reporter but, thanks to Bob Millar, I had developed a sharp news sense and loved the adrenalin bursts when challenged by an exciting story. The newspaper, housed in the Art Deco black glass building, nicknamed Lubyanka, at the bottom end of Fleet Street, was in its prime, matching its great rival, the *Daily Mail,* for mass circulation and scoops. Whenever there was a big story, the *Daily Express* would turn up mob-handed. If the *Daily Mail* beat us to the man at the centre of the story, the *Daily Express* would invariably get the wife! Competition was hot. Every quote appearing in a story in the *Mail* and missing from the corresponding *Express* story would lead to angry inquests by the news editor or the editor. Reporters survived by their fingertips, as one editor, Charlie Wilson of *The Times,* once famously said.

As a young reporter, it was not always easy to gain recognition. With such big names as Pincher and Hoskins on the pay roll, contributions to their big-headline stories often got lost, and a shared byline was a rare event.

Percy Hoskins was the nicest and gentlest of men who knew absolutely everyone in Scotland Yard. He was revered. He only had to pick up a phone to call the Yard and policemen, from the Commissioner himself down to the lowliest sergeant, would jump. But even the great Percy Hoskins was not omniscient.

On one occasion, I received a phone call from a lawyer I was acquainted with who told me he was acting for the head of the Vice Squad at Scotland Yard. His client, he told me, had been arrested and was being questioned for corruption. That was a huge story for the *Express*. I went straight to the news editor to reveal my scoop. He told me he would have to refer the matter to Mr Hoskins. A few minutes later, the news editor called me up to say I had been misinformed. Mr Hoskins knew nothing of any arrest. I spluttered that I had an excellent source and that I was convinced the story was true. The news editor said he was not prepared to run any crime story without the agreement of Mr Hoskins, and that was that.

Two hours later, Scotland Yard press office put out a brief statement that the head of the Vice Squad had been arrested and was being questioned. The *Daily Express* splashed the story the next day. The byline on the story was Percy Hoskins, crime correspondent. The news editor had the decency to apologise to me for not being able to include my name on the story. In those days there was no such thing as the Internet, so the story could not have appeared earlier than the following morning. With Scotland Yard's statement, all the papers had the same story. Nobody knew, except the news editor and Mr Hoskins, that a young, eager general reporter had been the first to get a whiff of the story. It made me more determined than ever to make my mark at the *Express*, so that in future a news editor might actually say to a new recruit: 'Sorry, that's a good story but I have to check it first with Mr Evans.' I hope I would have had enough grace to insist on including the other reporter's byline.

The 1970s were awash with some of the

best news stories for generations, including the Balcombe Street siege, the Spaghetti House siege and the Norma Levy call girl scandal which shook the Conservative Government of Edward Heath. I covered all three. It was an exciting period for me for other reasons, too: two of our three sons were born in that decade – Sam in 1974 and Christopher in 1978.

In the Balcombe Street siege in December 1975, four members of an IRA active service unit in London who had gone on a shooting rampage ended up taking a married couple hostage in a council flat. It produced my first genuine scoop which did me no harm in my ambition to advance my career as a Fleet Street news reporter.

John and Sheila Matthews, of 22B Balcombe Street, Marylebone, found themselves confronted by the four IRA men on their doorstep after a mad chase by police on foot patrol. They had been alerted on their radios to a shoot-up at Scott's restaurant in Mayfair.

The IRA, unlike more modern terrorists, never contemplated suicidal ends to their lives and always sought an escape route. This time, they appeared to have blundered and seized the hapless Matthews couple in the hope that the authorities would provide a plane to fly them and their two hostages back to their homeland across the Irish Sea.

They held out for six days in the council block surrounded by armed police and the finest reporters Fleet Street could rustle up. The IRA hostage-takers surrendered after a BBC radio broadcast hinted that the SAS was about to launch a rescue operation. The thought of the flash and grab boys from Hereford leaping through windows in their black balaclavas was one step too far for the IRA terrorists, and the siege was over.

My job was not to report on the daily dramas of the siege but to find a way to persuade the Matthews couple to tell their story exclusively to the *Daily Express* once they had been released. The news editor ordered me to find a close relative and present the paper's case for a scoop interview with John and Sheila Matthews. The whole world would want to know what they had to endure and how they had coped with having four IRA gangsters living with them. Every national newspaper was after the same thing. It was the big one.

After several days of fruitless searching, I had a tip-off that a family member lived somewhere in northwest London. Checking through the phone books – an old-fashioned reporting technique totally neglected today because of the Internet – I came across a Matthews in the right area and set off to the address, with little expectation that it would produce what my news editor was seeking. I knocked on the door and it was opened by a man peering at me in a somewhat unfriendly manner.

'I'm really sorry to bother you at this time,' I said. 'I know it must be a terrible time for you but I'm from the *Daily Express* and I just wondered if, when it's all over and John and Sheila are freed, you might be able to ask them if they would be happy to talk to me?'

It was an exceptionally long-winded opening gambit, but it worked. He invited me in. We sat in his front room and chatted about the siege, and I assured him that I would be very gentle with his relatives and that it might be helpful for them to talk about their experience. He promised to put a good word in for me. From the way he spoke it was clear he hadn't already done a deal with the *Daily Mail* or any other newspaper. I left the house and rang my news editor from a pay phone. The end of the siege was still two days away.

The surrender of the four IRA men was filmed and broadcast on every news channel. It was a major success story for the police, and in particular the Scotland Yard negotiators who had spoken each day to the hostage-takers, convincing them that the safe release of the couple was of paramount importance. John and Sheila Matthews were brought out and driven swiftly off to University College Hospital for a medical check-up. No interviews were allowed. The police wanted to debrief the couple before any Fleet Street reporter came anywhere near the hostages.

I used the oldest trick in the reporter's book in my next move to persuade the victims of one of the most dramatic sieges in London's history to talk to me and only me. I bought a huge bunch of flowers and attached a note saying I had spoken to a member of the family and hoped that my request for an interview had been passed to them. I wrote down my contact details.

The police were in force outside the hospital, preventing reporters from gaining access. But I spotted a delivery van outside. The driver got out, carrying a bunch of flowers. I ran across the road, handed him my flowers and asked him to take them to the hospital reception desk. The police didn't stop him from entering the foyer. I crossed my fingers, knowing that the flowers ritual had probably been used by all my rivals. But I was pretty confident that I had an extra ingredient in my favour – the chat with the family member. Sure enough, once the Yard's anti-terrorism officers had had their fill of John and Sheila Matthews, I received a phone call from the family to say that the couple would be happy to talk to me and to the *Daily Express*. It was a major coup.

But I nearly lost out despite all my reporting endeavours. The editor designated a grizzled veteran reporter, Bob McGowan, to carry out the interview. But this time the news editor stood up for me and I was told that I could also participate. McGowan had had no idea the part I had played in winning round the Matthews family. It was agreed that we would ask questions together, although McGowan would be the lead interrogator. Everything would be taped, partly because of concern by the paper's lawyers that we might publish something that could compromise or damage the prosecution's case in a future trial of the four IRA men.

The couple arrived in the morning and McGowan and I settled down for a marathon interview, knowing that the news editor wanted a big story for the following day's paper – a splash and at least two whole pages inside. The Matthews' story was to be spread over two days to gain maximum impact. As soon as the first edition came out, the *Daily Mail* and all the other papers seized on our material and produced stories for their second editions, even though our lawyers had placed a copyright stamp at the end of each page of our interview. Scoops always last for only one edition. That's the way it is in Fleet Street. Provided our rivals didn't openly plagiarise our copy and acknowledged, somewhere in their articles, usually at least half way down, that John and Sheila Matthews had been interviewed by the *Daily Express*, our lawyers would be reasonably flexible. We had to be because the next time it could well be the *Daily Mail* with a scoop that our night news editor would want to salami-slice into an *Express* version.

The story was published the following day, the two pages inside written in a question and answer fashion. This was not my favourite form of journalistic writing; I prefer a good long read with proper paragraphs and sentences. But it looked impressive. The *Daily Express* received a visit from Scotland Yard. Not because we had been guilty of contempt of court or had somehow annoyed the Police Commissioner but because McGowan and I had apparently squeezed more information out of John and Sheila Matthews than the combined efforts of the Yard's best interrogators. The two senior officers sent to Fleet Street wanted to know if they could see the full transcript of our interview, the second part of which was yet to be written up for the next day. The paper's security staff checked the officers' credentials to make sure they weren't *Daily Mail* reporters in disguise, and the editor agreed to hand over the taped interview. The couple hadn't been physically harmed but they had been terrified throughout their ordeal, which had lasted from the 6th to the 12th of December. For the paper, the story read like a television drama script.

More than two years earlier, on the 8th of March 1973, I was sitting in the *Daily Express* newsroom. It was a wonderfully old-fashioned editorial open-plan floor with fading yellow walls, piles of newspapers strewn across every desk and grumpy-looking news desk staff hating all the reporters for having more fun. Suddenly, there was a mighty explosion. It was a sound I had never heard before, clearly nothing to do with a car back-firing or the King's Troop Royal Horse Artillery celebrating the Queen's birthday with a gunfire salute. This was a thunderous but strangely muffled sound that rattled the *Express* windows and made every reporter jump from his desk. Frank Howitt, even more of a veteran reporter than Bob McGowan, keen on his lunchtime drinking but a highly capable newsman, grabbed a notebook and ran for the door. I needed no encouragement to follow suit. We ran together out of the building and into Fleet Street. The explosion had come from somewhere in the direction of St Paul's Cathedral. I could see the smoke.

'It's a bomb at the Bailey!' Howitt shouted.

It was a dash of only two minutes from the *Express*. We got there before the police. The scene was devastating. Every window had been shattered by the explosion; cars parked in the street outside the famous Old Bailey court were crumpled and twisted. Howitt ran in one direction, I headed off in another. The first victim I saw was covered in blood but didn't seem badly injured. He was suffering from shock. By the time the ambulances and police turned up to cordon off the whole street, Howitt and I had interviewed every witness we could lay our hands on and written furious notes about the destruction. There was no doubt this was the responsibility of the Provisional IRA, who spent much of the early 1970s causing mayhem in London with bombings and shootings.

Two ambulancemen came to where I was standing next to an injured woman and I helped carry her on a chair down the street. The police guarding the cordoned-off area must have thought I worked at the Old Bailey or one of the office buildings, now with mangled window-frames. I was aware of a flash of cameras from among the photographers and reporters grouped the other side of the cordon. The next day the photograph of the wounded victim being evacuated, with me walking at the back holding up one side of the chair, was splashed on the front page of the *Daily Telegraph*.

Howitt and I ran to a phone box to make our first and rushed report of what we had seen. I had been a general reporter for less than a year and had had no experience of such intense dramas, let alone dangerous situations. There was no time to formulate a properly structured story; it had to come blurting out of my mouth, a tidal wave of first impressions. I remember my opening description: 'It's like a battlefield!' Well, it was, as far as I knew. It was unquestionably, however, a poor cliché which a more rounded reporter would probably have avoided. But Howitt, bless him, raised his eyebrows and muttered, 'Very good.'

During the half hour or so I spent in the Old Bailey street, I had spotted someone I knew. He ran a wool shop round the corner which I had visited on a couple of occasions at lunchtime with my wife, who was then working as an assistant to the news editor of the *London Evening Standard*. He was wandering around in a daze with a bloodstained bandage around his head. I asked him if he was all right. He said he was fine. The next day, he was dead – the only fatal casualty of the Old Bailey bomb.

CHAPTER 2
CALL GIRLS AND GANGSTERS

In the same year, I was given an assignment with highly stressful responsibilities. Norma Levy, a Mayfair call girl with clients at the highest levels of government, became a *Daily Express* asset. Our senior news executives had persuaded her to tell her full story to the *Express* and someone had to look after her, to 'babysit' her and keep her away from the rest of Fleet Street while we built up the exclusive. I was selected because the news editor said I was one of the few reporters he could trust to conduct himself professionally with the most famous prostitute since Christine Keeler! In 1963, Christine Keeler had brought to an end the glittering political career of War Minister John Profumo after it was discovered he had shared the same call girl mistress as Yevgeny Ivanov, a defence attaché at the Soviet Embassy in London. Now, in 1973, the Norma Levy scandal also had huge political repercussions after the *News of the World* revealed she was sleeping with Lord Lambton, Undersecretary of State for Defence. Lambton was forced to resign from Government.

There were rumours that Norma Levy had slept with another minister. There was talk of a 'masked man' appearing at a party that prostitutes, including Norma Levy, had attended. The man in the mask was supposed to have been a member of the Cabinet. A second minister had already been caught up in the affair. Lord Jellicoe, Leader of the House of Lords, confessed that he, too, had consorted with prostitutes, although not with Norma Levy, and resigned. That was two ministers gone and a developing picture of seediness and debauchery in the British Establishment.

I was given my assignment late in the afternoon and my orders were bizarre: 'Drive south towards the coast and ring when you get halfway.' That was it. I grabbed some notebooks and spare pens and set off from Fleet Street in my company car, a brown Ford Sierra. After about an hour and a half of driving, I stopped the car and went to a phonebooth. I received my next instructions: 'Go to Eastbourne to the Wish Tower Hotel. You'll find Norma Levy there. Ring when you arrive.' It was about seven o'clock.

When I reached Eastbourne and found the hotel, I was in for a shock. Norma Levy was there – but so was her mother. I had two women to guard, and the mother appeared to be in no mood to cooperate. The call girl at the centre of the political sex scandal was dressed simply. She was slim, had a pretty face and spoke quietly. After all the lurid stories in the *News of the World*, with photographs of Lord Lambton in bed with her taken by her husband, Colin Levy, who had hidden in a wardrobe, this rather demure fresh-faced woman standing in front of me was not what I had been expecting.

The mother was demanding and I could see she was going to be a problem. But my job was to keep them happy and to make sure they spoke to no one except me. Terry Disney, a veteran photographer, had been assigned to join me to take pictures of the woman whose story was going to be plastered all over the *Daily Express*.

Fortunately, the mother didn't stay for long, and I spent a week with Norma Levy, talking to her, drawing out her story. On one occasion we walked together along the Sussex Downs, close to Birling Gap. I was looking at everyone walking by, expecting at any moment to be confronted by a rival reporter and photographer. But it never happened.

Norma Levy was not in a confessional mood. She hinted at the identity of the masked man in the sex party but did not directly name him. I became convinced who it was and said so to her. She didn't deny it. However, halfway through the walk, I discovered why she was behaving so warily with me; she said she thought I was from MI5 and refused to believe I was a *Daily Express* reporter.

However, when Terry Disney arrived, she agreed to have her photograph taken. We went to the beach at Birling Gap, along from the famous Seven Sisters cliffs, where she stripped off into a skimpy green-spotted bikini and posed for the photographer. She was stunningly slim and had an appendix scar.

The news desk rang and told me to take her for dinner at a Sussex restaurant called the Golden Galleon, which sits at one end of the

Cuckmere Valley. News executives from the paper would join us, I was told. I drove Norma Levy to the Golden Galleon for our rendezvous with the *Express* news bosses, one of whom was Brian Vine, an assistant editor in charge of home news and a rumbustious character. We sat down to dinner. Vine dominated the conversation. He was pleased that our scoop asset was still *Daily Express* property and that none of our Fleet Street rivals had tracked Norma Levy down.

However, I had another week of minding her ahead of me, and the stress levels were due to rise because I had to take her to London, find her a hotel and deliver her to Scotland Yard's Serious Crime Squad at Tintagel House on the South Embankment for questioning each day. This was the deal. The police knew we had acquired rights to her story but they informed the paper that she was to be brought to Tintagel House without fail, or there would be repercussions. I booked her in at the Park Tower Hotel in Knightsbridge and took a second room, next door, for me. The first night I was so scared she would run off I knocked on her door to make sure she was planning to go to bed. She said she was tired and would be going to sleep early. I believed her, and returned to my room. The following morning I discovered that as soon as I had closed her door she had rung a prostitute friend of hers called Brenda, who joined her at the hotel and stayed all night. It was a nightmare. Now someone I had never met knew where Norma Levy was staying and would probably ring another newspaper to destroy our scoop. I rang to warn the news desk and was told to get her out of the hotel fast and find her a flat. I took a taxi to Tintagel House to hand her over to the Serious Crime Squad for the day and went in search of a suitable flat.

I found a top-floor flat for her in Queensgate, west London, and moved her in after picking her up from the police. I begged her not to phone her friend again and she promised to behave. I spent a week worrying that she would vanish or call her friend again. But I faced only two major challenges: she wanted to go to the hairdressers and she also wanted her cat, which was being looked after by a friend. I managed both.

By the end of the second week, having successfully acted as Norma Levy's minder, I discovered that the story was to be written by Brian Vine without any input from me. All those cliffside conversations were to be ignored. I probably had more insight into the mind of this high-class call girl than anyone else but it was not going to be my name on the story. It was a bitter blow.

I went into the office on Saturday because I was told Vine was there writing the first exclusive story for Monday's paper. I went to see him and said I had masses of material from the two weeks I had spent with Norma Levy and felt aggrieved that I was not involved in writing the story. He told me to write up everything I remembered and to give it to him. The paper's intention was to start publishing the full story to coincide with Norma Levy's appearance in court, due that Monday. I went home on Saturday believing that my contribution would be included.

But nothing ever appeared. The *Daily Express,* like all other newspapers, ran a small story to go with a picture of her as she entered the court building. Some high executive with contacts in the Establishment and a personal acquaintance of Norma Levy's 'madam' played a role in suppressing the story. The editor of the paper was persuaded to spike the scoop. All my efforts were wasted. I was never given a proper explanation. Norma Levy continued to believe that I was working for MI5.

1975 was the year of two sieges in London. An earlier one, in September, three months before the Balcombe Street siege, erupted at a restaurant in Knightsbridge when three gunmen tried to rob it of its takings. When their plan failed to go as smoothly as they had hoped, they pushed and harassed nine staff members down into the basement and held them hostage. So began the Spaghetti House siege. As soon as word reached the *Daily Express* newsroom that a major story had broken, an A Team of reporters was sent to Knightsbridge to cover the drama. At that stage, I was not considered one of the A Team. Just like the Balcombe Street siege, this was to become a drawn-out affair.

The siege began late evening on the 28th of September, and it soon became clear that the desperate gunmen were not going to give themselves up. They claimed they were members of the Black Liberation Army and told police negotiators they wanted a plane to take them out of the country to Jamaica. The gunmen, like the four IRA hostage-takers, must have seen too many Hollywood films where the bad guys make demands for aircraft, helicopters and bags of gold. This was never going to happen. The Home Office told the Met Police to keep negotiating but there was to be no trip to Jamaica at the taxpayers' expense.

Franklin Davies, the Nigerian leader of the Spaghetti House gang, was the main contact man for the Met, but the siege soon settled into a familiar format, with the police sending in food for the gunmen and hostages, and the negotiations going nowhere. The *Daily Express* team of reporters set up shop in a nearby hotel and prepared for a round-the-clock watch, with four redoubtable hacks taking it in turns to man the police barricade. They also attended the daily press conferences, which elicited little information but helped to develop the dramatic story which looked set to run and run.

After several days of stalemate, word reached us that a mysterious figure may have been behind the siege gunmen – perhaps the organiser of the Spaghetti House raid – and that he could be found in a club in Soho. I was dispatched, along with Norman Luck, a crime reporter, to find the club and track down this mystery man. We arrived in Soho in the early evening and found the club, one of many seedy establishments in that infamous part of London. We climbed a steep set of stairs and entered a darkened room with low lighting. In the middle was a card table with green baize covering, and sitting there on one of four chairs was a fearsome-looking individual with a bald head and one mangled ear. It was not a cauliflower ear in the style of a rugby prop-forward, but a chewed sort of ear, hinting at a mighty fight in a dark alley or a wrestling ring with no rules.

He invited us to sit down opposite him and we asked him if he knew Franklin Davies. He gave us a look which indicated we were treading on dangerous ground. He pointed to his ear as if to warn us that a question too far might end up in another ear-biting incident – only this time he would be in the chewing game and we'd have a similarly mangled body part. We gleaned little from the card-playing gentleman but our crucial mission was successful. We had acquired a photograph of Franklin Davies, or so we hoped, and we needed him to confirm that we had the right picture. The man with one ear glanced at the photograph and nodded. The atmosphere throughout the interview was never less than totally intimidating and we extracted ourselves as soon as we felt it was safe to do so.

The siege had now been underway for nearly six days, and it was time for the A Team to be replaced by the B Team, of which I was to be a member. I went off to the *Daily Express* hotel to be briefed by the resident reporters and was volunteered for the late-shift rota.

I was at the barricades at around one in the morning on day six when a shot was heard from the restaurant. The police went into overdrive and rushed for the restaurant. It turned out that Franklin Davies, a skinny individual, had accidentally shot himself in the stomach. The siege had ended in a bizarre fashion. Davies and the two other gunmen were brought out of the basement in handcuffs. Davies had a superficial wound.

There were only a few Fleet Street reporters left at the barricades. We raced to the four-star hotel near the restaurant which had been used for six days as a communications hub for the whole of Fleet Street. With no mobiles available, the row of telephone booths in the foyer of the hotel had provided the perfect link with news desks. I ran alongside the reporter from the *Daily Mail* and the *Daily Mirror*. It was half past one. All of us were praying that a copytaker would still be on duty to take down our dramatic stories. When we arrived at the hotel, breathing hard, we were confronted by an extraordinary scene.

After six days of having aggressive reporters manhandling the phones and upsetting the clientele, the management had ordered the staff to build its own barricade right there in the foyer. There were chairs piled on top of each other to prevent access to the phone booths. But with such an amazing story in our heads, not even the highest mountain of chairs was going to stop us. All of us clambered up and over the chairs, knocking them in all directions. The night porter shouted that he would call the police but we ignored him. The police were far too busy – we hoped. We all got through to our newspapers at roughly the same time, desperately feeding money into the phone.

I will always remember the strangled voice of the *Daily Mirror* reporter. 'What?! What you mean there's no one there? Shit, can anyone take down my story? Anyone?!' He was out of luck. The *Daily Mirror* had closed down for the night. The *Daily Mail* reporter suffered the same fate. The last edition had gone to bed, the night news editor had packed up and the late copytaker had left.

Imagine their horror and fury when they heard me say, 'What? The copytaker is still there? Stop him, stop him – the siege is over! There's been a shooting! Quick, quick!' The late-night copytaker was on the point of leaving when the night news editor rang him to say I was on the phone and needed to put over a few paragraphs. I shouted everything I knew down the phone. At one point the copytaker asked in a bored, I-want-to-go-home fashion, 'Is there much more?' I spilled the facts, the end of the siege, the shooting, the arrest of Franklin Davies and his fellow hostage-takers and the safe extraction of the restaurant staff. I had already told the news editor that the photograph of Davies was fine to use in the paper.

The *Daily Express* ran a late, late London edition, with the picture of Davies stretched from the top to the bottom of the front page – the paper was still a broadsheet size in those days – along with my breathless prose! Mine was not the only byline because my contribution topped up the story sent over earlier in the day for the first edition. However, the *Daily Express* was the only Fleet Street paper to have the story of the end of the siege, and it was because a copytaker just happened to be around at half past one in the morning. It was a scoop but it was not an exclusive. My friends on the rival papers had the same story but no way to impart it to their readers. A night of agony for them, a night of triumph for me.

CHAPTER 3
MOVING UP IN THE REPORTING WORLD

The *Daily Express* in the 1970s was full of Fleet Street characters. The way of life was totally different from the Google-based, Wikipedia-helped, sit-at-your-desk reporting so prevalent today. Reporting stories then required ingenuity, cunning, long hours of 'door-stepping', chasing leads and outfoxing rivals. The sense of competition was overwhelming. In between the story-writing, there was a ritual, at least for the older reporters, that was repeated without fail every day of the week. Fleet Street was full of newspapers and pubs and the two were inextricably linked. Lunchtime boozing was accepted.

The Old Bell, just across the road from the *Express,* was the paper's favoured watering hole. Further up Fleet Street was the King and Keys, the *Daily Telegraph*'s lunchtime venue. The famous Cheshire Cheese was an alternative, especially for those who fancied a plate of steak and kidney pie and the pub's wondrous stilton. But reporters tended to stick to their own dives.

Express reporters of the drinking variety would start looking at their watches around lunchtime and then head off while the news editor looked busy. The news desk always knew where to find reporters if an emergency arose. There were no mobile phones to ring, but the barmen at the Old Bell knew the rules. If the phone rang they would answer it, and within seconds a name would be shouted: 'Frank!' 'Norman!' 'O'Flaherty!' The pint would be downed, not too rapidly, and the chosen reporter would exit reluctantly and return to the Lubyanka. Those not required would stay until three in the afternoon, drink three or four pints without food and then wander back across Fleet Street to see what, if anything, was going on.

Sometimes, the older reporters would stay in the pub on the basis that if the news editor needed their services he would ring. There were legendary moments when reporters returned to their desks after long sessions in the Old Bell. Frank Howitt arrived back in the newsroom on one occasion and stood shakily looking at the backbench, the long line of desks where the assistant editors and chief subeditor and other executive types performed their duties to get the paper to bed. Howitt then swept his right arm in their general direction and informed them that they were all 'c**ts'. Amazingly, no one intervened or even disagreed, let alone called security. This was one of Fleet Street's finest with a pint or two too many in his belly, and he was discreetly ignored.

On another occasion, Michael O'Flaherty, another fine reporter with an exquisite turn of phrase, returned to the newsroom in such an unfit state that we all knew there was going to be trouble. He duly proceeded to visit the managing editor's office, on the same level as the newsroom. He crawled into his office on all fours and succeeded in biting the executive's ankle. He escaped the sack but it must have been a close call.

When I started my Fleet Street career as a reporter on the *Daily Express* I wrote my stories on an old typewriter, using eight sheets of lightweight paper backed by carbon. I kept one copy for myself; the rest were delivered to the news desk and then distributed to the relevant people, including the subeditor designated to get my piece down to the printers below the newsroom. For a reason I never understood, the subeditor would then rewrite my story using a pen or pencil and small sheets of paper, with one paragraph on each sheet. When completed and given an appropriate headline, the sheets of paper were rolled up and placed inside a plastic tube. The night editor would then shout, 'Down the hole!' as he slipped the tube into a cut-out hole in the desk. It would tumble helter-skelter style to the waiting printers. In those days, when the newspaper printer was king and paid huge salaries, there was probably one man whose sole duty was to grab the plastic tube and hand it to a comrade, who took it to another comrade, and so on until it arrived at the huge iron printing press. It was truly a production line of effort. One of my most startling discoveries in those heady days of Fleet Street was when I entered the printers' domain late one evening and watched in disbelief as a mass of brown-overalled employees stood shoulder to shoulder, helping to guide the quires of tightly-stringed copies of the newspaper down a conveyor belt. The bundles of newspapers were quite capable of moving on their own. But these gentlemen – oh yes, all gentlemen, no ladies – were paid every night to place their hands on the batches of folded newspapers, which included my stories, before they were carried to vans queued up at the side of the building. So much tender loving care for my daily few hundred words, sliced and packaged and sometimes wondrously improved by old-style subeditors.

The night news editor for many years was Ben Vos, a tall, white-haired, gentle character who smoked a pipe and liked to drink Guinness with a shot of port. But he always remained respectably sober and treated his night reporters with courtesy and old-world charm. During my general reporting days, I had more than my fair share of night shifts and appreciated his quiet leadership. Many nights in the early 1970s were spent chasing around London in the aftermath of yet another IRA bomb explosion.

Night shifts, viewed by reporting stars as the graveyard rota, were more often than not filled with drama and excitement in the 1970s. Under the tutelage of Ben Vos, front pages were rewritten as the nocturnal IRA attacks swept the first-edition splashes to the inside pages, and the Michael Evans byline was slotted under the late-breaking stories.

I was promoted in 1977 from general

reporter to home affairs correspondent. My speciality subjects covered a vast array of issues including prisons, immigration, social services, local government and nuclear power. In fact, anything which no one else wanted to write about ended up on my desk. I shared a secretary with Chapman Pincher and several other specialists, the middle-aged and immaculately groomed Yolande Brooke. She told me once of the importance of thanking people formally if they agreed to be interviewed. She said Pincher always wrote letters of thanks. When I interviewed the head of Marks & Spencer for an article about business achievements, I wrote to him and duly thanked him for his time. He replied to my letter, expressing his pleasure and surprise at my courtesy and wished other Fleet Street reporters followed my example. It was good advice from Yolande.

Harry Chapman Pincher had always been an eminent loner in the office. He spent every lunchtime meeting lofty contacts in town. He once told me that when he lunched with a senior Russian diplomat in L'Ecu de France, his favourite restaurant, he suspected his table had been bugged. He was certainly not a Fleet Street pub frequenter; he was far too busy writing his latest spy scoops. But, towards the latter end of his illustrious career, his journalism tended to be less sensational and more geared towards writing about senior figures in the military. The *Express* ran a number of stories which were effectively profiles of generals and admirals who had been chatting to Pincher in their clubs.

When Pincher retired after four decades on the *Express*, he just left. There was no farewell party, no traditional 'drumming out' of the office (a great Fleet Street tradition when the whole staff come out to bang on the desks with hands or mugs). For Harry, there were to be no career-summing-up speeches. He wanted to leave by the back door and that was it. He came to me and said, 'Well, old boy, I'm off. Sorry I can't give you any of my contacts – that's the way it is.'

I had never really expected to be handed the most treasured contacts book in Fleet Street. Contacts are personal; they cannot be passed from one reporter to another. Contacts have to be nurtured and, above all, they are developed through trust. Pincher had spent his reporting life entertaining his contacts at expensive restaurants. It was one of the most important lessons I learnt at the *Daily Express*. Pincher and Percy Hoskins could raise an individual at the top of his or her profession, whether in the military, intelligence, political or police world, at any time of the day or night. That was an achievement I wanted to try and emulate. From the moment I became a specialist reporter on the *Express*, and later when I joined *The Times*, I worked industriously to fill my contacts book with influential names of people who would trust me enough to give me all of their telephone numbers. That included phones in their car, weekend cottages, Caribbean villas and, eventually, when they arrived to transform a reporter's life, their mobile numbers.

I was the home affairs correspondent for five years, during which, among my more notable assignments, I was commissioned to investigate how easy it would be to build a workshop atomic bomb. The *Daily Express* actually paid a scientist to do just that, based on my research, without the nuclear fuel, of course – although I spent a week investigating the routes British Nuclear Fuels' transporters might take when carrying radioactive fuel to the plutonium reprocessing plant at Dounreay in Caithness. I expected another visit from Scotland Yard, but not this time!

In 1980, our third son, James, was born. Having three sons was the most exciting part of my life, never mind working for a national newspaper. I told them stories every night and, as soon as I could, I taught them how to play cricket, another of my life's great loves. All three turned into talented cricketers. In 1982, six weeks before the Falklands War erupted, I applied for a new job on the *Express*: to be the next Chapman Pincher. But in addition to being defence correspondent I suggested I should also be diplomatic correspondent. The editor, Christopher Ward, a former *Daily Mirror* executive who was my seventh editor in twelve years at the *Express*, seemed surprised that such a role was necessary. Once Chapman Pincher had retired, I think he felt the job had retired with him. I persuaded him otherwise. At a time when nothing really exciting was going on in the defence world – the Cold War was the only 'war' in town – I was duly appointed as the defence and diplomatic correspondent.

Then, on the 19th of March, a small party of Argentine scrap metal men, led by Constantino Davidoff, landed at Leith on South Georgia in the South Atlantic. So began one of the most extraordinary events of that era, and one of the most exciting stories for a nascent defence and diplomatic correspondent who had no experience of war. My only military experience had consisted of time spent with the Combined Cadet Corps at Christ's Hospital, and firing a .303 rifle, with some degree of accuracy, at the Bisley shooting range in Surrey.

The landing of the scrap metal men meant little to me at the time. The Foreign Office tried to play it down. Officials indicated that the unlawful arrival of Argentine civilians on the British-owned island in the South Atlantic, where scientists of the British Antarctic Survey shared their lives with four species of penguins, was irritating but not a sign of something more sinister cooked up in Buenos Aires. Little did they know. Indeed, Lord Carrington, the charming and old-school foreign secretary, was so unmoved by the Argentine upstarts that he made it clear he intended to fulfil a longstanding travelling engagement to Israel.

As the newly-appointed diplomatic correspondent of the *Daily Express*, I was invited to fly with him, along with other 'dip cors', as we were always known. This meant pitting my wits against the illustrious John Dickie of the *Daily Mail*, an impeccably-dressed veteran correspondent who went nowhere in London or, indeed, around the globe without a red carnation or rose in his buttonhole. I travelled all over the world with him and he never failed to refresh his buttonhole, even in the most unlikely places. John Dickie's pursuit of the carnation-seller was as rigorous and as determined as his pursuit of a story. He was going to be a redoubtable rival and I felt distinctly nervous – even more so when I met another Fleet Street 'dip cor' legend, the regal Hella Pick of *The Guardian*.

I was the new young kid on the Fleet Street block and expected to be treated, if not with disdain, at least with a certain indifference. The opposite was the case. John Dickie said he was delighted that the *Daily Express* had appointed a 'dip cor' at last and offered his assistance and knowledge. Hella was less forthcoming with her long experience of diplomatic affairs but was also charming, if somewhat patrician. The biggest surprise for me came when I first introduced myself to Lord Carrington. He was immediately interested and told me, I believe genuinely, that if there was anything he could do to help, I should ask him. Over all the years of dealing with British foreign secretaries and defence secretaries, Lord Carrington was one of the nicest.

So, at the end of March 1982, we all flew off to Israel for a visit that was to last only twenty-four hours. We left behind increasing anguish in Whitehall over the Davidoff affair and tried to focus our minds on the Israeli/

Palestinian conundrum. In those days, the British Government still had sufficient influence and sway for its opinions to be listened to with respect in Tel Aviv and Jerusalem. During the brief visit, Lord Carrington was asked, in my presence, what was going on in the South Atlantic. He must have regretted his reply. He described the Davidoff affair as 'a minor incident a long way from home'. Within days he was to resign as foreign secretary. I was at the press conference after he had tendered his resignation. He looked sad but made it clear he knew it was the right and honourable decision.

On the Israel trip, as we rushed from one meeting to another in the footsteps of the foreign secretary, cables from London and from the British Embassy in Buenos Aires began to paint an alarming picture. It was clear to all of us that the minor incident 8,000 miles away was about to move into a different diplomatic stratosphere. As we flew back to London, there were strong indications that the Argentine military junta in Buenos Aires was planning an invasion of the Falkland Islands.

About 600 Argentine commandos arrived early on the 2nd of April, and occupied the Falklands after a brief but brave flurry of military action by the detachment of sixty-eight Royal Marines in Port Stanley, the capital. This provided Margaret Thatcher with her first Churchillian moment. She had to decide whether to listen to the doubts and misgivings of half of her Cabinet who opposed the idea of sending an army to liberate the Falklands, or to side with the military. In particular, the bold and insistent Admiral Sir Henry Leach, First Sea Lord and Chief of Naval Staff, who informed her that he could form a Royal Navy Task Force within days and ship troops and fighter aircraft off to the South Atlantic to take on the Argentine occupiers.

This was to be my first war, but not as a reporter in the field. The editor decreed that my role would be to cover the war from Whitehall. This entailed attending all the Ministry of Defence briefings and press conferences, and, in the early stages of the diplomatic war and America's attempts to prevent a conflict, to follow the moves and moods of the Foreign Office. Bob McGowan was selected to head off to the Falklands on a Royal Navy ship and write dramatic accounts of battles when he got there. Little did he know – little did any of us know – that by the time the war correspondents from all the papers arrived in the South Atlantic their attempts to send back daily files of events as they occurred would be lost/spiked/mislaid/delayed by an overbearing, insufferably frustrating censorship process that meant stories heading for Fleet Street front pages never got past the minders on the warships.

While poor Bob McGowan, like most of the other reporters, found himself engaged in a battle that had nothing to do with the ongoing dramas between the Argentine and British forces, my fellow defence correspondents and I were treated to daily briefings, which sometimes provided the sort of material McGowan would have died for. It was brutally unfair. But it turned out that staying in London was infinitely more productive than being embedded with the British military in the freezing South Atlantic. There were exceptions, of course, that have been well documented. Max Hastings, then writing for the *London Evening Standard*, had the military on his side, and managed to file wondrous copy, using a unique form of communication with London that was reliant on the technical expertise of the SAS, thus bypassing the MoD censorship minders. Good for him, but the special treatment he received not only angered his fellow war correspondents but drove them to despair.

Meanwhile, my byline appeared on the front page of the *Daily Express* pretty well every day for six weeks. It was a sixteen-hour day every day throughout the war. *Harpers & Queen* magazine cottoned on that the war in the Falklands, once it began in earnest, was mostly being recounted from Whitehall, and sent a writer to interview Fleet Street's defence correspondents. The fashion magazine described me as 'the nattiest dresser' in the MoD briefing room. I was photographed standing on the steps of the MoD, wearing my favourite dark brown velvet jacket. The caption under the photograph read: 'Man in velvet mufti: dapper Michael Evans of the *Daily Express*.' I never lived it down.

While the deadpan but delightful Ian McDonald, middle-ranking civil servant at the MoD selected as war-bulletin spokesman, droned on each day before the cameras, informing the world's media of the most recent developments in the South Atlantic, much juicier morsels of news were being handed out in unattributable background briefings. These took place in upstairs rooms at the ministry, where the defence correspondents gathered in front of senior civil servants and military top brass who were prepared to reveal more than Mr McDonald. Sir Frank Cooper, the MoD's permanent undersecretary, was even drafted in to brief us on occasions.

After weeks of disaster suffered by the Royal Navy and Royal Fleet Auxiliary, which lost six ships and dozens of sailors to the fearsome, French-made, sea-skimming Exocet missiles, Sir Frank was brought in to play the role of arch schemer. This was before the ground war began. He informed us off the record that we should expect to see a series of 'smash and grab raids' taking place to harass the enemy.

'There will be no D-Day landing of troops,' he said with a straight face.

We all rushed off to write our front-page stories. The *Daily Express* headline screamed: 'Smash and grab raids'. The strapline underneath informed the readers there would be: 'No D-Day invasion'.

On the 21st of May, a few days later, 3,000 British troops were offloaded from ships in San Carlos Water onto the beaches to form a bridgehead from which the liberating land force launched its offensive against the dug-in Argentine military occupiers. Sir Frank must have been pleased with his deception. It fooled us and, presumably, fooled the Argentine military who, even if they didn't read the *Daily Express*, certainly followed the BBC's World Service, which carried the same story.

In comparison with the 1944 D-Day landings in Normandy, the 1982 South Atlantic version was small scale. The 3,000 troops landed with negligible opposition. We never confronted Sir Frank with his deception but we remained wary of him. None of us enjoyed being unwitting partners in the MoD's black propaganda scheming. However, this type of deception was not repeated, and, for the most part the relationship between the defence correspondents and the MoD improved during the Falklands War. The opposite was the case with the poor war reporters 8,000 miles away. They continued to struggle against censorship and communications glitches. Often, by the time their stories arrived at their papers in London, the war had marched on apace, and their filings were out of date.

In the Crimean War of the 1850s, the great *Times* correspondent William Howard Russell wrote his dispatches from the front but never expected to see them in print for weeks because of the time it took for his vivid accounts to reach London. A century and three decades later, the war correspondents filing their stories from warships off the Falklands coast never imagined that they would find themselves in the same position as their legendary predecessor who, strangely, was not impeded by government censorship but merely by the constraints of nineteenth century communications.

Writing about the war when so much was happening almost every day proved a challenge, especially because news of major developments often broke late at night. There was one evening when the now close-knit group of defence correspondents decided to go to a Chinese restaurant in Soho for a meal together. We ordered a generous amount of food, waited twenty minutes for the dishes to arrive and picked up our chopsticks for what we thought was a well-deserved feast, all on expenses. The first mouthful coincided with the sound of the restaurant phone ringing. Another ship had been sunk. The plates of delicious food had to be abandoned as we all rushed back to the MoD.

The sinking of *HMS Sheffield*, the first warship to be hit by Exocet missiles, happened one weekend while I was away visiting friends in Bristol. I spent the whole day upstairs sitting on their double bed ringing the MoD and writing the front page splash for the following day's paper.

When the yomping by soldiers and marines across the length of the Falklands finished, and the battles had been fought and won, there was a sense of national pride in Britain which, for the younger generation, unused to war, was a revelation. Jingoistic headlines in the tabloid newspapers, especially *The Sun*, often went over the top but they summed up the mood of the country. British troops had travelled 8,000 miles to a country few people had bothered to think about in their lives and had prevailed over an enemy that had made the mistake of imagining that Britain would have neither the motivation nor the will to respond to the invasion of such remote islands.

Thanks to the vision of Admiral Leach and the political grit of Margaret Thatcher, the 1,800 inhabitants of the Falkland Islands could return to their lives without the sound of Argentine military boots on their streets. A total of 255 British military personnel sacrificed their lives for them.

After it was all over, I was summoned to the office of Baron Victor Matthews of Southgate, the businessman with slicked-back hair who in 1977 had bought the *Daily Express* and the rest of the *Express* group, which included the *London Evening Standard*. At the same time, the *Daily Express* was transformed from a broadsheet into a tabloid format. When I knocked on his door, Max Hastings was there standing next to the boss, a man of humble origins who had started life as an office boy and had risen rapidly to his fortune through the Thatcher era. Max and I were handed a glass of champagne, and Lord Matthews congratulated us for our coverage of the Falklands War. Poor Bob McGowan, who went on to write a hilarious book about his experiences, was on his way back from the South Atlantic and was not included in the celebrations. Hastings, of course, was the superstar in the room but I had probably written as many words as he had.

Hastings didn't really know me. At one

point, he bent down from his great height – and I'm 6ft 2in – and asked me to explain the story I had written about the supposed secret arrival by submarine of Special Boat Service commandos in Argentina in the early stages of the conflict. He appeared to be accusing me of making it up. I remembered the story; it had been a splash in the *Daily Express*. But I had not written it. It had in fact been written by Michael Charleston, our correspondent in the West Country. Hastings looked confused when I told him.

One issue arising from the conflict that even to this day is the cause of intense debate was the order by Mrs Thatcher, backed by her war cabinet, to sink the Argentine cruiser, the *General Belgrano,* which resulted in the loss of 368 sailors. It brought to an end any remaining threat posed by the Argentine navy. The sole aircraft carrier in the Argentine fleet never played a role in the war. The impact of the torpedo attack by a submerged Royal Navy nuclear-powered submarine on the *General Belgrano* was enough to keep the rest of the Argentine navy in port.

In October, four months after the war was over, I approached a senior Royal Navy officer in the MoD and asked him if he could tell me everything about the lead-up to Mrs Thatcher's order, why it was felt necessary to take such action and who were the key figures involved. My source was an admiral closely linked to all the decision-making during the conflict. He knew the whole story, and he revealed it to me.

It made a riveting story and the *Daily Express* put it across pages six and seven, more than 2,000 words.

The basic facts were well known. The Argentine cruiser with two destroyer escorts was steaming towards the British-imposed 200-mile naval exclusion zone around the Falklands on the 2nd of May, posing a clear threat to the Royal Navy warships scattered around the South Atlantic. Buenos Aires had been told that any hostile warship entering the zone would be vulnerable to attack. The cruiser appeared to be heading for the zone with the intention of ignoring Britain's edict. But the decision for the Royal Navy commanders monitoring the movements of the cruiser was not simple because it was being steered somewhat erratically, at one moment skirting the perimeter of the exclusion zone and the next, turning away and heading in the opposite direction.

The key military men with a decision to make were Admiral Sir John Fieldhouse, Commander-in-Chief of the Fleet, based in the Royal Navy bunker at Northwood outside London, and Admiral Sir Terry Lewin, Chief of the Defence Staff. My source described the scene when the two men met on the morning of Sunday the 2nd of May:

'It was about nine o'clock on Sunday morning. Admiral Fieldhouse, with only a few hours' sleep, had been joined by Admiral Lewin, who had called in for a situation report. The picture looked alarming. Not only was the *General Belgrano* in a potentially threatening position, along with her two destroyers, but there were now also two other Argentine ship formations north and northwest of the Falklands. To the two admirals, it looked like a classic pincer movement. The target was obvious – *HMS Hermes* and *HMS Invincible* [the two British aircraft carriers] upon whose survival the whole of the South Atlantic campaign [codenamed Operation Corporate] depended.'

If the two carriers, laden with Harrier jump jet aircraft, were seriously damaged, British hopes of recovering the Falklands from the aggressors would be lost. Admiral Fieldhouse, I was told, was the first to speak. 'The rules of engagement will have to be extended,' he said. 'The lives of our men are at risk.'

What he wanted was this: the rules of engagement for submarine commanders – different from those given to surface ship commanders – had to be extended to allow an attack on certain designated Argentine warships that posed a threat to the Task Force, irrespective of the 200-mile exclusion zone. Admiral Lewin agreed and immediately left the Northwood HQ in his official car and asked his driver to take him to the Ministry of Defence in Whitehall. Before going to Chequers, the prime minister's country retreat, to consult Mrs Thatcher, he had to call a meeting involving all the chiefs of staff to seek their opinions.

My source said there was no argument from the service chiefs, including Admiral Leach. With time running short, Admiral Lewin left for Chequers where, fortuitously, the War

Cabinet was meeting. When he arrived, it was about half past noon – half past eight in the South Atlantic.

'An urgent message was passed to Mrs Thatcher that Admiral Lewin was waiting outside,' my source told me.

She and her War Cabinet colleagues – Defence Secretary John Nott, Foreign Secretary Francis Pym, who had succeeded Lord Carrington, Home Secretary William Whitelaw and Tory Party Chairman Cecil Parkinson – left the Great Hall, where they were having pre-lunch drinks, and moved into the Hawtrey Room for what was to be an historic meeting. Admiral Lewin did not waste words. He told them of the threat from the three-pronged Argentine ship formation. Mrs Thatcher, who had from the beginning delighted the military chiefs with her forthrightness and determination, did not take long to make up her mind and to persuade her colleagues that action had to be taken immediately.

At four o'clock in the afternoon South Atlantic time, eight o'clock in London, the nuclear-powered submarine *HMS Conqueror,* which had been tracking the *General Belgrano* as it steamed back and forth before appearing to head once again for the exclusion zone, fired three torpedoes at the armour-plated hull. One of them missed. The *General Belgrano* was at that point slowing down and turning away from the exclusion zone, and when two torpedoes hit the cruiser, one on the port bow and the other in the stern, the ship was thirty-six miles outside the 200-mile circle and heading in the opposite direction. But the changed rules of engagement, agreed by the War Cabinet during the interrupted pre-lunch drinks meeting at Chequers and signalled to the submarine skipper, Commander Chris Wreford-Brown, provided the authorisation for the attack.

Soon after my article appeared, I travelled with John Nott to the Falklands to see for myself what these islands so far from home were like. When I walked towards the spot where the 2nd Battalion Parachute Regiment had launched its attack on the settlement of Goose Green, defended by more than 1,000 Argentine troops, I was staggered by the terrain. I had imagined, back in Whitehall, that there were steep hills for the soldiers to hide behind, providing protection before they crept up on the enemy positions. But the terrain was almost flat; there was a bit of a rise and fall here and there, but nothing to protect the Paras as they moved forward. It emphasised for me their incredible bravery. This was highlighted by the seemingly suicidal dash by their commander, Lieutenant-Colonel 'H' Jones, who had tried to take out an Argentine machine gun post which had been belching out withering fire at the British troops, preventing them from advancing. It was a classic act of self-sacrifice to help the men under his command complete their mission and to score the first ground victory against the Argentinians. But his death, the highest-ranking fatality of the war, was a bitter blow for the whole British Task Force. When I saw the terrain where he had hurled himself against the Argentine machine gun position, it struck me that this momentous incident, for which he was posthumously awarded the Victoria Cross, was an act of heroic madness.

All the other famous battlegrounds, such as Sapper Hill, Mount Kent, Wireless Ridge, Mount Longdon and Mount Tumbledown, were in a different geographical category. As their names implied, they were hills, providing the Argentine troops with crucial raised ground from which to defend against the advancing British expeditionary force. Visiting the lonely spots, battered by cold winds, the slopes still covered with Argentine detritus, was a sombre experience.

The only incident to lighten the mood was an anecdote from one of the British soldiers involved in clearing up the battlefields, removing scattered ammunition, live rockets, artillery shells and bodies. Argentine corpses were referred to by the soldiers as 'Alberts'.

A visiting three-star British general had made a trip earlier to the Falklands and had questioned the soldiers about what they had found that day. One of them replied, 'Quite a lot of ammo, General – oh, and a couple of Alberts.'

The general asked what he meant.

'They were Argentine soldiers, General,' the soldier replied.

'Good lord, fancy them both being called Albert,' the general mused.

CHAPTER 4
TRAVELLING FIRST CLASS WITH THE ROYAL AIR FORCE

One of the perks of being a Fleet Street diplomatic correspondent was instant membership of one of the most exclusive flying clubs, a seat on a Royal Air Force VC10 in the company of the foreign secretary and all the trappings that go with VIP travel: glasses of champagne when required, the tastiest of canapés before dinner, steak cooked to your preference and guaranteed inclusion in the minister's police-escorted convoy into the capital of this and that country. Maybe not in a limousine but in a perfectly presentable minibus, with 'Travelling Press' written on the front.

Newspapers in those days had the money to send their 'dip cors' around the globe wherever the foreign secretary chose to go. It was like being part of the British delegation, except that we weren't. We had privileged access and were allowed to sniff the rooms where the host and visiting ministers would sit for their chats. But as soon as they had finished talking about the weather and the charming city they were in, we were always shuffled off to wait in the corridors or be taken off to be briefed by officials of the host country, who would underline how important it was to have dialogue between the two countries. Well, quite.

Similar conversations could be held in almost every part of the world, whether Middle East, Asia, Africa or North America. There were exceptions: the Soviet Union and China always seemed to offer the unexpected. Not always pleasant, sometimes downright hostile. Travelling with Her Majesty's foreign secretary did not guarantee deference on the part of the visited government, especially towards the press. You didn't mess with the heavy Kremlin boys, and we learned never to underestimate the sheer determination of Chinese security men to stop us carrying out our job.

In Peking (before it became Beijing), in April 1984, I was presented with a scoop of a unique kind. I had travelled with Sir Geoffrey Howe, the foreign secretary, for a round of negotiations in China over the transfer of sovereignty of the British colony to the Chinese, due to take place in 1997. For us 'dip cors' there was a lot of waiting around, but being in Peking for the first time provided such a culture shock that every minute was exciting. The sheer numbers of Chinese people dressed in communist blue Mao 'fashion' uniforms and caps cycling around the city, the smog from the power stations and factories and the monumental size of the government buildings hit you in the face as soon as you stepped out of the hotel. John Dickie, my carnation-wearing *Daily Mail* competitor and colleague, suggested there was one thing we had to do before leaving Peking for Hong Kong. The famous Parisian Maxim's had just opened a restaurant in the Chinese capital.

'How about lunch at Maxim's?' he said.

It was an outrageous invitation that I could not possibly turn down. We took a taxi to one of the most famous restaurant names on the planet and had no trouble getting a table. The place was nearly empty. The average Peking resident could not have afforded the prices, and the more well-to-do were probably wary of indulging in capitalist-funded gastronomic pleasures. This was 1984, after all, before China started developing its own capitalist tendencies.

John Dickie and I sat down at a table in the centre of the restaurant and ordered what would prove to be an exceptional feast. I can't remember who spotted her first – I think it was Dickie – but at a table in the far left corner was Elizabeth Taylor, accompanied by her latest fiancé Victor Luna, a wealthy Mexican lawyer. Eating a three-course meal at Maxim's, set in the most unlikely city in the world for a Michelin-starred restaurant, while one of the most famous film stars of any generation was doing likewise a few tables away, was a unique experience. Even as I placed each delicious mouthful between my lips, I was devising a story in my mind for the *Daily Express* William Hickey column, the much-read daily diary of showbusiness and political gossip.

We couldn't hear what they were talking about until Ms Taylor summoned a waiter and informed him that they had to leave. But she said she wanted to taste some of the items on the dessert menu. The waiter informed her that he would box up some selected pastry morsels for her to take away. The woman with the legendary violet eyes smiled and muttered something to her fiancé.

After a few minutes, the waiter returned with ten small white cake boxes, each with a brightly-coloured looped ribbon, and proceeded to follow Ms Taylor and her Mexican fiancé, soon to be ex-fiancé, out of the restaurant, holding the boxes in each hand. She didn't look in our direction but we watched as the procession moved elegantly towards the door.

The headline in the William Hickey column was not so elegant but it summed up the scene at Maxim's: 'Food-mad Liz bags the ultimate Chinese takeout.'

Thanks to Elizabeth Taylor, I felt it was justified to put my Maxim's lunch on expenses. No one quibbled back in London. It's not often you get a scoop on a plate!

After three days of secret talks between Sir Geoffrey and the Chinese negotiators, we travelling press had gleaned little detail of the progress or lack of progress. Hong Kong was going to be switched to the communist Chinese whether Sir Geoffrey liked it or not, but he was doing his best to fix a deal that would not damage or destroy the island's prosperous reputation or agree to anything which the people of the colony might feel was a sell-out to Peking.

I had two regrets as I left Peking for Hong Kong: I hadn't had time to visit the Great Wall of China; and, during a state banquet at Peking's Great Hall of the People, I ate sea slugs, which disagreed with my tender Western stomach. I was sitting at a round table in the vast dining hall with nine Chinese officials. In front of each of us were six small glasses, containing liquid of varying colours, from off-yellow to bright orange. One of them was rice wine and I had been warned to treat the drink with respect. In other words, sip it carefully or pour the contents into a flowerpot, if there was one conveniently available. But there was no flowerpot near my chair, and when my Chinese table companions picked their rice wine up and slugged it back in one movement and then looked at me, nine pairs of eyes willed me to follow suit.

I was a guest in the Great Hall of the People, representing, as it were, Her Majesty's Government as an unofficial delegate in Sir Geoffrey's entourage, so clearly I had no choice but to do likewise. I managed it without spluttering. But then the first course arrived. It was a large soup bowl with grey-coloured liquid and lumps of fat floating on the surface. My Chinese companions tucked in heartily and in a matter of minutes the lumps had been swallowed and the soup sucked up with extravagant licking of lips. I had no idea what the floating bits were and had made the decision that I would try to spoon up the liquid and leave the uninviting lumps to sit at the bottom of the bowl, hopefully unseen by the others around the table. But, again, I had to make a sacrifice for Her Majesty. My table companions informed me that the lumps were sea slugs and that they were a Chinese delicacy. They had to be eaten by a visiting foreigner. It was a privilege, they said. There were three sea slugs. They entered my stomach with the sound of muffled retching in my throat, which I tried to cover up by smiling enthusiastically and seizing one of the glasses, hoping it was water. But it turned out to be something even stronger than the rice wine. My near-death experience caused much amusement around the table.

I was ready to leave, but then the second course arrived, consisting of a plate of rabbit droppings. Well, they looked like rabbit droppings and for all I knew they tasted of rabbit droppings, having never indulged in this form of gastronomic eating before, but I didn't need to ask the obvious question. They were already nodding their heads. 'Yes, another Chinese delicacy,' they said.

Poor Sir Geoffrey. I assumed he had been through the same experience. What's more, he had to make a speech without vomiting across the table as President George H.W. Bush did so spectacularly during a visit to Japan eight years later, in January 1992, when he was violently sick into the lap of Japanese Prime Minister Kiichi Miyazawa during a state dinner. The British foreign secretary stood up to make his speech and pronounced that he was satisfied with the progress made in the negotiations with his Chinese hosts. He made no mention of the delicious food before him.

It wasn't until we arrived in Hong Kong that

Sir Geoffrey revealed that the Chinese leader, Teng Hsiao-Ping – or Deng Xiaoping, the more common spelling – had promised the British foreign secretary that the colony would be allowed to retain its capitalist system for fifty years, once Britain's lease had run out in 1997. During his talk with the Chinese leader, Sir Geoffrey had to remember one important fact about Xiaoping. He was totally deaf in one ear, but officials in the British camp seemed a little confused over which ear it was. When they sat down next to each other for the pre-talks appearance in front of the press, Sir Geoffrey ended up sitting to the left of the tiny Chinese leader. We all hoped that bending Xiaoping's left ear would prove fruitful. The key to the ear situation was to watch the interpreter; when he started whispering into Xiaoping's left ear, we knew Sir Geoffrey was sitting in the correct chair.

The Chinese press were totally deferential to their leader. We were largely ignored. In Hong Kong it was a different matter. Hong Kong's indigenous journalists were like piranhas preying on a lone swimmer. Every press event arranged for Sir Geoffrey's visit was like a mass attack; microphones were thrust forward in the most aggressive fashion and every question was repeatedly shouted for good measure. Sir Geoffrey, a reserved, gentle soul who liked to choose his words carefully, like a good lawyer, dealt with the hordes as competently as he could. But, after his three-day trip to China, no one in Hong Kong believed he had negotiated a deal that would benefit anyone in the colony.

Sir Geoffrey was Sir Geoffrey because he had been knighted in 1970, before his appointment as Solicitor-General in the government of Edward Heath. But his Chinese and Hong Kong hosts never worked out what to call him. So, throughout his Far East trip he was called 'Sir Howe'. No British diplomat had the courage, it seemed, to put them right.

It wasn't the only point of confusion in the trip, which also embraced a visit to Japan. We all went off to visit the giant Fujitsu plant in Numazu City where 'Sir Howe' was asked to address a computer – which, our Japanese hosts disclosed, was the first of its kind in the world capable of answering back. The computer was supposed to take a voice print from something said by Sir Geoffrey and then give an appropriate response. In his usual slow, modulated way of talking, he uttered the word 'Paris'. The Japanese officials said the computer screen would instantly show the French flag flying over Paris. But instead, it displayed the German capital, Bonn. The Japanese blamed it on the 'strange way' Sir Geoffrey spoke.

Three months later, I was in Moscow with Sir Geoffrey. Soviet-West relations were not good. Sir Geoffrey fell foul of the odious Soviet Foreign Minister Andrei Gromyko, the Kremlin veteran, then seventy-four, whose face sunk into itself with disapproval and ill temper on every occasion he met the foreign secretary. The issue that had driven even more ice into the Cold War was the famous Star Wars speech by

President Ronald Reagan, in which he appealed to America's scientists to come up with a way of creating a space-based shield capable of protecting the United States from a mass nuclear ballistic missile attack by the Soviet Union. Margaret Thatcher thought the Reagan vision was pie-in-the-sky, but Moscow saw it as a ploy by the man in the White House to undo decades of East/West deterrence based on the notion of Mutual Assured Destruction (MAD).

All conciliatory moves made by Sir Geoffrey were spurned by his Soviet counterpart who, when not launching a tirade against the West, just answered questions with his favourite word: 'Niet'. Gromyko was in an angry mood throughout the trip but he wasn't all sourpuss. To us travelling press he could be chatty and even amusing. Standing in his familiar Homburg hat and heavy coat, he seemed to enjoy a little banter, and generally spoke in perfect English. But not with Sir Geoffrey, who looked like he had been hit by a cruise missile every time he emerged from a session with Mr Niet.

Gromyko was a born and bred Cold War warrior. But whether he truly believed the US wanted to attack the Soviet Union, like most Russians appeared to believe in those days, or whether he just enjoyed playing the grumpy old man on the world stage, was always difficult to tell. But, in September that year, he stood up at the United Nations General Assembly in New York and accused the US and its NATO allies of 'pushing mankind towards a nuclear abyss'. The language was as dire as when Nikita

Khrushchev threatened to 'bury' the West in a speech in 1956 in front of Western ambassadors in Moscow.

Little did we know that Gromyko's days were numbered. In March 1985, Mikhail Gorbachev became the new Kremlin leader after the death of Konstantin Chernenko. During Sir Geoffrey's ill-starred trip to Moscow in 1984, the travelling 'dip cors' were allowed into the Kremlin to see Chernenko. As the head of a nuclear superpower, his entry into the room was truly shocking. He had aides on either side of him, holding him up as he took tiny steps towards Sir Geoffrey. His face was puffed up and red and he was clearly having trouble breathing. For the brief appearance before the press, the Soviet leader stood behind a chair, his hands gripping the top to maintain his balance. The fact that he survived another eight months was some sort of miracle, although with the Soviet Union in the Cold War it was never certain when a leader actually died. The public announcement of a death did not necessarily coincide with the leader's last breath. With the death of Chernenko, the Old Guard, including grumpy Gromyko, was swept away, although the former Foreign Minister was pushed upstairs to the ceremonial position of head of state before he retired in 1988.

The arrival of the apparently charming Mikhail Gorbachev in the Kremlin caused the West to reassess relations with Moscow. A month after Gorbachev took over as Soviet leader, Sir Geoffrey made a trip to Eastern

Europe, accompanied by Fleet Street's 'dip cors', to test the waters in Czechoslovakia, Poland and East Germany.

In Prague, he was involved in an extraordinary plot to hoodwink the Czech secret police to enable two senior Foreign Office diplomats to meet in secret with leading dissidents from Charter 77, an underground reformist movement. The subsequent drama which caused celebrations in the British delegation and furious reaction from the Czech authorities was duly splashed all over the front page of the *Daily Express* the following day, with the headline: 'Howe's amazing Czechmate foils Reds.'

Sir Geoffrey played his part in the deception of his hosts. He went carousing with Bohuslav Chnoupek, the Czech foreign minister, at a bar in Prague called The Seven Angels. They ate and drank and were entertained by a bunch of gipsy musicians. Two of his key officials went missing. While the Czech foreign minister and his close aides were all enjoying themselves, Derek Thomas, political director of the Foreign Office, and John Birch, head of the Eastern European Department, slipped away from the entertainment and climbed into a car that took them to a private flat where they met the dissidents.

They returned shortly after midnight, without the Czech security men realising what was going on.

Sir Geoffrey had been waiting anxiously to hear whether the plot had been successful. So, when Mr Birch passed him a written message which read simply, 'mission accomplished', the foreign secretary was so excited he invited his hosts to join him in a rendering of *Good King Wenceslas* and *It's a Long Way to Tipperary*. Sir Geoffrey was not a man to let his hair down, not in public at least, but the coup by his two senior advisers gave him something to celebrate. He even had copies of the lyrics with him to hand out to the Czechs.

My source in the British delegation told me Mr Chnoupek had a fruity baritone voice, and the revelry continued until nearly one in the morning.

As soon as my front page story appeared in the *Daily Express* just before midnight in the first edition, the BBC Radio's Today programme rang me, desperately trying to get hold of Derek Thomas and John Birch. Both officials were shocked to discover their secret visit to the dissidents had been disclosed, and kept away from any further media exposure. The *Daily Express* gave the story the space and coverage I felt it deserved. Poor John Dickie had also written the story, but the *Daily Mail* failed to react properly and hid his piece away. It was probably a bit tabloid for Hella Pick of *The Guardian*. Whether she had written a story or not, the fact is that my splash was effectively a scoop because the *Daily Express* was the only paper which gave it the big treatment. John Dickie, being a gentleman, was the first to congratulate me.

The mid '80s was a momentous period to be a

diplomatic correspondent. There were repeated trips to Geneva to follow the superpower talks on arms control – always events of great theatre. The Russian negotiators moved around the Swiss capital in huge Zil limousines, escorted by stocky KGB men attired in loud Chicago-style suits that never fitted because of their oversized pectorals and biceps. With Gorbachev in power there was a new generation of younger officials in Moscow, but the KGB never changed. They eventually acquired a new name, a brand makeover to convince the world that the KGB was a different beast. But the establishment of the SVR and FSB, the new acronyms, couldn't hide the fact that while the Kremlin Old Guard had been pushed into retirement, the Russian intelligence boys were still the KGB in reality. The same old faces kept on turning up. Geneva was packed with them and they looked as unwelcoming as ever.

South African apartheid was also big news in the '80s. Sir Geoffrey Howe was handed the job of presenting a new European Economic Community (EEC) five-point plan to the governments of southern Africa. He had to go twice because the first time, President Botha of South Africa refused to see him, saying he was on holiday. On the second trip, arriving first in Lusaka, capital of Zambia, in late July 1986, President Kenneth Kaunda, the Zambian leader, was not in a good mood and gave Sir Geoffrey a hard time. The first thing he said was that he loved the Queen but was only prepared to speak to Her Majesty's foreign secretary because he was a human being. He would not welcome him to Zambia as a representative of the British Government. He and other southern African leaders were of the view, quite wrongly, that Thatcher supported apartheid in South Africa because she was opposed to economic sanctions. Thatcher felt they wouldn't work and would harm the South African people, black and white.

President Kaunda, a strong supporter of sanctions, was so insulting and rude to Sir Geoffrey that the temptation must have been almost overwhelming to answer back in kind and waltz out of the room. I asked Sir Geoffrey later why he hadn't stormed out.

He replied, 'The problem is, if you walk out it's very difficult to walk back in again. That's a lesson I have learnt. It's better to stay in the room and take the punishment.'

He was right, of course. Kaunda was playing to the gallery for domestic reasons. Sir Geoffrey later revealed that the Zambian president put on an apron and served everyone tea.

The Zimbabwean leader, Robert Mugabe, a man who, probably for good reason, trusted no one, didn't insult the foreign secretary when we arrived in Harare. But he also made it clear he rejected the British Government's stand against economic sanctions and threatened to pull out of the Commonwealth Games in Edinburgh. It wasn't the mightiest of diplomatic sticks to wave but it was another prod to Sir Geoffrey that his peace mission appeared to be heading nowhere.

Meeting leaders of different shapes and

sizes on a fairly regular basis is another perk of travelling with the foreign secretary. You acquire what one might call a lack of awe for most of the government leaders one comes across. There were exceptions, of course: Helmut Kohl was awesome because of his sheer gargantuan size; Bill Clinton was mesmeric as soon as he walked into a room; Ronald Reagan had old-fashioned charm and wit; and Menachem Begin, though small and intense, was stuffed full of his past life as the leader of Irgun, the Zionist 'terrorist' organisation that targeted the British in Palestine in the 1940s. I saw Israel's sixth prime minister in action in the Knesset during a visit to Jerusalem. When he left the chamber, I headed off quickly and ran through the building to where I knew his car was parked. I was told something unusual would happen and I wanted to witness it without scaring the Shin Bet security-service bodyguards.

I reached the car before him. No one stopped me. It was an old limousine with a leather bench seat in the back. The passenger side rear door was wide open. A minute or so later, the Israeli prime minister came through the doors, looked neither to his left nor his right, and then hurled himself head first, belly-flop fashion, into the back of the waiting car. A Shin Bet bodyguard slammed the door and the limousine accelerated away. Pretty impressive for a man in his seventies but a good example of the indignity sometimes required of a leader under constant threat of assassination.

The Commonwealth heads of government

conference in the Bahamas in October 1985 brought together an eclectic mix of leaders, representing countries as far apart as Australia, Mozambique and Sri Lanka. The Queen was in attendance, having travelled to the Bahamas on board the Royal Yacht *Britannia*. However important the issues before them – and apartheid was at the top of the list – all the Commonwealth leaders were looking forward to one event: dinner with the Queen on board the *Britannia*, to which they were all invited. I was covering the conference.

The media present had also received invitations, although only for pre-dinner drinks. We all duly turned up in our best suits and were introduced to the Queen on the deck about half an hour before the dinner was due to start. She was smiling and seemed relaxed, and was quite happy to chat about this and that. But then a royal aide came to see her to pass on a message. Thirteen of her guests, including Rajiv Gandhi, the Indian prime minister, and President Kaunda, had gone missing on a riverboat trip. They had chosen to reach the *Britannia* on board a chartered pleasure boat called the *Gran Mudder*. The excuse given later was that they wanted to avoid demonstrators who had gathered to shout at Sir Lynden Pindling, the prime minister of the Bahamas, who was being accused of corruption. But they also wanted to enjoy the local beauty spots from the river. They ran into some windy weather, and, as a result, they turned up an hour and twenty minutes late.

The Queen was not amused. As we sipped

our cocktails, she began drumming her white-gloved fingers on the wooden rail of the quarterdeck. Her smile had gone. She looked, if one might be so bold as to suggest, mightily pissed off! When the pleasure boat eventually emerged from the darkness, the Queen resorted to waving her hand at them, as if to say, 'Hurry up, the saddle of lamb is getting cold!'

During the same conference in the Bahamas, the Commonwealth leaders held a get-together with the press in the gardens of an official residence. Most of the reporters surrounded Bob Hawke, the irascible Australian prime minister who had been quoted as saying that a 'Gang of Four' – Gandhi, Kaunda, Canada's Brian Mulroney and Hawke himself – was plotting to 'corral' Mrs Thatcher into changing her mind and agreeing to impose economic sanctions against South Africa. The plot failed after British officials made it clear that 'the lady is not for corralling'.

While my fellow reporters buzzed around Mr Hawke, I spotted an exceptionally tall gentleman in a long white robe standing all on his own at the side of the garden, and thought he needed company. I walked towards him, smiled, introduced myself and asked who he might be.

'I,' he replied from his lofty position, 'am the president of Bangladesh.'

There was no hint in his voice of any form of irritation that I had failed to recognise him.

CHAPTER 5
NEW LIFE ON THE THUNDERER

In 1986, I had to make a difficult decision. The *Daily Express* had changed editors yet again, and the new man, Nicholas Lloyd, had plans for me. He wanted to turn me into the paper's chief feature writer, and his deputy, Bernard Shrimsley, talked of trips to Washington and elsewhere. It all sounded exciting and I was tempted. But my friend John Dickie had once advised me that the best job at a newspaper was a specialist reporter. Feature writers and general reporters came and went as the mood of the incumbent editor varied, but a reporter with a specialist subject and an impressive contacts book was invaluable. Not immune to the whims of an editor, of course, but perhaps less vulnerable, provided the exclusive stories kept on coming. I had been a specialist reporter on the *Daily Express* for many years and felt this was my natural habitat. I suggested to Nick Lloyd that he could appoint me chief specialist writer, but even as I uttered the mouthful I knew it didn't sound right. I was grateful to Nick Lloyd for his ambitions for me, but the job he had in mind wasn't really what I wanted.

By a stroke of fortune, I received a phone call during this period of indecision and doubt from Michael Hoy, a pipe-smoking young Australian who was the managing editor of *The Times*. He asked if I would be interested in joining the newspaper. I had been recommended by two senior members of *The Times'* news team who had recently moved to the paper from the *Daily Express*. John Jinks, a senior news desk executive, and Jack Crossley, assistant editor (news), were both longstanding friends of Charlie Wilson, who had been appointed editor of *The Times* in 1985. A former Royal Marines boxing champion, this tough-looking Glaswegian didn't fit the stereotype to run 'the Thunderer' (the favourite nickname for the newspaper), but he was one of the best editors I ever worked for.

Jinks and Crossley had spoken to Charlie Wilson about me. The timing was impeccable – although, having been a reporter on a popular newspaper for so long, I was nervous about moving to such a serious paper as *The Times*. I assumed, quite wrongly, that the journalism on this famous newspaper would somehow be different. But the presence of Jinks and Crossley on the news desk was enough reassurance for me. I told Mike Hoy I was interested and a date was fixed for me to see Charlie Wilson.

I met Charlie Wilson at the Waldorf Hotel in the Aldwych, but as soon as I arrived he said he needed a walk, and off we went towards Covent Garden.

'So what do you want to do at *The Times*?' he asked.

The question threw me because I had assumed he was about to offer me a particular job.

'You can't be defence correspondent because we've got one of those,' he went on.

I said some form of specialism where I could make use of all the Whitehall contacts I had made during my time at the *Daily Express* would make sense. I was no Chapman Pincher but I had phone numbers in my blue book of senior civil servants and military people which had proved productive over the years. Charlie Wilson, his face thrust forward in a pugilistic sort of way, thought for a moment and then suggested, 'So you could be Whitehall Correspondent?'

Neither he nor I knew what that really meant, but as we wandered among the tourists in Covent Garden, it had a certain ring to it, and it meant I would remain as a specialist reporter. I nodded my head and we shook on it. Within days, I received a letter from Mike Hoy outlining my job on *The Times*. So I went to see Nick Lloyd to tell him I had decided to resign. When it became known on the *Daily Express* that I was leaving for *The Times* to be Whitehall Correspondent, everybody had the same opinion: I was mad. My friends warned me that with such a general title I would end up stepping on other specialist writers' toes and would not be able to identify any specific areas of reporting which I could claim to be mine.

I joined *The Times* at the News International building, which had become known as Fortress Wapping after the eruption of violent protests following Rupert Murdoch's decision to sack all the printers and set up the new production plant east of Tower Bridge. It was one year later but there were still small groups of angry sacked printers shouting and waving their fists at anyone who looked as if they were on their way to the plant. I had to travel from Waterloo to Wapping in a 'battlebus', a coach whose windows were protected by grills. It was an unreal situation but one I got used to. It did not affect my excitement at working at *The Times*.

However, for the first two months on *The Times*, sitting at my desk in the old rum warehouse that was home to the paper inside Fortress Wapping, I scrabbled around, snatching this story and that story, and struggling to get anything into the paper. One of my first pieces was about immigration and I remember selecting the longest words I could muster to demonstrate that I was no longer working for a popular newspaper. I received a message from John Dickie, congratulating me on getting a story published in *The Times* but noted that I appeared to have adopted a somewhat posh writing style. It didn't take me long to realise that, in fact, my time working for the *Daily Express* – learning how to write concisely, ensuring that the whole meat of the story could be summed up in the first paragraph if necessary – was invaluable. Two words were always better than four, and short, simple sentences were more effective for any newspaper reader, whether of *The Times* or the *Daily Mirror*.

While that discovery was comforting, my growing concern over my role on the newspaper was matched, it seemed, by the news editor, David Tytler, who came to me one day and said, 'What are you supposed to be doing exactly? I have no idea what stories to throw in your direction.'

I acknowledged that I needed time to bed in but that eventually stories would begin to flow. He was remarkably understanding and went away apparently reassured.

I was saved by Peter Wright, a retired senior MI5 officer whose dynamite memoir, *Spycatcher*, caused mayhem in the British intelligence world and panic in the government and throughout Whitehall. The retired spy, living in Tasmania, provided me with my first real story for *The Times*. It also sparked what would become for me an abiding interest in the whole business of intelligence and espionage. As soon as the story broke that Wright was hunting for a publisher and that *Spycatcher* was full of juicy details that drove a seventy-ton tank through the Official Secrets Act, I went to the news desk and said, 'This story is mine.' No one demurred. It was November 1986. My career at *The Times* took off.

Peter Wright's book famously claimed that MI5 bugged and burgled its way around London. However, in November 1986, the story was not so much about the content of the book, which was as yet unpublished, but the desperate attempts being made by the government to stop publication in Australia. Wright had a wooden shack in Tasmania and the only photograph available of him showed him wearing a broad-brimmed hat with corks dangling around the brim to keep off the flies. He'd obviously gone native. Sir Robert Armstrong, Cabinet Secretary, had been selected to present the government's case in the New South Wales Supreme Court.

All Sir Robert's efforts in court seemed doomed to fail. One way or another, Peter Wright was going to have his insider revelations published. The momentum was unstoppable. Everyone wanted to read *Spycatcher*, especially Fleet Street hounds like me.

Some of the unauthorised disclosures had already been published in 1981 in another book, *Their Trade is Treachery*, by my old colleague Chapman Pincher. Peter Wright had been his prime source for the bestselling book, which, among other things, claimed that a former head of MI5, Sir Roger Hollis, had been a KGB spy. Peter Wright was a paranoid individual and he imparted all his conspiratorial musings to Pincher, although his involvement in the Pincher book was not widely known at the time of its publication. I rang Pincher when the *Spycatcher* story broke and asked him about Wright's role behind the scenes for his book in 1981. I wanted to know whether he had paid the former MI5 officer for his contributions to *Their Trade is Treachery*. He told me that Thatcher's Government had known Wright was the main source for his book and that ministers had acquired a copy of his book prior to publication. The British Government, he said, could have taken legal action to serve an injunction on his book, which he freely admitted breached the Official Secrets Act on every page. No action was taken. Pincher then admitted to me that Wright had received fifty percent of the royalties on the book. The money was to be paid to a front company of consultants. But there was only one consultant, and that was Peter Wright.

The extraordinary collaboration between Pincher and Wright began with a meeting at a secret address in Britain in 1980. A mutual friend, Lord Victor Rothschild, who was himself a former senior MI5 officer, had arranged for Wright to fly to Britain from Tasmania. It seemed Lord Rothschild may have paid for the flight. This led to a second meeting, this time in Tasmania, where Pincher spent two weeks debriefing Wright about his allegations that MI5 was filled with traitors. All of these secret goings-on were revealed in a front page story I wrote for *The Times* on the 24th of November 1986. It provided a new angle to the British Government's fight to stop the publication of *Spycatcher*. If Thatcher's Government knew Wright had spilled all his secrets to Pincher six years earlier and taken no action against him, why were they making such a fuss in an Australian court to prevent the world from reading the revelations in his own memoir? Well, of course, it's one thing for a journalist to write about claimed treachery in MI5, whatever the source for the material, but quite another for a former member of the Security Service to pen his personal allegations from his own experience while working as a government employee.

Wright read my story in Tasmania and issued a statement, which he sent to *The Times,* claiming that the report in the paper about him receiving fifty percent of the royalties for the Pincher book must have been 'placed in the public domain by the British Government in an effort to discredit me'. But my only source for the story was my friend Pincher, who was more than happy to talk to me. In his statement, Wright very kindly confirmed for me that Lord Rothschild *had* paid for his trip to Britain in 1980. 'He sent me a first-class air ticket,' Wright wrote. He also revealed that it was Lord Rothschild who had suggested approaching Pincher to write a book about Sir Roger Hollis that might then force the British Government to launch an investigation.

'We had dinner with Pincher and discussed it. I was terrified of getting into trouble. Victor assured me it was going to be all right. He told me that he would arrange for his Swiss banking facilities to pay me half of the royalties from the book. He knew I was in financial difficulties and I was grateful for this assistance. It was not the motive behind my helping Pincher, rather a helpful incidental benefit,' he wrote in his statement.

I later learnt that that first meeting in Britain between Pincher and Wright had taken place at Lord Rothschild's home. *The Times'* disclosures about the Pincher/Wright collaboration in 1980 and the involvement of such a distinguished and respected figure as Lord Rothschild added spice to the theatrical drama going on in the New South Wales court.

Wright was a strange creature. Whitehall saw him as a traitor – not an espionage traitor, of course, but someone who had betrayed the rules of secrecy. But buried in his head was a crusading yearning to put right what he believed was an injustice, the failure of the British Establishment to accept that a senior member of MI5 had worked for the Russians. He was convinced beyond doubt that Sir Roger Hollis had been a Russian spy. But he had no real evidence. What he did have was a series of circumstantial bits and pieces which he believed pointed the finger of suspicion at Sir Roger. Pincher had become convinced of Wright's arguments and followed the same line. No one else fitted the bill, according to their argument, and if there was a spy at a senior level in MI5 it had to be the man at the top.

The trouble is, when chasing shadows in the intelligence world it is often too easy to start with a preconception, then surround it with a mass of circumstantial evidence, and before you know where you are you have a guilty man. A touch of paranoia adds to the soup of suspicion. James Jesus Angleton, the counter-intelligence chief in the CIA at the same period, was in a similar mould to Peter Wright, convinced that traitors were everywhere. The KGB had been brilliant at recruiting some of Britain's intelligence officers during the Cold War but there was never any hint by Russian spy defectors or other persuasive sources that Sir Roger Hollis had been anything but a loyal servant of his country.

In Wright's shack in Tasmania there was a framed Latin quotation on a wall which read: '*Dilexi justitiam et odi iniquitatem, propterea morior in ixilio*' ('I have loved justice and hated iniquity, therefore I live in exile'). By the time his book had burst into print, despite all the attempts to stop the publication of his insider memoirs by Her Majesty's Government, Wright was a sick old man in his seventies who needed a stick to support his slow, painful steps. When I eventually acquired a copy of *Spycatcher,* delivered to my desk via a roundabout route that began in the US, I found it a riveting read. It was not written for the general public and was scorned by discerning book reviewers, but for curious journalists like me it unravelled an extraordinary world of conspiracy, darkness and intrigue.

My growing fascination with spooks, past and present, was cemented by a special visit to the headquarters of MI5, the domestic Security Service, in the company of Charlie Wilson. He had been invited to lunch with Patrick Walker, who had taken over as director-general of MI5 in 1987, and he asked to bring me along. MI5 was then based in Gower Street in a rather dilapidated building not far from University College Hospital. There were numerous other MI5 offices dotted around London, but Gower Street was where Patrick Walker and his board of directors were housed. We were escorted in an ancient lift up to the third floor to a door marked 'Directors' Dining Room'. The editor and I were introduced by Walker to his board of directors and we sat down for lunch. I remember one of the directors sitting opposite me looked exceedingly pasty-faced, with dry hair that may never have been shampooed.

Another director had a watch chain straddled across his waistcoat. The lunch menu reminded me of school. The conversation was carefully scripted. No secrets were divulged – but I hadn't exactly expected to come away with a notebook of future splashes. It was all off the record, unattributable, between Charlie and me and the four walls. Visiting the Gower Street headquarters on that occasion made me feel like I was entering a slightly musty gentleman's club where people wandered the corridors burdened by state secrets.

Some years later, this all changed when MI5 moved from Gower Street into the interior-modernised Thames House overlooking the river, down the road from Parliament Square. Apart from the overdose of security, the new premises are like any other modern office building, full of young, fresh-faced people in shirtsleeves. Gower Street was positively Dickensian by comparison, an old, creaking building with dark corners, redolent of a different and more mysterious era. No wonder Peter Wright became so paranoid.

In 1987, I was appointed defence correspondent on *The Times* after the previous incumbent had decided he wanted to return to the part of the country he loved most, Cheshire, and to be the paper's northern correspondent. Charlie Wilson called me up to his office on the first floor of the old rum warehouse to give me the news. I had already been writing a number of defence-related stories in my capacity as Whitehall correspondent. I told Charlie

Wilson that I wanted to hang on to intelligence issues as part of my remit in the new job. I was reluctant for someone else, perhaps my successor as Whitehall correspondent, to grab the intelligence coverage. The editor agreed, and in fact I was not immediately replaced as Whitehall correspondent. The role lay dormant.

The paper was blessed with some of the best specialist writers in Fleet Street: Robin Oakley, political editor, later succeeded by the inestimable Philip Webster; Frances Gibb, queen of the legal affairs correspondents; Nigel Hawkes, who had moved from *The Observer* to be science editor; and Michael Binyon, a longstanding foreign correspondent who was diplomatic editor and also one of the ablest and quickest leader writers in the business. Over the years, I worked with and became friends with a host of other talented specialists, including Jill Sherman (politics and Whitehall), who joined *The Times* the same week as me, Richard Ford (home affairs), Stewart Tendler and Sean O'Neill (crime), John O'Leary and David Charter (education), Dalya Alberge (arts) and Rosemary Bennett (social affairs).

Getting contacts in the right places was key to all our jobs. My intelligence beat was one of the most difficult to crack. Although MI5 was a publicly-acknowledged service, it was still an agency that thrived in the shadows. The Secret Intelligence Service, MI6, was still officially non-existent. When I started writing about intelligence issues, MI6 was housed in a building almost as old and unsightly as its sister service's headquarters in Gower Street. Century House, a relatively modest tower block that was a shortish walk from Waterloo Station, was the hub of MI6's overseas spying operations. It was only in 1992 that the Thatcher Government put it on record that it had an overseas espionage service. The chief of SIS was announced, a man who wrote every missive in green ink and signed, simply, 'C'. It took another two years for MI6 to be enshrined in the statute books.

This was when the service became subject to parliamentary scrutiny and greater accountability. With the passing of the Intelligence Services Act, MI6 moved from its backwater office block, Century House, to an exotically designed 'palace' at Vauxhall Cross, close to Vauxhall Bridge. The building, which had not been designed for MI6 but was available, quickly became known as Ceausescu Towers. This was in memory of the architectural extravagance of Nicolae Ceausescu, the former autocratic communist leader of Romania who built himself a vast palace in the centre of Bucharest.

The late '80s and early '90s were filled with intelligence stories, and I took full advantage of the contacts I continued to make, especially at the Foreign Office, Home Office and Ministry of Defence. Bizarrely, the only intelligence service with a press office was GCHQ, the Government Communications Headquarters at Cheltenham, perhaps the most secret of the three agencies. But the responsibility of its press officers was to comment on aspects that affected the local area, such as employment and building plans, rather than on the operations and functions of GCHQ's staff.

CHAPTER 6
AND SO TO WAR

From 1990 onwards, it was war. In August, we had planned as a family to go for a two-week holiday to the Greek island of Zante. Our three sons were growing up fast; Sam was fifteen, Chris, twelve and Jamie, ten. The holiday was paid for and we were all set to go when President Saddam Hussein invaded Kuwait. It became clear very rapidly that this was a step too far by the ambitious Iraqi dictator in the eyes of the Western alliance. Saddam had been supported during his eight-year war with his Iranian neighbour in the 1980s but was now seen as a dangerous despot thumbing his nose at the West. He must have calculated in his Baghdad cocoon, surrounded by advisers who didn't dare to raise doubts about his strategy, that he could get away with snatching Kuwait's northern oil fields, which he had always felt belonged to Iraq. From the moment the Iraqi troops advanced across the border into Kuwait, my life became overwhelmed with the prospect of a full-scale land war between Iraq and a coalition of nations persuaded by the US to join an alliance to liberate the Kuwaitis from their Iraqi occupiers.

My holiday plans had to be scrapped. Although the build-up of coalition troops in Saudi Arabia, the proposed launch-pad for the US-led assault on the Iraqi invasion force, was going to take a long time, Simon Jenkins, who had succeeded Charlie Wilson as editor of *The Times* in 1990, decided he couldn't do without his defence correspondent, even for two weeks. *The Times* covered the costs of the cancelled holiday and my family went off to the Isle of Wight with friends. I stayed chained to my office desk and then ventured off to Saudi Arabia to report on the arrival of troops from so many different countries that the Saudi desert became a pageant of individual military camps, each with their national flags and customs.

The Iraqi invasion had begun at two o'clock in the morning on the 2nd of August. Within about twelve hours of crossing Kuwait's northern border, the Iraqi troops, led by the Republican Guard Corps, fiercely loyal to Saddam, had taken control of most of the capital. Around 30,000 troops, the equivalent of two divisions, including armoured brigades equipped with Soviet-made tanks, were used in the main attack across the desert towards Kuwait City. It was a ruthless, well-planned operation. It was the first time in modern history that an Arab nation had invaded another to take total control. Within twenty-four hours, there were warlike noises emanating from Washington. The White House was, rightly, fearful of the prospect of Saddam's forces marching south into Saudi Arabia. President George H.W. Bush started ringing around alliance capitals to gauge enthusiasm for taking on the Iraqis. But Pentagon and US Army officials were quick to point out the challenges ahead if a liberation force were to be assembled to drive the Iraqis out of Kuwait. A US Army official I spoke to said: 'It would be a logistical nightmare. We have no infrastructure in the region.'

Despite all the misgivings, Saddam forced President Bush's hand. He had deployed seven divisions, the equivalent of about 120,000 troops, on Iraq's southern borders, far more than was needed to carry out the lightning strike into Kuwait. With two of the divisions occupying Kuwait City and other key sites, that left between 80,000 and 90,000 troops poised on the border. Saddam might have had his eye on Bahrain or Qatar or the United Arab Emirates, but the jewel in the crown for him was clearly Saudi Arabia.

Saddam in control of Saudi's oil wealth was not a prospect that could be contemplated by the West, which largely relied on the Royal Kingdom for its energy supplies. The swift decision by the Saudi rulers to allow American troops to be based in the country to defend the kingdom against possible attack provided an instant solution for the US. It must also have delivered the biggest shock to Saddam since he had begun to plan the invasion of Kuwait. Saudi Arabia, Custodian of the Two Holy Mosques of Islam, at Mecca and Medina, allowing American troops with their western morals and values onto such sacred territory? Saddam surely could never have envisaged that happening. It put him off his stride; when the US, backed by Britain, started flying troops into Saudi Arabia,

Saddam hesitated. Instead of ordering his huge invasion force on the border to advance into Saudi Arabia, seizing his moment while the West stuttered and prevaricated, he played a waiting game.

The Saudi decision was so crucial that the Iraqi dictator must have spent his days raging at his advisers for failing to warn him that Riyadh was capable of such treachery to the Muslim world. Saddam's hesitation proved fatal, and a blessing to the US and its burgeoning coalition. It provided the time so desperately needed to stuff the Saudi desert with troops and tanks and armoured personnel carriers and all the other paraphernalia of war.

In September 1990, I flew to Saudi Arabia to take stock of the coalition's preparations for war with Saddam. I was particularly interested to see how enthusiastic the Arab components of the coalition were in facing up to the man they all feared and hated. Saddam Hussein was suffering from domination disease. He wanted to be the supreme leader of the Arab world. Were Saudi and Egyptian troops, for example, going to play a crucial role in stamping on Saddam's ambitions? Were they deployed in the desert as a symbolic gesture of togetherness with the Americans or would they be genuine fighting units, ready to fire on their Arab brothers?

In Dhahran, southern Saudi Arabia, which was a hive of American military activity, a huge US public relations organisation had acquired a fleet of battle buses to take reporters from all over the world up to the frontline. I travelled in one of these buses with an assortment of reporters. It was like a jolly day out. It was baking hot but we were well supplied with water bottles. Our destination was about thirty miles from the Saudi-Kuwaiti border. The driver, a skinny Saudi, had looked blankly at us as we all scrambled in to grab a seat in the sweltering, dusty heat. After about an hour of driving along a precarious raised-up sandy track, with a steep fall on either side, several of us noticed that the driver's head was beginning to flop to one side. Then his body began to sway, and at the same time, the bus swerved from left to right, dangerously close to the steep incline. The bus, with at least forty reporters on board, was heading for a premature and potentially fatal journey's end. We all cried out with alarm and shouted at the driver to stop. His head jerked upright. Suddenly aware that he was still in charge of the battle bus, he slammed on the brakes, and the vehicle came to a halt across the track. We were in a desert wasteland, not a tent in sight. There was an explosion of voices as the reporters, relieved that they were not the first casualties of war, began to wonder what the hell to do. A Swedish reporter at the back of the bus provided the answer. A cool dude with long blond hair, he informed us that he had an HGV (heavy goods vehicle) licence and could take over driving the bus. We all instantly approved, and the Swede moved up to the front and pushed the driver into another seat. The Saudi could speak no English, but he got the message, and within seconds he was fast asleep. Our Swedish colleague settled into the driver's seat and off we went.

A few hundred yards off the desert highway running northeast from Hafar al-Batin to the Kuwaiti border, we found the commander of the Saudi Arabian 20th Armoured Brigade. He was in a jovial mood but was anxious to underline the fact that while the brave Saudi troops were positioned relatively close – about forty miles from the nearest crescent-shaped line-up of Iraqi tanks the other side of the frontier – the Americans were much farther back. Brigadier-General Turki al-Nefie pointed southwards and said, 'The Americans are far, far away.'

With the threat of an Iraqi armoured invasion of Saudi Arabia appearing to recede, it was sound politics for the Saudi commanders and their Arab comrades-in-arms to distance themselves from the Americans both militarily and geographically. General Turki addressed us from a roughly-hewn lectern inside his tented brigade headquarters, which consisted of a bunker with chipboard walls and bright yellow, flowered cloth across the ceiling. He was responsible for up to 15,000 Saudi troops located in two positions on the frontline, one stretched out beyond his brigade HQ, and the second one about twelve miles farther north. Their nearest neighbours in this northern province of Saudi Arabia included units from Syria, Egypt, Morocco and the Gulf states. When I went to visit the Egyptians I found an encampment of about 2,000 soldiers. All the troops I saw were walking around with fixed bayonets, as if ready for anything that might emerge through the desert haze. 'Whatever orders I am given, I will carry them out,' declared their commander, Colonel Abdel Rahim Mohammed.

The long period of troop build-up meant that for months there was a strange sense of ambiguity and uncertainty among the men in uniform scattered around in their campsites. The main focus to begin with was to provide protection to Saudi Arabia. The British force, which initially consisted of an armoured brigade with Challenger 1 tanks, was deployed in a defensive capacity, to deter Saddam from any further land-grabs in the region. The troops and armoured vehicles were not deployed to fight the Iraqis in Kuwait, although it was clear that it would only take a decision by Thatcher and her war cabinet to switch the mission from defensive to offensive. Saddam will have made that calculation, even if he hadn't read *The Times'* daily reports. As a result, he poured more of his Republican Guards into Kuwait as a challenge to the West. Stories began to emerge of Iraqi acts of brutality inside Kuwait as the occupying forces trampled on the Kuwaiti citizens and destroyed their properties. Saddam hated the Kuwaitis.

I went with Patrick Bishop of the *Daily Telegraph* to Khafji, a town on the Saudi/Kuwaiti border, to interview refugees who had been escaping from Kuwait, and witnessed a bizarre sight. Coming through the border checkpoint was a long line of expensive Chevrolets, Buicks and Mercedes. I described them as 'limousine refugees'. For some reason, the Iraqi occupiers had allowed them to make the seventy-five-minute drive from Kuwait City to the border unimpeded. However, there was a catch. When they reached a checkpoint about six miles from the border, they were ordered to hand over their passports, driving licences and any other documents which proved they were Kuwaiti citizens.

It was an ominous move. Baghdad wanted Kuwaitis to leave their country, never to return. It was President Saddam Hussein's version of the final solution, seizing, robbing, threatening and finally exiling Kuwaiti citizens from their own country.

Saddam referred to Kuwait as the '19th Province', and he was making it clear to the US and its coalition partners that he had every intention of absorbing Kuwait into Iraq's fold. By now Saddam had at least twenty-five divisions either in Kuwait or in an area of southern Iraq within relatively easy reach of the Kuwaiti border – a total of 300,000 troops and about 3,000 tanks; a formidable force.

It was not surprising that many of the refugees I spoke to said they couldn't understand why the multinational force spreading out in the Saudi desert did not launch an attack to save Kuwait from being plundered by the Iraqis. But setting up a coalition, sorting out the command structure, drawing up the battle plan and ensuring a huge support framework was in place to fuel and feed an army on the move all took time, and the Kuwaitis had to be patient.

There was little doubt in my mind in September 1990 that the coalition was being formed to drive the Iraqis out of Kuwait. Mrs Thatcher, with the Falklands War under her belt, was never going to be satisfied with just protecting Saudi Arabia while leaving the poor Kuwaitis to their fate under the boot of Saddam's troops. She didn't know, of course, that in a matter of two months she was to be ousted as prime minister, deserted by her senior Cabinet ministers. The Gulf War, as it became known, was not to be her war after all. She made many of the key decisions about Britain's military contributions to the coalition, but it was to be John Major, her successor, who donned the robes of war once the decision was taken to liberate Kuwait. The tears she shed in the back seat of her prime ministerial car as she was driven out of Downing Street were not just for the loss of her job after eleven years at Number 10 but also, I suspect, because of the timing of her ousting by her erstwhile colleagues. She was responsible for sending men and women in uniform to war, and I'm sure she would have dearly wanted to remain their political leader to see it through to a successful conclusion.

Despite the Egyptian commander's claim that the Americans were 'far, far away', I found them in the northeast of Saudi Arabia: three brigades from the famous 82nd Airborne Division. They, like everyone else in the desert, were training hard every day, trying to acclimatise in the sweltering conditions, and waiting for the politicians to make up their minds. Among them were two British soldiers, a captain and a sergeant, who were on secondment to the division. The Americans were lucky to have them. Both had served in the Falklands War and knew what it was like to come under fire. Because the Cold War was never a war as such, the vast majority of American and other NATO troops had never experienced combat. Young officers had become generals without firing a shot in anger. So these two men had tales to tell and their young American comrades-in-arms were fired up by their Falklands experiences. The captain, who gloried in the name of Giles Orpen-Smellie, had been injured in the right elbow by a ricochet while brewing tea on Mount Longdon during the assault by the 3rd Battalion Parachute Regiment (3 PARA) on the key Argentine position in the Falklands. Sergeant Stephen Bardsley, serving with 2 PARA, saved a soldier's life while attacking Argentine machine gun bunkers during the battle for Goose Green, for which he was awarded the Military Medal.

The 82nd Airborne was the first American unit to deploy to Saudi Arabia. Thirty-year-old Captain Orpen-Smellie and thirty-three-year-old Sergeant Bardsley were, as a consequence of their secondment, the first British combat soldiers to arrive in the desert. The British ground forces assigned for Saudi Arabia had yet to deploy. Like all British soldiers, the two men loved their tea and the captain had brought out his own supply of Earl Grey. The American soldiers, much to their disgust, only drank coffee. 'I may be with an American unit but I've stayed totally British,' Captain Orpen-

Smellie said with a smile.

The only way to find the Syrian forces was to drive twenty or so miles into the desert, following intermittent signposts consisting of small white wooden arrows on a blue background attached to a dented oil drum. On the day I visited them it was the first time the Syrians had allowed western journalists into their encampment. There were men there, including Brigadier-General Deeb Mohamed Dhaher, the brigade commander, who had fought the Israelis on the Golan Heights in the 1973 war, and again in a famous tank battle in Lebanon at Ain Dara in August 1982. Like most of his men, the general wore a skull and crossbones badge on his jacket to denote 'danger and death', as well as a golden parachute with wings and a star on top as proof of many freefall drops. These were tough-looking men from Syrian special forces, but it was not clear what their role was to be. The general said they were there to protect Saudi Arabia, but would they join a US-led, Western-dominated force into Kuwait to attack the Iraqis? The 2,000-strong brigade only appeared to be armed with AK47 Kalashnikovs. 'If we are given orders to go on the offensive then we are ready to do so. But we hope that Saddam will die soon,' the Syrian general said.

The Syrian presence, located about fifteen miles east of Saudi Arabia's 20th Armoured Brigade in the northern province, may just have been symbolic. But the Americans were counting on having as many coalition partners as possible, especially from the Arab world, to demonstrate to the doubters in the international community that this upcoming war was not some half-baked Washington-inspired plot to topple an unpopular Arab leader but was focused on a just and justifiable mission, backed by Arab leaders, to liberate Kuwait from Baghdad's brutal occupiers. 'It is difficult and embarrassing to have to fight the Iraqis,' the Syrian commander told me, 'but they took the law into their own hands and that is why we felt obliged to come here and to defend the Saudis.'

The desert in Saudi Arabia is staggeringly beautiful. During the day, in the intense heat, it is impossible to spot a single cloud in the sky. Just when you think you have seen one, it turns out to be a dust cloud. Travelling across the desert, the dust was so thick that the tanks, tents and lorries that appeared regularly on the horizon vanished. Then it cleared again and the shimmering outlines were once more visible and recognisable. At night, the vast sky was emblazoned with so many trillions of stars that it looked as if they were having to jostle for space. Saudi men would drive every night out of Dhahran in their vehicles and sit around on the sand, gazing at the spectacle, oblivious of the gathering armies around them.

Having so many Americans pouring into Dhahran posed quite a problem for Saudi Arabia. Not that the country had been devoid of US nationals. There had been about 80,000 Americans working and living in Saudi Arabia before the arrival of combat troops. The main difficulty was that some of the soldiers were women and they used to wander around the foyers of the hotels in Dhahran in their uniforms. Saudi women were not even allowed to drive, let alone don combat uniforms and fight for their country. The Americans and their Western comrades were all warned to beware of stepping on cultural sensitivities. Apart from a supposedly private event in which four scantily-clad dancing girls performed 'for the boys' at the US consulate in Dhahran, which was disclosed by CNN to its viewers, including the inveterate watcher of the American TV channel, Saddam himself, there were few incidents to worry the authorities.

The main sensitivity was over the command of the rapidly-growing multinational force settling into positions across the Saudi desert. It was clear that war was coming. The US had selected the biggest man they could find to command the American forces in Saudi Arabia: General 'Stormin' Norman' Schwarzkopf. He was actually the automatic choice for the job because he was commander of US Central Command, whose security responsibilities included Saudi Arabia and Kuwait. But it somehow seemed appropriate that the huge task of commanding a mighty coalition should be placed in the hands of a man built like a giant with a thrusting chin, a voice capable of mastering any parade ground and the swagger of General Patton.

Stormin' Norman was already secretly

planning what was to become known as the 'left hook' strategy – a cunning plan to deceive the Iraqis and deliver a blow of such proportions to Saddam's so-called 'elite' Republican Guard that he hoped they would all run home to their mothers rather than confront him with the 'mother of all battles', which the Iraqi dictator had boasted about so often.

The command fix was sorted out. General Schwarzkopf would take charge but work alongside his Saudi counterpart. Of course, Stormin' Norman was the dominating personality. The British Government eventually appointed Lieutenant-General Sir Peter de la Billière to take command of the UK force. He had spent twelve of his thirty-eight years in the military with the SAS and was more decorated than any other soldier. But, perhaps as a consequence of his many years in covert operations, he was no Schwarzkopf. He was a quiet, hard-thinking man with a quizzical expression on his face; not an easy commander to get to know and with none of the dash and presence of Stormin' Norman. It was probably a good choice, nevertheless. He had to work intimately with the Americans, who had always loved and admired the SAS. Sir Peter arrived in Saudi Arabia already endowed with the mystique of the British Army's most famous regiment.

I returned to London convinced that within the next few months there would be a land war, possibly including classic-style tank battles between the US-led coalition and Saddam's forces. As with the Falklands War in 1982, I was to cover the proposed Kuwait liberation campaign from London. Simon Jenkins wanted his defence correspondent to be always at hand and to be ready to pull together the mass of material that would come out of Kuwait, as well as commentating on developments and providing insight and guidance as the campaign progressed. Richard Beeston was to be the courageous reporter to write from Baghdad, and others, including the veteran war reporter Philip Jacobson, were to be dispatched to cover the war embedded with military units.

The politics and diplomacy continued in the hope that Saddam might pull back his troops from Kuwait. Saudi Arabia had been saved from occupation by the rush of Western fighter aircraft and troops to defend the Saudis from the same fate as the Kuwaitis, but the Iraqis were still on the rampage in Kuwait City, destroying and plundering with impunity. Saddam's forces were also digging in in southern Iraq in huge numbers, indicating that he was prepared to take on the Americans and their allies.

In November, President George H.W. Bush announced that significant reinforcements had been sent to Saudi Arabia, including three more aircraft carriers, up to 200,000 more troops and 700 additional tanks. No one in the Pentagon had any real doubts about being able to defeat Saddam, but with the war of words going on between Baghdad and Washington there was an element of unease creeping in. What if something unpredictable happened? What if Saddam ordered a chemical and biological attack? Reinforcements would add not just additional firepower to the coalition forces but also put new pressure on Baghdad. Britain followed suit and announced a doubling of forces, bringing troop numbers up to a full division of 25,000 men. The man responsible for commanding the division – the 1st Armoured Division – was possibly the British Army's best-looking and most glamorous officer, as well as being an astute tactician and brilliant strategist. Major-General Rupert Smith spoke in the tones of an upper-class gentleman. He was so charismatic he made Lieutenant-General Sir Peter de la Billière, his overall boss, look dour by comparison.

As the war drums increased in volume, I went to Paris to cover a summit of the thirty-four-nation Conference on Security and Cooperation in Europe (CSCE) which was to sign a treaty heralding the end of the Cold War and a new era of democratic freedom and market economies spreading throughout eastern Europe. It was an historic event. Everyone was there: Bush, Gorbachev, President Mitterrand and Thatcher.

None of us covering this symbolic glad-handing had any idea that we were to witness another historic event. Thatcher and her summit companions were all due at a fancy dinner in the evening but, first, she was driven to the British Embassy to discover how the first round of voting had gone back in London for her continued leadership of the Tory Party, and thus, her continued life as Britain's prime minister. I was purely an observer. My colleague from the paper's political team, Nicholas Wood, had the task of reporting the event from the embassy, but he filled me in on the mathematics which made it possible that the Iron Lady would not gain the outright majority she needed to win the first round of the leadership challenge and eliminate the need for a second. Her cabinet colleagues, headed by Michael Heseltine, the only man in living memory to have walked out of a Cabinet meeting in high dudgeon before resigning, were ganging up against her, and she had made the tactical, though understandable, error of being away when the vote was being orchestrated across the Channel. She had wanted to participate in the Paris gathering, but the timing could not have been worse for her.

I joined the collection of reporters and photographers at the embassy, but I was too late to get a close-up view of events and was stuck at the back. But, being over 6ft, I still had a good view of what was about to happen. I was hemmed in by frustrated and pushy photographers from around the globe who had also arrived late but desperately needed a good vantage point. They began setting up their stepladders and each climbed to the top rung, balancing precariously with their multiple cameras swinging from side to side. The rest of us were jostled and jabbed and generally pushed out of the way. I sympathised with their frustration. The early boys were all encamped below and to the side of the steps leading down from the embassy building, ready for the electric moment when Thatcher was expected to emerge and make some form of statement.

Nothing happened for about fifteen minutes. John Sergeant, the BBC political correspondent, with his instantly recognisable hang-dog face, was standing around at the bottom of the steps, in prime position. As we all waited for the appearance of the Iron Lady, a baby started to cry. It seemed bizarrely out of place. Hundreds of reporters and photographers were crammed into the limited space, like a packed auditorium in an outside theatre. The sound of a baby perhaps reminded everyone that the impending drama was taking place in an affluent, relatively quiet residential area where other people were carrying on their normal lives.

Suddenly, there she was, flanked by suited aides. She was wearing an elegant dark green jacket, ready for her evening out. She seemed taken aback by the assembled crowd and the thunderclap of camera flashes. She took what I can only describe as faltering steps downwards, heading roughly in the direction of John Sergeant who, because he was carrying a microphone, seemed to the prime minister to be the obvious person to head towards. It wasn't a pre-planned situation. So often, after an important meeting involving prime ministers and presidents, the media are informed beforehand that there will be a photographic and/or reporting opportunity, and sometimes individual correspondents will be delegated to ask a question. This event, however, wasn't just impromptu, it was totally unscripted and fairly chaotic. Thatcher had been told that she had failed to get sufficient votes in the first ballot to win the leadership challenge outright. It was a mighty blow for her. She must have realised that the axe was falling on her career. But, keeping her eye on John Sergeant, she moved close to him and he shoved his microphone towards her. He asked for her reaction to the news from London. There was a total hush. The baby had stopped crying and the photographers on their step ladders were frozen, waiting to take the picture as she spoke. In true 'lady-not-for-turning' style, Thatcher told Sergeant and the rest of us craning our necks forward to pick up her words that she would 'fight on'.

Nick Wood started running down the road to file his report in time for the first edition. For once, I was under no pressure and stuck around to absorb the atmosphere. Thatcher had gone back into the building to review her future and to decide whether it was dignified to keep her name on the list for the second ballot. She was about to head off to a dinner for which she probably had little appetite. It was to be her last banquet as Britain's prime minister.

CHAPTER 7
SHOCK AND AWE

Just over a month before the US-commanded forces began to batter the Iraqi troops in Kuwait with sustained bombing from the air, I was back in the Saudi desert to spend time with the Desert Rats, the legendary name given to the British Army's 7th Armoured Brigade, led by Brigadier Patrick Cordingley. He was an incredibly nice man, almost too nice to command such a tough unit, courteous to a point, softly-spoken, relaxed, even-tempered and, to his undoing, too trusting. He was in the midst of final training for a full-scale land war and felt he had a duty to spell out to his visitors from Fleet Street that this might not be a walk-over. The Iraqis had built massive defences and it was known that Saddam possessed chemical weapons.

Before I had left London, *The Times* supplied me with an NBC (nuclear, biological, chemical) kit. It consisted of a bright yellow rubber suit and gasmask, which had been bought from some wise-guy 'specialist' military shopkeeper in East London for a few hundred pounds. I tried it on in the office but never managed to pull it up fully over my clothes. It clung to me like some sort of sadomasochist bodysuit. Everyone in the office had laughed their heads off, although it was in fact a serious business. I took it with me to Saudi Arabia. During the weeks I spent there before the war started, there were three chemical attack warnings while I was in the desert. But I gave up trying to engineer my body into the yellow S&M suit and just hoped for the best. Fortunately, all the alarms were false ones. The military had given me what looked like a large pen that, when instructed, I was supposed to stab into my leg. It was an antidote to nerve agents. Saddam was feared to have operationally-workable biological weapons and there were concerns he might pre-empt the US-led liberation invasion by launching some of them in our direction. I couldn't imagine ever having the courage to stab my leg, but I carried the pen around with me as if my life depended on it. I took the unused yellow bodysuit back with me to London and stored it in a box under my desk where it stayed for a couple of years and then mysteriously disappeared. I don't think *The Times* ever got its money back.

Brigadier Cordingley took the journalists into his confidence and what he said was potentially headline-making stuff. It was the sort of warning which the British Government and his bosses at the Ministry of Defence in Whitehall did not want to hear, let alone see splashed all over the front pages of the national newspapers. What he said was that he feared the British public was not prepared for the horrors of war and that 'under the worst scenario, British casualties could be high'. We all realised the significance of his remark, and unless it was written in context, it would look alarmist under a bold headline. The brigadier was doing what he sincerely felt needed to be done, to stop the 'Oh What a Lovely War' atmosphere back home and to remind people that soldiers were going to die.

'It seems to me that we have to prepare the British public for a particularly unpleasant war. There are going to be a lot of casualties and inevitably one has to be prepared for unpleasant things to unfold,' he said, speaking at the Desert Rats' headquarters about thirty miles west of Jubail, Saudi Arabia's main northeastern port.

His forthrightness was then made worse by a prediction from his chief of staff, Major Ewan Loudon, that if the 7th Armoured Brigade, and the 4th Armoured Brigade on its way out to Saudi Arabia, were used to tackle the Iraqi defensive positions in Kuwait, casualties among the fighting force could be as high as fifteen percent. For the British component, building up to a force of 25,000 troops, that could mean around 1,500 casualties 'under the worst scenario'. The word 'casualties', of course, covers both dead and injured, but that tends to get lost in the rush to paint as dramatic a picture as possible for the folks back home. Brigadier Cordingley added one more decisive point, but that also got lost in the excitement. He said that with any two armies 'of this size and with this sort of firepower, it's inconceivable that the casualties will not be large. *Hopefully it will all be one way* [my italics]'.

The trouble was that not all the reporters present when he made the remarks quoted him in full but selected the most damaging elements. What inevitably happened was that the majority of the stories published focused on his remark that there were going to be 'a lot of casualties'. I don't blame the reporters, the brigadier said what he said, but when he had finished speaking to us he made a special, perhaps rather naïve, request. He asked us not to get him into trouble and to write our stories carefully. We all liked him but the momentum for a big headline was unstoppable.

Unfortunately for him, his honesty was not appreciated either by ministers or by his military superiors, and when the headlines duly appeared the next day, he received a phone call and the biggest reprimand of his career. What had seemed right to him standing in the desert not far from the frontline looked defeatist in Whitehall. When we saw him the next day he seemed chastened and disappointed that, with some exceptions, including *The Times,* reporters had neglected to mention that he had expressed a hope that most of the casualties would be on the Iraqi side. It was a tough lesson for him. If he wanted every reporter to get that message across to the newspaper readers, he should have started off his casualty warning from a different angle, i.e. warning the Iraqis that they were facing huge casualties because of the awesome strength of the coalition forces, with an added note that there could be casualties on the coalition side, too. I don't think Whitehall would have minded that sort of message.

However, Brigadier Cordingley's burst of realism was eventually accepted in high places.

The Chief of the Defence Staff himself, Marshal of the Royal Air Force Sir David Craig, uttered a similar warning only two weeks later. Speaking to senior Russian officers at a military academy in Moscow, Sir David rejected the view that a war with Iraq could be over swiftly, and he, too, predicted that there could be 'substantial casualties'. His words added to the growing perception that, as the 15th of January – the United Nations deadline for Iraq to remove its forces from Kuwait – crept ever closer, the coalition of mix-and-match units lined up in the Saudi desert faced the prospect of a war lasting months. But in the lead-up to a war, no one really knows what is going to happen. For all his bluster, Saddam had no idea whether his Republican Guards would be a match for the Americans, and he had to make assumptions about how General Stormin' Norman would attack.

The American general's war plan was top secret. But Saddam and the rest of us presumed that there would be a full frontal attack on the Iraqi defensive positions in southern Kuwait, and probably a US Marine Corps assault on Kuwait City from the sea. That was the way it looked. But would there be a surprise? Every commander, however predictable the battlefield might seem, always wants an element of surprise up his sleeve. Stormin' Norman had the advantage on the surprise side. Unless the Iraqis launched forth en masse from their defensive positions to attack the coalition in Saudi Arabia, the US commander could choose when to start Kuwait's liberation. After the 15th of January deadline passed, the sense of anticipation in the Iraqi ranks must have been almost overwhelming. 'The Bear', as General Schwarzkopf was also known, kept them waiting for a couple of days and nights.

Operation Desert Storm began on the 17th of January. Night-time air raids were conducted by hundreds of aircraft, including America's mighty B52 bombers, F117A Stealth fighters and F15E bombers, Royal Air Force Tornado GR1s and Saudi F15s, as well as Tomahawk land-attack cruise missiles fired from US warships in the Gulf. Back in London, it was an awesome spectacle, but it also looked unreal. After five months of building up to war, the fact that it was actually happening and that the huge flashes in the sky were coming from the most modern bombs designed by the most sophisticated military coalition in history took time to grasp.

From the beginning of Operation Desert Storm, I found myself writing between 2,000 and 3,000 words a day. More by accident than design, I began to produce a daily commentary, having the luxury of benefiting from the mass of briefings and announcements from both sides: General Schwarzkopf's personal progress declarations complete with swagger stick and battlefield map, and Baghdad's desperate propaganda pronouncements claiming that every bomb dropped was landing on a children's hospital or baby milk factory.

Richard Beeston, filing from the danger zone

inside Baghdad, had the challenging task of telling the world where the bombs were falling while trying to distinguish between reality and Saddam's information henchmen who poured out their daily accusations. Baghdad's claims of victory against the US-led coalition reminded me of the constant statements from Buenos Aires during the Falklands War, which included claims that the Royal Navy had lost an aircraft carrier. Admiral Sir Terry Lewin, the Chief of the Defence Staff, had warned Thatcher that in the worst scenario she might have to endure the possibility of the loss of one of the two aircraft carriers sent out to the South Atlantic. But it never happened. Beeston in Baghdad and the rest of us in London were fully aware that Saddam would be exploiting whatever propaganda tools he had at his disposal to undermine the statements from Stormin' Norman that the campaign was progressing as planned.

General Schwarzkopf's secret plan, a left-hook advance to the west, coming round into southern Iraq to take the Republican Guard by surprise from the rear, effectively brought Baghdad's promised mother-of-all-battles to an end. The expected US Marine amphibious landing to attack the Iraqis in Kuwait City was a feint. As the Iraqi troops faced one way, their enemy skirted round their flank and popped up behind them.

In London, the band of defence correspondents had been tipped off about the left-hook tactic the day before it was launched

– but strictly on confidential operational grounds. We were not to write a word until the plan had been effectively accomplished. Robert Fisk, the veteran Middle East correspondent, in Saudi Arabia as a 'floater' (the name given to journalists covering the war without being attached to any military unit), was unaware of the secret plan and spotted a huge movement of troops and armoured vehicles heading off in a westerly direction. His story was published the next day in *The Independent*. Fortunately, either Saddam failed to read the report or considered it a propaganda move to deceive him.

When Operation Desert Storm ended with Baghdad's surrender, Martin Ivens, foreign editor at *The Times*, said he wanted to reward me for all my work by sending me off to Kuwait. I was a little surprised, as everyone else who had been working seven days a week had started planning their holidays. But it turned out to be an inspired decision. First of all, it gave me a chance to witness the aftermath of the war in Kuwait, and secondly, I came across a story that revealed what could have been a disaster for General Schwarzkopf and his planning team. I flew to Kuwait City airport in a C130 Hercules. The last few miles were like a scene from Dante's Inferno. Every oil well in sight was burning, torched by the Iraqis as they retreated, and the sky was filled with dense black smoke, which wrapped itself around the Hercules like a thick cloak. As the pilot steered his way through the swirling pollution and started to lose altitude, the airport came into view. It looked as if there was nowhere to land. The runways were pitted with craters, still smouldering, and the terminal building was blackened and twisted.

We landed safely and the next day I met up with a British Army captain to go off into the Kuwaiti desert in a Land Rover to do a battlefield trip – except that this was not like visiting a Second World War site. This was an area that, only a few weeks before, had been the location of the Iraqi Republican Guard defensive positions. The whole desert was littered with hundreds of detonated – and unexploded – cluster bombs, rockets, artillery shells and every munition imaginable that had been hurled at Saddam's troops from northern Saudi Arabia and from the air. Stepping round the cluster bombs as we walked across the desert was probably not the safest way of spending a day out, but here before me was the end result of all those flashes in the sky we had seen on television. But more interesting than the desert graveyard of bombs was the network of underground bunkers built by the Iraqis. The officers' bunkers were extraordinary. There were panelled oak doors and walls, leather armchairs and tables. Once the bombs started to fall I don't suppose these little comforts helped much to assuage the fear as they cowered twelve feet beneath the desert surface, but they provided an intriguing insight into Baghdad's officer class.

Over the next few days, I went in search of the British 1st Armoured Division, which was still encamped in the Kuwaiti desert. General Rupert Smith gave me a Sandhurst-style lecture on the war's tactics, an intellectual *tour de force* which filled my notebook with elegant phrases. But having written so many thousands of words on the campaign during the war, I felt the readers of *The Times* probably didn't need another splurge of military tactics. It was still fascinating to sit in his HQ and listen to the commander who had led a whole division into battle. I assumed he would one day become the chief of the defence staff. He had charisma and style and now the combat experience that so few of his fellow generals had enjoyed. He was a natural for Britain's most senior military appointment. But for a reason I never quite understood, he failed to make it to the very top. Instead of being promoted, in due course, to chief of the general staff and then chief of the defence staff, he was hived off to become Deputy Supreme Allied Commander Europe, a NATO job based in Mons, Belgium. That was his final posting. Sitting with him in Kuwait, it was easy to predict a more glittering career than a senior post in NATO – albeit an important one.

A genuine scoop presented itself while I was chatting with another British commander at his HQ in the Kuwaiti desert. Brigadier Christopher Hammerbeck, commander of 4th Armoured Brigade, part of 1st UK Armoured Division, and I were talking about the left-hook tactic and the participation of the British troops. The officer said it was a stroke of luck that the secret plan had not been prematurely exposed to Saddam's forces. He revealed that the theft of a laptop computer in Britain had led to fears that an undercover agent had betrayed the left-hook plan to Saddam.

I immediately knew what he was talking about. Months earlier, a Royal Air Force wing commander working at RAF's Strike Command in High Wycombe in Buckinghamshire had left his laptop in the boot of his car while he visited a car showroom in Acton, west London. When he returned he discovered that the windows of his Vauxhall Carlton had been broken and the rear seat pulled down. The laptop was gone. The RAF officer, Wing Commander David Farquhar, reported the theft. His job at the time was personal staff officer to Air Chief Marshal Sir Patrick Hine, who, with General Sir Peter de la Billière, was joint commander of the British forces in the Gulf. Wing Commander Farquhar was also the liaison link between Sir Patrick and General Schwarzkopf's staff in Riyadh. He was later court-martialled for the grave offence of leaving a sensitive piece of equipment unattended.

I had written about the theft at the time, although it was not that much of a story then. But now there was a sensational new ingredient. Brigadier Hammerbeck, chatting to me in the Kuwaiti desert, casually revealed that the stolen laptop had contained all the details of the 'left-hook' battle plan and the fake amphibious assault by the US Marines! For three weeks, General Schwarzkopf and his fellow British commanders had been on tenterhooks, wondering whether the theft had been carried out by an opportunist, without any ulterior motive other than stealing something from the boot of the car, or by an Iraqi secret agent looking out for the chance of grabbing the laptop of a senior British officer. 'The plan was frightfully secret. I wasn't allowed to bring my staff in the know. It was the best secret I've ever kept, and I'm a naturally garrulous person,' the brigadier told me.

Their fears were only assuaged when the thief posted the laptop to the Ministry of Defence with a message suggesting that the man responsible for the loss should be hanged. The thief, known as 'Andrew', was the only person in the world, outside the inner circle of military officers involved in the great left-hook plan, including Brigadier Hammerbeck, who knew that Saddam was going to be in for a shock. But all that came out much later, in June 1991, when the court martial took place.

However, I found out about the story in March 1991. It was such a good tale, I bade farewell to the commander and the Kuwaiti desert and got a lift back to Kuwait City airport in the hope of hitching a ride in a C130 Hercules to Dhahran in Saudi Arabia where I could book into a hotel and write my scoop. When I arrived at the airport, there were no planes heading for Dhahran in the next few hours. There was no electricity at the airport, so I couldn't file my story from there. I had to get to Dhahran.

It was late morning. I needed to reach Dhahran by late lunchtime to ring the office, warn them of the scoop and then write it. I knew they'd love it. I made my way across the destroyed airport until I reached one of the main exits. I hoped there would be a flow of traffic, so that I could stick my thumb out and get a lift to the nearest taxi rank in Kuwait. The road running alongside the perimeter fence of the airport was totally empty, both ways. I waited ten minutes. Then, in the far distance, I spotted through the heat haze some sort of vehicle approaching.

I stuck out my thumb, but the vehicle took a long time to reach me. It was a road sweeper! I just needed a lift into town, and with not a single car, lorry, truck, bus or tank in sight, I decided to thumb down the road sweeper. The turban-swathed driver looked down at me from his perched-up sitting position and grinned. I grinned back and said, in slow English, 'Journalist. I want taxi to Dhahran. Lift with you?' He kept grinning but, having apparently grasped what I wanted, beckoned me into his cab. Away we went – at 2mph – all the way to the nearest taxi rank. It was now lunchtime, but the time difference with London was in my favour. So, I thanked my road-sweeping friend and hopped out after he had swept up alongside a row of Cadillacs. Within minutes, I was on the road to Dhahran, travelling at a wonderful 60mph. The story was duly written in plenty of time and appeared on the front page of *The Times* the following morning.

One of my final trips before leaving the region was to Mutla Ridge, twenty miles northwest of Kuwait City. The road from the capital up towards Mutla Ridge was the escape route for thousands of Iraqi troops and civilians. As the US-led coalition advanced rapidly through Kuwait and westwards into southern Iraq, this route had become a traffic jam of panicking human beings, in and out of uniform. But American M1 Abrams tanks formed an armoured blockade at the end of the road, cutting off the escape route. As the convoy of vehicles headed north, US Apache attack helicopters and ground-attack aircraft opened up a relentless barrage of fire, like heavily-gunned American Wild West sheriffs, destroying, killing, burning and wounding for a period of several hours. The slaughter became a 'turkey shoot'. Nothing could survive the withering hail of cannon fire and exploding bombs.

The grossly charred bodies sitting in the driving seats and the passenger seats had been removed, although, bizarrely, there were two seemingly unaffected bodies lying across the road behind a fence. But the road to Mutla Ridge, which led to the southern Iraqi city of Basra, was a highway graveyard of blackened, twisted, crippled vehicles. It was the most gruesome sight I had ever seen. The smell of death was lingering in the air. The stink of defeat and fear rose from every gutted car, truck and bus. Standing in the total silence of death, it was impossible not to feel emotional about what had happened here. Was such carnage necessary? The convoy included many military vehicles, filled with Iraqi troops who had committed murder and torture in Kuwait during Saddam's occupation. But this vengeful ambush on a retreating army seemed, to me, unwarranted.

The mass killings, described in apocalyptic fashion by CNN and other broadcasters, compelled President George H.W. Bush to call a halt to the war. Victory had been achieved; it was now time to show compassion. As a result, the war came to an abrupt end. Any thoughts of continuing the march up to Baghdad and toppling Saddam were cast aside. President Bush's view, not shared by many senior military commanders in the coalition, was that this was a campaign to liberate Kuwait, not to bring regime-change to Iraq. That ambition was to return at a future date, when another President Bush – George W. – was in the White House. The war between England and France in the fourteenth and fifteenth centuries had lasted one hundred years. The war with Iraq in 1991 lasted exactly one hundred hours. Such was the awesome display of modern firepower.

CHAPTER 8
BALKANS GO UP IN FLAMES

In the winter of 1992, a group of British defence correspondents flew to Zagreb, capital of Croatia, in the first stage of a journey into Europe's new war zone. After the division of Yugoslavia, and with ex-Tito territories seeking independent status, war seemed inevitable, spurred by decades of religious, political and social hatreds in the region. Under the masterful dictatorship of the old communist marshal, these hatreds had been held in check. Now they were to explode. In the early 1990s (and until 1995, when the Dayton Accord enforced a retreat from all the murderous ethnic cleansing and brought about a form of political settlement), the region of Europe that had for long been a favourite tourist destination was a hotbed of tribal conflict. Into this dangerous mess marched United Nations peacekeepers, including British soldiers, to bring humanitarian aid to the civilian victims of the wholesale bloodletting.

For defence and war correspondents, the presence of so many different nations involved in the mission provided an opportunity to cover this complex and unpredictable conflict from a number of angles. But whether you were a British or an American or French or Swedish correspondent, it was imperative to do your homework before setting off for the danger zone. Some grasp of the cultural and political sensitivities and a feel for the historical context behind the ethnic killings were vital both for your own safety and for an appreciation of the story you had to write. Nevertheless, for my first visit to this region under fire, it was impossible to be fully prepared for what lay ahead.

The sense of dread and heavy anticipation affected all of us as we sat in a hotel bar in Zagreb and pondered why we had left the comforts of Whitehall to be immersed in a war where reporters not only had no protection but were already becoming targets of the fanatical ethnic cleansers. David Fairhall of *The Guardian,* Mark Laity of the BBC and David White of the *Financial Times* were among those in the bar who shared the same sense of foreboding as I did. Our destination the following day was Split in Croatia, then a day of preparations, including hiring a car, before travelling up through the mountains into Bosnia-Herzegovina, where Bosnian Serbs, Croats and Muslims were all killing each other. It was a war of families against families, of artillery shells and snipers' bullets against women and children. Rape was being carried out systematically as a weapon of war. We humble defence correspondents were veterans of covering wars but not in the line of fire. This was to be our first foray into a real-time battlefield, but one that was so complex, we knew it was possible that one wrong turn in the road could lead you into an unexpected ambush where a 'Press' card in the hand or a sticky 'Media' label on the side of the car provided no guarantee of safe passage.

When we eventually arrived in the Croatian coastal resort of Split, geographically relatively close to the war zone but a million miles from the death and destruction in neighbouring Bosnia, the sense of anticipation was put on hold. There were pavement cafés and restaurants, expensive cars and hotels and all the trappings of normal life. Only the airport gave a hint of what lay over the border. Military helicopters were parked everywhere, and UN trucks and white Toyota Land Cruisers drove in and out of the peacekeeping HQ outside the town. I always had feelings of déjà vu hopelessness when I saw UN peacekeepers all gathered together at their HQ. A carpark was stuffed with new Toyota four-by-fours and myriads of soldiers in varying uniforms wandering around like lost souls, with only their light blue berets to unite them in the common cause.

I went to Hertz and asked to rent a Russian Lada Niva. Journalist friends back in London said these were the best cars for Bosnia: tough, no fancy bits and a reliable engine for steep mountain tracks. They were boring and as invisible as you can get – not the sort of car an ethnic cleanser might take a fancy to. But every Lada Niva had already gone. The only car left was a dark blue executive Audi 80 saloon. I was desperate. I was due to set off early the next morning for Bosnia. Without thinking of potential consequences, I signed up for the Audi. The Hertz man asked me where I was planning to go and I replied that I would be driving around. He said I wouldn't be allowed to enter any war zone. But when I signed the paperwork and studied the insurance exclusions there was no specific reference to driving into Bosnia. I took the car and drove to my hotel to make final preparations for my journey the next day.

One visit was to the bank. I handed over 200 pounds and, in return, received a huge brick of freshly printed dinars. That was my first mistake. Well, actually, as I was to discover to my cost, my first mistake was the Audi. As soon as I arrived in Bosnia, I found that no one wanted dinars. They just dealt in US dollars. It's one of those golden rules for war correspondents: wherever you are in a war zone, take US dollars.

However, with my brick of Croatian currency in my jacket pocket, I went to see a man about a helmet. Richard Owen, the foreign editor, had supplied me with a flak jacket but no helmet. The Croatian had been recommended as the most reasonable helmet salesman in town. He handed me a standard helmet. Some reporters and photographers turned up with helmets that were shaped straight downwards over the brow like Second World War German models or Turkish Army headgear.

The next morning, at seven o'clock, I was in position outside the UN HQ, ready for the long drive through the mountains to reach Vitez, where the first detachments of British soldiers were already operating – or, at least, trying to operate against the worst possible odds. Their UN mission was being hindered every day by intransigent Bosnian Serbs who had carved out their territory and had little time for the well-meaning peacekeepers who wanted to deliver food to their enemies. The Audi 80 made it up the hills with relative ease. At the top, there was a huge expanse of flat terrain with lakes dotted around. There were no signs of warfare. Bosnia, I was to discover, was a beautiful, mountainous country with large areas unaffected by the civil war. But the journey down to Vitez, through Tomislavgrad and Gornji Vakuf, provided the first glimpse of what was tearing this country apart. Gornji Vakuf was like a Wild West town. You could feel the tenseness in the air. It was easy to imagine gunmen hiding behind the curtains of every house.

Gornji Vakuf was at the heart of the British supply route to Vitez, known to everyone as the Ho Chi Minh trail. A company of British soldiers from the 1st Battalion Cheshire Regiment as well as a squadron of Royal Engineers, were due to set up home in Vitez. But the Serbs had their eye on Gornji Vakuf, and if it fell into their hands, the British supply route would be vulnerable to attack. The Serb frontline sloped southwards into central Bosnia, not far from Vitez. With their artillery positions in the mountains of Vlasic and Komar, Vitez itself could just be in reach of their shells.

Tomislavgrad was a Croat town. Passing through in the Audi 80, I could see truckloads of Croat troops looking with hostile curiosity at my fancy car.

The main purpose of my first trip to Bosnia was to witness the arrival of the British Army's heavily armoured vehicles, which were to provide protection from indiscriminate or deliberate shellfire and small arms fire as the soldiers went about their business of escorting convoys of humanitarian aid around central Bosnia. But their arrival was not to be for another few days and I spent the time acquainting myself with the area.

One of the first visits was to a refugee camp in Posusje, southwest of Vitez, close to the Croatian border. There is no such thing as a happy refugee camp, and as soon as I saw old Muslim women queuing up outside the makeshift toilets that provided neither privacy nor dignity, it was impossible not to share in their anger and shame.

However, there was one extraordinary individual present in the camp who, at least in our eyes, provided some relief from the gloom and desperation that was so visible everywhere. The individual was an eleven-year-old girl called Jasmina. A refugee for five months, she had a clean, pretty face and shiny hair tied in a ponytail. Unlike the old women crying in the toilet queue, Jasmina shed no tears. With her large, innocent eyes, she gave us her life story. We had just arrived from our homes in England, where normal comforts were taken for granted, and here was a girl whose home was a crumbling, smelly, abandoned school, sharing her life with 700 Muslim refugees, sleeping on mattresses crammed into unheated classrooms, stairways and landings. She and her fellow refugees had been driven from their homes in northern Bosnia by rampaging Serbs. Jasmina was no longer an innocent child, yet she somehow seemed untouched by all the horrors she had already experienced in her eleven years. One of my journalist friends with me started weeping. He couldn't stop himself. He said he could hardly bear to talk to the girl.

Jasmina came from Prijedor near Banja Luka, a Serb stronghold in northern Bosnia. Her home had been ransacked and burnt to the ground. Her father, who owned a supermarket, was seized and thrown into a Serb concentration camp. Approximately 800 men were killed in her town. Of her father, she said, 'I know he's still alive. That's all. I want to see him again.' There were still no tears.

In a place of weeping, angry women, men with fear in their faces and children looking confused but resigned, Jasmina was an extraordinary example of the human spirit surviving against all the tragic odds thrown at her and her family. We all wanted to give her money, food, anything to brighten her life, and yet, to do so, somehow, would be like trying to rid ourselves of guilt, because soon we would be leaving the camp and she would wait for the next visitors to tell her sad story. My colleague who had cried remained inconsolable. I felt strangely uplifted, as if meeting Jasmina would help me to understand better what was happening to her country. Her sweet face and big eyes would stay with me as I wrote about the Bosnian War over the following three years.

When we left the refugee camp and drove

into the town of Posusje, it was like entering a different world. This was still Bosnia-Herzegovina but there were cafés with people drinking coffee and eating sandwiches. A black BMW cruised by. People were shopping. For them, the refugees in their midst might as well not have existed.

I returned to Split in Croatia the following day to witness the arrival of the British cavalry, represented by the 9th/12th Lancers, whose nine-tonne Scimitar armoured reconnaissance vehicles were being offloaded from a cargo ship in the Croatian port. The Lancers were to climb the mountain track into Bosnia the next day and position themselves along the route on picket duty, to await the arrival of the heaviest armour to be sent to Bosnia, the thirty-tonne Warrior infantry fighting vehicles. I decided to join the cavalry. Driving behind the Scimitars, all flying the British flag as we climbed up through the mountains, was so exhilarating I already had the story I planned to write once we reached Vitez. It was the cavalry coming to the rescue. We drove past a farm where a man and a woman were toiling in the fields. They glanced at us briefly, then returned to their work. Did they know there was a war on the other side of the mountain?

Nearing the top of the mountain track, it was the Scimitars, not my Audi 80, which began to slip and slide. One slid right off the track and ended up pointing downwards, dangerously close to the precipice.

The next day, it was the turn of the Warriors

to make the trip up over the mountain, but the journey took longer than planned. The armoured vehicles had to spend the night on the mountain because of the icy conditions. The drivers had a perilous time slipping and sliding on the track. At least the soldiers, who would normally be squashed into the back, eight at a time, were saved from a night on the mountain. Serving with the 1st Battalion Cheshire Regiment they were transported to Vitez by coach.

Soon after the Warriors started arriving in Vitez, there was a thunderous bang. It was a huge explosion that filled the air. I was sitting in the British military media office, consisting of a couple of rooms in a house opposite the camp. I had been writing the story of the Warriors' arrival and had been on the point of filing the piece, using the military satellite phone linked to my Tandy computer. Inexperienced as I was, and urgently needing to file my copy to make the first edition, I changed the introductory paragraph to say that the Warriors had arrived and had immediately come under fire, dramatically reminding the soldiers that this was a war zone.

Within minutes of sitting back relaxing after the relief of sending my story to the office, I asked what damage the explosion had caused. The reply was surprising.

'Oh, that was just Nora. She always goes off at this time of the evening,' a know-it-all media press officer told me.

Nora was the nickname of a mighty Bosnian Croat artillery piece, located not far from the

British camp in Vitez, which had fired off a shell in the direction of Muslims several miles away. The bang was outgoing, not incoming. It made a huge difference to my story. I looked at my watch. There was just time to change the intro. I grabbed the phone and got through to the foreign desk. David Watts, a former foreign correspondent, was on duty. I asked him to change the intro. 'The shell was not incoming, so the British soldiers had not been under attack,' I said. Watts, the nicest and calmest of men, was somewhat surprised that as a defence correspondent I hadn't been able to distinguish between incoming and outgoing.

To my shame, I replied, 'It's incredibly difficult to know what's happening; this isn't bloody Wimbledon, you know.'

He was courteous and sympathetic and promised to do as I asked. I vowed that I would never again jump to conclusions, even if a deadline was only minutes away. I had to be sure of my facts, *then* file.

Many of us were staying in a bed-and-breakfast. Early one morning, a worried-looking David Fairhall knocked on my door and told me my car seemed to have been stolen. My precious Audi 80 with the comfy seats, and with my flak jacket and helmet in the boot, was no longer in its parking spot. It had survived in the war zone for just a few days. I rang the office to let them know what had happened. I heard someone calling out to anyone interested, 'Mike's had his car and everything stolen.'

But sympathy in London was of no use to me.

I had to get to grips with the setback and work out how I was going to cover the war without the basic requirements of wheels and body protection. First, however, I made a fruitless visit to the local police station and filed a theft report. The Croat police chief asked me to sign a document in Serbo-Croat and informed me without a hint of a smile on his face that he was sure I would get my car back. Of course I never did. I had been the only correspondent to arrive in Bosnia with a family saloon, and as soon as it was spotted by the local community, which included Bosnian Croat military commanders who were treated like Mafia godfathers, it must have been the trophy everyone wanted.

I was also one of the few reporters to enter the war zone without a properly protected vehicle; the BBC had a mammoth armoured beast, the *Daily Telegraph* had an armoured Land Rover and ITN had a similarly impressive fortress vehicle. A German reporting team arrived with a mighty battle bus. David Fairhall had been one of my passengers in the Audi, so my problem was also his problem. Later, he was given a creaking-looking Citroen which had been driven across Europe to be *The Guardian*'s war vehicle. No one would want to steal it but it was as vulnerable as my Audi to accurate sniper fire and exploding landmines that littered some of the roads. In future trips to Bosnia over the next three years I always managed to hire a Lada Niva. But *The Times* never supplied me with an armoured vehicle. I didn't mind. I grew quite fond of the Lada. The snipers always missed, and approaching a checkpoint in a normal car, rather than a menacing-looking armoured beast, somehow seemed safer. Climbing out of a Lada with a smile on your face and an outstretched hand generally worked well.

However, for my first trip, in November 1992, I was dependent on my comrades from the BBC to drive me around when there was a spare place in their monster vehicle. Kate Adie, the redoubtable news reporter, was the first one to offer help when she heard of my problem. She was a great lady, fearless, stubborn, professional and never satisfied unless she was in the right place for the big story. Another BBC reporter that offered help was Malcolm Brabant, always a good companion. Covering a war with colleagues is a special experience. Friendships grow quickly and although we all worked as rivals you learnt pretty fast that heading off on your own for a scoop may sound exciting but is probably too dangerous. You need someone with you, if not in your car, at least in a car behind or in front. Safety in numbers is a golden rule. Scoops are great but death before the story is written means no story!

It's a war reporter's duty to take risks in order to get the story but it's imperative to stay alive! Yet these basic rules for covering a war were forgotten every day in the Bosnia civil conflict. Photographers, in particular, took excessive risks for the picture that would make the front pages. Many brave photographers died in Bosnia. Reporters, too, were killed. A BBC correspondent died when a madman armed with an anti-aircraft weapon fired at his armoured vehicle from the top of a nearby hill.

Every night, we went to bed to the sound of mortar and artillery fire. Every morning, we awoke to the sound of ammunition rounds and the deep-throated spatter of heavy machine gun fire. After a few days, this mayhem became normal. This was what life was like, it was exciting, and when the stories were published most days, it was all worth it.

At one point I had to move from the house where I had been living and found a café owner willing to let me sleep in the back in an empty room. It was basic but more than adequate, and the coffee in the morning – strong, gritty liquid served in large china mugs – made the long day ahead seem surmountable. The one drawback was that the café was a little way out of Vitez. I had to beg a lift to reach the British camp, and then make sure I had transport arranged for my return in the evening.

One evening, I had been drinking in a bar and got chatting to a large Croat farmer who offered to drive me to the café. I climbed into his battered old car and we headed off down the road in the right direction until, suddenly, he swung off the road down a dirt track. I asked him with growing alarm where he was taking me but he just shook his head and refused to stop when I demanded to be let out. After five minutes, we arrived at his farm and he invited me to get out. A group of people were gathered around a spit with a whole pig roasting in the fire. I was not going to be raped and shot;

instead, I was to be the farmer's guest for an evening of barbecued pork and Slivovitz, the delicious but deadly plum brandy which the Croats swigged back with increasing frequency as the fire died down and the evening turned cold. The farmer later drove me to my café home. He was too drunk to understand that I was trying to tell him how sorry I was to have misinterpreted his sudden left turn off the road. I collapsed into my sleeping bag on the floor in the back of the café and woke only when the smell of strong coffee reminded me I had a war to cover.

Every day a choice had to be made: either stick with the British troops and follow them wherever they went, or find out from intelligence reports what was happening. If there was 'action', as the photographers loved to say, off we all went. Often, we'd arrive at a firefight well before the British troops turned up in their Warriors. On one occasion I was in Turbe, about twelve miles from Vitez, when a burst of gunfire filled the air with bullets. Two Warriors from the Cheshire Regiment had just arrived and set up positions on either side of the street. I sought the cover of one of them and kept low as the bullets continued to fly in all directions. There seemed to be no real purpose behind the gunfire other than to create trouble.

I settled down to wait and then, totally out of the blue, the sound of Barbra Streisand singing *A Woman in Love*, one of my favourite songs, blasted from a loudspeaker. It was wonderful, bizarre and surreal. Barbra Streisand at full volume can drown out the sound of bullets fired in anger. Bosnia was like that. A country split by centuries-old hatreds, but also blessed with passionate, hospitable people. The war didn't stop when Streisand's stunning voice echoed around the streets, but the song reminded those of us cowering behind military vehicles that normal life could continue. Whoever had the inspired idea to switch on Streisand at that particular moment clearly intended to demonstrate that firing guns would solve nothing, and that at some stage this bitter, angry, anarchic war would come to an end.

The British Army had an extraordinary officer in charge of the UN humanitarian-aid convoys in central Bosnia during my first trip to the war. Lieutenant-Colonel Bob Stewart, commanding officer of the Cheshire Regiment, was to become famous worldwide in April the following year for his outrage after discovering the bodies of 103 people in the village of Ahinici – Muslim men, women and children, slaughtered by Croat 'troops' in one of the worst ethnic-cleansing episodes of the war. Colonel Bob, as he was known, was instantly likeable, but back in Whitehall his publicly expressed anger towards the Croats caused alarm. Here was a British officer in charge of a UN operation, involved strictly in escorting aid convoys, seemingly taking sides and venting his wrath against the Bosnian Croats.

But it was impossible to remain neutral in this tidal wave of murderous ethnic cleansing. Colonel Bob was voicing the anger we all felt and it was entirely understandable and appropriate for a soldier in his position to tell the world what a horrific sight he had witnessed. It was not politically correct and did not conform to the regulations laid down for an officer wearing the light blue beret, but Bob Stewart was a man of emotions as well as being a disciplined soldier, and his outburst was symbolic of the despair that flooded the length and breadth of Bosnia for more than two years. He was brilliant at public relations, and journalists like me, Robert Fox of the BBC and Chris Bellamy of the *Independent* who got to know him well felt protective towards him.

When he fell in love with the local International Red Cross representative, a slim, pretty, dark-haired woman, we knew it would cause trouble for him, but I never wrote a word about it even when the affair broke in London and there were interviews with his wife. I received a phone call from a reporter on *The News of the World,* who asked me to confirm who the woman was and to give my view of the relationship. I claimed ignorance. We were all in the war together and had to stick together.

My most traumatic moment during my first trip to Bosnia in 1992 came on the road from the town of Tuzla, in the north of the country. Bob Stewart was determined to get aid to Tuzla, which had been cut off by the fighting. Tuzla was a Muslim town but to reach it you had to drive through Serb-held territory. For months, the Serbs had refused to allow anything past their heavily-gunned checkpoints. Now they had relented, but the journey was going to be tense, potentially dangerous and, as everywhere in Bosnia, unpredictable. A bunch of reporters set off with the aid convoy and the Cheshire Regiment to try and reach Tuzla. I travelled in an armoured Land Rover with Mark Laity of the BBC. It was a great story, British soldiers relieving the starving town of Tuzla. When we all arrived, the first people to greet us were children. Kids in war zones are the most resilient. They kick footballs around houses shattered by rockets and artillery shells, and carry toy guns, shooting whoever comes near them. It's the only world they know, and somehow they lead as normal a life as possible. Their faces lit up when the soldiers climbed out of their armoured vehicles and held out their hands. Not for food, but for basic gifts, especially pens and pencils, and notebooks. A pen for a child in Bosnia was like a packet of Marlboros for the checkpoint militias.

It had taken a long time to reach Tuzla, so I rushed off to find electricity to link up my Tandy. I found a socket in an abandoned warehouse but never really expected it to work. I plugged in my computer and attached it to a large fan-shaped satellite system. After a few agonising moments, I saw on the screen, 'Welcome to News International'. It was a truly wondrous moment. I typed out my story and sent it.

By now it was late afternoon. Another golden rule in a war zone is not to travel at night, but to get back to base before the sun goes down. We all climbed into our vehicles and set off with a Spartan armoured vehicle ahead of us. Suddenly, a pick-up truck travelling fast towards us struck the side of the Spartan and the glancing blow lifted it right up into the air. It hurtled towards the Land Rover in which I was a passenger and then came crashing down onto the road, with a terrible sound of tearing metal. We all leapt out, reporters and soldiers. The sight before us was horrific. There were two men in the truck. The older one had had a leg torn off and blood was pouring from the wound. The younger one, who had been the passenger, had received a massive blow to the head and was also bleeding.

Kate Adie took charge. She called to a few of us to grab the man with the severed leg. She shouted, 'Hold the leg up!' The leg had been ripped off just below the knee and shards of bone were sticking up like stalagmites.

We carried him to a bench, holding up the remains of his leg. The second victim was clearly suffering from concussion and was wandering around looking dazed. Both men stank of alcohol, and when I checked their truck, I found a half-empty bottle of Slivovitz lying on the floor. In minutes, a makeshift ambulance arrived and took both injured men away. Carrying a man with a severed leg was a shocking experience, and yet all of us rallied round as if it was a natural occurrence. This was Bosnia.

There was no time to stand around. We had to leave. The sun was setting and within a few minutes it was going to be dark. Either we stayed in Tuzla or we risked driving across the mountains in the dark. We decided to take the risk. A convoy of reporters' cars set off towards the mountain route that went through thick forest. I was, once again, in the BBC Land Rover. It became dark almost immediately and all of us switched on our lights. Within minutes, there was the sound of guns firing and bullets started whizzing through the trees. The convoy of vehicles travelling through the mountain forest with their headlamps on must have looked like fairy lights. We were an inviting target for the Serbs watching us from below.

Almost simultaneously, everyone switched off their lights. As the bullets continued to fly around, we drove on, relying only on what ambient light was available through the thick forest. It was nerve-wracking, scary and yet – bizarrely – exciting. After ten minutes, the Serbs got bored with firing into the dark. When we thought it might be safe, we switched on our lights once again and headed for the nearest town. We were not going to make it back to Vitez and had to find somewhere to eat and sleep. The town of Kladanj was our refuge that night. We found a hotel that was empty but open, and begged the owners to give us food. About fifteen of us gathered round a long table in the hotel dining room, feeling overwhelmingly relieved that we had survived, but still unable to forget the drunken truck driver with his severed leg. We drank bottles of local red wine and relived the day with increasing boisterousness and laughter. We staggered off to our rooms just as a heavy machine gun started opening up at the side of the hotel. I knew by now that it was outgoing and closed my eyes, untroubled by the noise.

Before returning to London after my three-week stint, I was invited to be a guest at a truly British event. Colonel Bob was determined to celebrate a regimental dinner, complete with silverware and military band. A large marquee was set up in the Vitez camp, and members of the Cheshire Regiment assembled for the dinner. Colonel Bob sat at the head of the table. On his left was Claire Podbielski, the young Swiss Red Cross worker. It was his statement to all of us present that his chief guest that evening was also the woman he hoped to marry. He left his wife and married Claire in January 1994. But that evening, the seating arrangement at the regimental dinner was bold to say the least. He trusted us to respect their relationship. She was delightful and her diminutive figure surrounded by Cheshire Regiment officers in combat uniform reminded us that war can bring people together, and sometimes it can inspire feelings of love in an environment that is otherwise filled with hatred and violence. In a longstanding British military tradition, a goblet of port was brought to Colonel Bob. After sipping from it, he passed it to Claire. It was another gesture of romantic defiance. Unfortunately, the regimental dinner was reported across two pages in one of the national newspapers, and Colonel Bob received a roasting from his superiors.

Returning to Split, I had to inform Hertz that the Audi had been stolen. I was asked whether I had taken it into Bosnia at any stage. I said I had, but insisted that the car had not been stolen because I was in a war zone. The Hertz man smiled and replied in a resigned voice, 'Oh well, these things happen.' I had given them my American Express card details when I rented the Audi. I signed a document confirming the theft of the car and that was it. However, a week later, back in London, I received an American Express bill for 13,000 pounds. I was staggered. Hertz was charging me for the loss of the car. I rang them but was told I had breached the rental agreement by taking the car into a war zone. Hertz said the insurance I had taken out had stipulated that I would not be covered if I drove the Audi into Bosnia. I had no memory of that.

I went to see the managing editor, Peter Roberts, and presented the bill to him. He was reasonably phlegmatic, reassuring me that *The Times* would pay. But I told him I would fight the charge because I was sure I had not been warned in writing that I was forbidden to drive into Bosnia. All I remembered was the Hertz man asking me casually: 'You're not going to go into Bosnia, are you?' To which I had replied, 'No, I doubt it.'

I wrote to the head of public relations at Hertz and explained why I thought it was wrong for them to charge me for the cost of a new Audi 80. He replied, dismissing my argument. So I wrote to the president of Hertz and pointed out that I had seen nothing in writing which had made clear I would not be covered by insurance if I drove into Bosnia. I had a reply a week or so later that brought a huge smile to my face. The Hertz president agreed. He had investigated and found that the warnings about driving in a war zone had been inadequate. He concluded that I should not be liable to pay for a new Audi, but should merely pay for the mileage I had covered while in Bosnia for three weeks, a total bill of around 2,000 pounds. I went upstairs to give the managing editor the good news.

CHAPTER 9
ENDLESS SLAUGHTER

I was back in Bosnia in May 1993, to discover that the country had deteriorated so dramatically that nowhere was safe. In November the previous year, I had been able to wander around Vitez in relative safety. Now the town was under siege, with Muslims in the old quarter surrounded by hostile Croats. The streets were empty. It was more like Sarajevo, the capital of Bosnia, where daily artillery fire from the mountain ridge overlooking the town and snipers' bullets from the top floors of apartment blocks tore the lives of the population to shreds. On a much smaller scale, but reminiscent of the daily mayhem in Sarajevo, men, women and children in Vitez who needed to come out of their houses during the day dashed across the street with looks of fear on their faces, desperate to avoid the snipers sitting menacingly at vantage points.

The Cheshire Regiment had completed its six-month tour and was being replaced by the 1st Battalion Prince of Wales's Own Regiment of Yorkshire, commanded by Lieutenant-Colonel Alastair Duncan. He knew what to expect during his six months' tour. Colonel Bob and his men had come across so many harrowing scenes during their tour of duty, including the execution of women and children. Whole families had been killed. In one Muslim house, a mother, father, three children and other relatives were found sitting up against a wall inside their house. All had been killed.

Colonel Duncan was a different kind of character, less emotional and passionate than his predecessor. However, soon after he arrived in Bosnia and before he took over command in Vitez, he was given a taste of the appalling scenes he and his men would have to confront during their tour of duty. He helped remove the charred remains of a Muslim family, including a three-month-old baby, from a village burnt by Croat soldiers. I interviewed Colonel Duncan and already he was feeling pessimistic about the future. His challenge, he realised, was not with the Serbs, who were better armed and trained than their rivals, but with the Muslims and Croats who had followed the Serbs into ethnic cleansing on a grand scale. Pointing on the map to the valley running from Turbe in the southwest, through Vitez to Kiseljak, about twenty miles west of Sarajevo, he said, 'There's a terror campaign [between Muslims and Croats] underway and my worry is that it's going to get very nasty. If it blows up again between the Croats and Muslims, a lot of people are going to be killed, and we can't give aid to dead people.'

Chasing the ethnic cleansers was a grim business and became a daily venture for me and my Lada Niva, a trusty vehicle which was sufficiently robust to master the rough and often treacherous routes, and adequately comfortable for normal driving. But I never drove anywhere without wearing my dark blue, excessively heavy personal flak jacket and helmet perched loosely on my head. Wearing a flak jacket that goes below the waist – not like the neat little fitted ones everyone else seemed to have – while driving means that the weight of the ceramic plates, front and back, bears downwards, and also causes the shoulders to ache. The helmet was always slipping sideways.

I used to follow a British Warrior up the muddy tracks to check on reported ethnic cleansing. It was difficult to imagine such brutalities were going on because everywhere I looked there were scenes of peaceful farming. It was only the constant rattle of machine gun fire and the woomph of mortar rockets looping up into the air in the distance that spoiled the idyllic environment. Occasionally I would drive through a village that had been literally burnt to the ground. Chapels and mosques had been desecrated. Cemeteries were not just for the dead, they were also minefields.

One of the most dramatic stories led to a classic front page *Times* headline in May 1993. The editor, Peter Stothard, wrote me a personal letter of congratulations for when I returned from Bosnia. The headline, taken from a quote by a British Army officer in the story, was, 'I'm not prepared to get one of my soldiers shot for the sake of a few sacks of flour.'

A group of soldiers from C Company 1st Battalion Prince of Wales's Own Regiment of Yorkshire, based in Vitez, had decided to help terrified Muslims take several sacks of flour across the road running through the town to their enclave where a few families still lived, surrounded by vengeful Croats. Vitez was largely a Croat town. The Muslim families were often too afraid to venture out to buy food, even though they were theoretically protected by a Muslim sniper team perched on a hilltop promontory overlooking Vitez. The snipers, however, aimed at anything that moved down the road in the expectation that they would kill Croats. The only open garage was half a mile down the sniper road, so my journeys to get petrol required a racing start (well, as racing as the Lada would allow), driving in helmet and flak jacket and speeding past the sniper point. Bullets would fly all over the place, but fortunately hitting a fast-moving target is always difficult, even for a professional sniper, and the Muslim gunmen on that hilltop were reassuringly inaccurate.

However, on the day when the soldiers resolved to escort the Muslim civilians – four women and two men – with their flour across the road, a bizarre incident occurred which illustrated the sheer madness of Bosnia. I came across the soldiers and the group of frightened Muslim civilians by chance and asked if I could join them. The soldiers agreed, warning me it would be highly risky. The Muslim civilians had a rusty farm wheelbarrow laden with sacks of flour, which they pushed slowly across the road and into the enclave, guarded by soldiers from the regiment, with a Warrior armoured infantry vehicle in front and taking up the rear. Throughout this risky manoeuvre, we were being watched by six Croat gunmen, one of them only a teenager, who had taken up residence in a house that used to be the home of a Muslim family before they were driven out.

The Croats came tumbling out of the house with their Kalashnikovs waving in the air, shouting at the soldiers and threatening the six Muslims, who scattered to take shelter. Then suddenly three shots rang out, not from the angry Croats but from the Muslim snipers on the hilltop who had spotted their enemy talking to the British soldiers and opened fire, putting everyone at risk. We dived for cover. It was at that moment when the young officer in charge, Major Vaughan Kent-Payne, said, 'I'm not prepared to get one of my soldiers shot for the sake of a few sacks of flour.' He ordered a rapid retreat. But the flour was left for the families. The mission had been accomplished.

I had been given some useful advice before I ventured to Bosnia for the first time in 1992. 'Take Marlborough cigarettes with you; that's what they love and it's the best gift to get you through checkpoints.' I never went to Bosnia without 200 Marlboros. On one visit I drove through a checkpoint without realising it. It was a solitary guard in a remote location in north Bosnia, Serb and Croat territory. When I looked in my rear-view mirror I saw the gunman standing in the middle of the road with his Kalashnikov raised and pointing in my direction. I had two options: accelerate fast in the hope that he would miss, or stop and reverse. Life and death decisions are often made in a split second, especially in a war zone. I braked hard and reversed. The sentry maintained his position with the Kalashnikov steady in his hands. I stopped and got out with a welcoming grin on my face.

'Sorry,' I said, *'novina angliski.'* (English journalist) I told him I hadn't seen him but my Serbo-Croat was not up to the task. So, I reached into my anorak and grabbed a packet of Marlboros. The Kalashnikov was lowered rapidly and he eagerly accepted the gift. The rest of his sentry duty would be less tedious for him. I drove on.

On that trip to Bosnia I had a new companion. One day, when I was in Vitez, a scruffy-looking bloke with long hair and a beard and a backpack turned up. He looked as if he needed a welcome, so I started to chat to him and recommended he stay at the same house I was in, run by a Croat woman called Viktorija. I introduced him, and set him up. He said he had spent three years with the British Army's Royal Green Jackets as a junior officer, but had left and was seeking a new career as a photographer. His name was Anthony Loyd. We got on well and we used to travel together in my Lada Niva. He took pictures as I covered stories, and I suggested he try and sell them to *The Times*. He learnt his new trade rapidly and soon switched from photography to war reporting. He was to become a justifiably celebrated war correspondent for *The Times*, reporting from Bosnia, Kosovo, Iraq, Afghanistan, Syria and other hotspots.

By now, NATO was talking seriously about launching a bombing campaign to stop the

Serbs from killing and raping their way through Muslim and Croat territories. But the reality was that while the Serbs were viewed in the West as the 'enemy' in Bosnia, the extremist Croats and Muslims were just as bad, and as equally brutal. The British and other international soldiers had arrived with heavy armour and an abundance of firepower but were unable to do anything about it. They were not in Bosnia to shoot people but to protect aid convoys. Ethnic cleansing continued unabated.

On the 19th of May 1993, Vitez itself was at the centre of a furious ethnic-cleansing operation, Croats against Muslims. I awoke at dawn in the bed-and-breakfast owned by Viktorija and her husband Milan; a hail of high-velocity bullets, mortar shells, 12.7mm machine gun rounds and rocket-propelled grenades were exploding over the rooftops. It was all happening a few yards from where I had been sleeping. The Muslim community housed in a pocket of Vitez called Bazen was being exterminated. The Croats had been threatening to drive out the Muslims from Bazen for months. What houses survived were ransacked, then torched.

Being rudely awoken by a cacophony of explosions may sound like a terrifying experience, but by my second trip to Bosnia, gunfire, artillery explosions, mortar rockets flying overhead – even the shock of the sniper's bullet – had become a normality. Life in Bosnia was a series of explosions, distant and close, and, therefore, such daily dramas were to be expected. Being awoken by a rocket-propelled grenade was irritating, even inconvenient, but not surprising. Provided, of course, it wasn't being aimed at my bedroom. Rushing out to discover what was happening, all I could see were burning houses. The Muslim survivors had vanished. Only one body was found, lying close to a pool of blood in a courtyard, but others may have been removed.

The massacre of Muslim families at Ahinici a few weeks before I arrived for my second stint in Bosnia had become a symbol of the country's ethnic tragedy. I felt drawn to the village, to see for myself what was left of a once peaceful community, not that far from Vitez. I drove there. Standing in the devastated village, my one thought was that someone, or some people, should be arraigned for a war crime for the systematic slaughter that had taken place. British soldiers had found the village full of bodies and burnt houses on the 23rd of April. At the centre of Ahinici were the remains of a mosque, its minaret lying broken on the ground. The village was totally quiet, except for the sound of flies buzzing around, hunting for remnants of human flesh. Although the charred bodies had been removed, there was still a smell of death in every shattered home. Ninety Muslims had died, but there were probably more bodies trapped under the ruins. Fifteen Muslims were still missing.

At the top end of the village, I discovered a few Croat families hanging out their washing in the sun, still prepared, it seemed, to live in Ahinici as if nothing had occurred. They looked away when I approached them and refused to answer my questions. They may not have understood my faltering Serbo-Croat but you could see from their tight lips and hostile eyes that they knew exactly what I was asking. How could they live in a village where the majority of their neighbours had been brutally murdered by men claiming to be soldiers?

Before leaving Ahinici, I discovered one sign of life that brought at least a suggestion of a smile to my face. Among the ruins and wrecked cars I found a small dog, cowering in a shed, barely able to stand, yet managing to wag its tail. After some encouragement, the dog accepted some canned beef, but nothing would persuade it to venture out from its dark haven into the sunlight.

The Ahinici massacre was the responsibility of the Croats. However, the artillery pounding of the beautiful 500-year-old city of Maglaj, also mostly populated by Muslims, was the work of the Bosnian Serbs. A shelling offensive by Serb guns up in the hills surrounding Maglaj had begun the previous August. A second wave of attacks had started eleven days before I drove into the city in my Lada, a journey that included a nerve-wracking stretch through a long, dark tunnel. In the past, the tunnel exit had been targeted by the Serbs who opened fire on anything that emerged from the darkness, whether British Army Land Rovers or reporters' cars. Maglaj was about fifty miles north of Vitez. Although I managed to drive through the tunnel without being targeted, within five minutes of arriving in the heart of the city, a shell landed about 300 yards away.

The east Bosnian towns of Srebrenica and Zepa had been shelled by the Serbs until the Muslims were forced to lay down their arms, and now Maglaj was being reduced slowly to rubble. It was another Serb triumph of destruction and death. Twenty minutes before I arrived in the city, a married couple walking across the bridge over the River Bosna that ran through the middle of Maglaj had been seriously injured by an artillery shell. Another shell had landed in a school, wounding four children. Half of the buildings in Maglaj have been damaged by artillery. The main street was a mass of broken glass and shattered buildings. A burnt-out police car lay in the middle of the road. A few people still walked around the streets but, with at least fifty shells hitting the city every day, most families stayed in their cellars.

Maglaj may have been a largely Muslim city, but it was being defended by a joint Croat-Muslim defence force. Such was the complexity of this civil war that enemies in one part of the country could be allies in another. Maglaj was so dangerous that UN food convoys were rarely to be seen. Locals complained there had been no food aid for a month. In the eleven days since the second phase of artillery strikes had been launched, eighteen people had died and sixteen injured. The Serb plan was to slice through Maglaj and to create a corridor from Banja Luka in the northwest down to Pale, their stronghold south of Sarajevo.

After leaving Maglaj, I drove up into the hills across from the Serb positions in order to look down on the city. Half a dozen shells landed in the city as I watched. The Croat-Muslim defenders replied with mortars that whistled over my head.

Another area where the Muslims and Croats had forged an alliance against the Serbs was in and around the city of Brcko, in northeast Bosnia. Some of the heaviest fighting in Bosnia was taking place there. A British Army captain who was keen to find out what was happening in Brčko offered me the chance to go with him to the city. I was in my Lada, he was in a Land Rover. My second tour of Bosnia was supposed to be over. I had promised my family that I would be leaving within a day or so. But with the chance of a trip to Brčko, I postponed my return home and set off on the long trip.

The day before, I had been travelling in the back of a truck through Vitez, facing rearwards, when a car accelerated towards me. Two young firebrands were in the car, one with a silver pistol in his hand, which he aimed out of the passenger window at my head. I shouted, somewhat melodramatically, 'He's got a gun!' I never knew whether he pulled the trigger and it jammed or whether it was just bravado, but the car raced past. In Bosnia you could never count on gunmen just play-acting. There was too much anarchy around to trust anyone with a gun. The experience, all over in seconds, stayed with me as I drove up towards Brčko, constantly on the look-out for danger.

Brčko was a real frontline in the war. Up to 10,000 Serb fighters, backed by forty tanks, heavy artillery and multiple rocket launchers, were embedded in the area around the city, which they had seized the previous year. Every village, every square inch of cropland, was being defended by the combined Muslim-Croat force. We stopped off at Tuzla to pick up a squadron of Light Dragoon Guards who had offered to take me into the war zone. Leaving my Lada at their headquarters, I travelled in the back of a Spartan armoured vehicle for the rest of the journey to Brčko. We arrived at Bajiki, a heavily shelled village about 500 yards from Serb positions. The only inhabitants of the village were members of the Bosnian Muslim 3rd Battalion 108 Brigade. The houses were so shattered the soldiers relied on hedgerows to block the Serb gunners' line of fire.

The Light Dragoons, who had replaced the 9th/12th Lancers for the role of forward reconnaissance, had ventured farther north than any other British Army unit since the UN operation began. We were within view of the Serb positions and had no idea how they would react at the sight of uninvited foreigners in their midst. We climbed out of our armoured vehicles and stood on open ground, with the Serbs hidden in a forest to the north. We spotted some Muslim soldiers looking at us nervously and when we went over to them, they warned us that thirty artillery shells and eighty rounds from Bofors guns, a highly effective Swedish-made 40mm cannon, had fallen on the village that morning.

The Light Dragoons squadron commander, Major Marcus Browell, was keen to move on but the Muslim soldiers wanted him to meet their battalion commander. Standing there in the open, it was easy to imagine the Serbs watching us from the protection of the trees. It was not a pleasant sensation.

'This isn't a very safe place, is it?' I asked Major Browell.

'No, this isn't a safe place,' he replied, looking around him.

Before he had finished uttering the last consonant, there was a huge explosion, followed by a second. Two 82mm mortar shells had been fired on either side of us from across the field. They hit the ground about seventy yards from us. When the first explosion broke the silence, we all dropped to the ground, but when the second mortar shell exploded on the other side of us, it was pretty clear what the Serbs had in mind. The third shell would land in the middle. Major Browell ordered an immediate exit. I was picked up by the scruff of my neck by one of the soldiers, force-sprinted to the back of the Spartan and literally thrown into the back. The driver was so anxious to leave he reversed straight into a ditch. But by then we were out of the line of Serb fire.

Six miles from the Serb gun positions in Brčko, where a full-scale war was underway, the town of Maoca had become a first-line casualty centre. The nearest hospital was in Tuzla, much farther south, so the wounded victims of Serb artillery and mortar fire were being brought to a house in Maoca, just off the main street. The basement of the house was converted into an improvised operating theatre. As I approached the house, after driving to the town, a nurse rushed out and hung about thirty pairs of surgical gloves along the fence to dry in the sun before the next casualties arrived. Clearly, a full team of doctors was working at full stretch to carry out emergency surgery.

But down in the basement, in stifling heat with flies buzzing as close to the patients as they dared, a single surgeon was bent over the anaesthetised body of a soldier whose right leg had been brutally injured, with a compound fracture so complex it was difficult to see how the bones could be set back into their rightful positions. The chief surgeon, who spoke with a gravelly voice caused no doubt by exhaustion, was on his tenth casualty when I was led into the cramped basement.

General Ivan Hudolin glanced up at me and invited me to watch. The casualty was a young Muslim soldier. The general was screwing long steel pins upright into his shattered femur to try to knit the bones together. I looked at the soldier. His face was deathly white. General Hudolin wiped the sweat from his forehead and told me he had carried out 7,000 operations on war casualties in the last twelve months. There was no reason to disbelieve him.

The wounded arrived on stretchers in the back of Opel Estates. Nearly all of them were young men who had been sent to war with little training but with a burning desire to protect their homes and farms from the rampaging Serbs. Maoca was a town of desperation. General Hudolin and his team were doing their best to save lives, but the drivers bringing the wounded from the frontline were running out of fuel for their makeshift ambulances. It took half an hour to drive from the front to Maoca, and on the morning I visited the town, they had just twenty litres of fuel left. The nurse on surgeon glove duty ran back and forth throughout the morning, grabbing the clean dry ones from the fence and laying out recently washed ones. The sight was reassuring, showing that the surgeons were being meticulous about cleanliness, and yet, the heat and flies in the basement, the lack of a plumbing system and the constant flow of people going in and out of the operating room told another story.

Not only the injured were being brought to Maoca. Across the road from the improvised hospital, the town's mosque, severely damaged by Serb air raids, was being used as a mortuary. Outside, a hosepipe connected to a wooden frame was sluicing water over a body, washing away the blood, before it was wrapped in a blanket and taken inside. I was invited inside the mosque and there, lying on stretchers, were seven dead soldiers, their faces and bodies covered with blankets or bloodied sheets. For some of them, the blankets were not quite long enough and their toes stuck out over the edge of the stretcher. Men and women, some with clutching children, waited respectfully in a queue to see if a family member was among the dead, lined up so neatly. A middle-aged Muslim woman in a blue dress lifted up the blanket from one stretcher and let out a piercing shriek. She had recognised her son. She couldn't stop screaming: 'He was nineteen, he was only nineteen!' Suddenly, there was a burst of gunfire outside the mosque. But it was just Muslim soldiers returning from the front, firing their Kalashnikovs into the air. They had survived one more day.

Everywhere in north-eastern Bosnia, there was evidence of destruction and death. Villages were being wiped out, their residents driven south or slaughtered. Brod, a frontline village hammered by Serb shells day after day, looked as if it had been hit by a hurricane. There was nothing left of what less than a year before had been a flourishing community. The commander of the largely Muslim defence force, whose headquarters was in a shell-damaged house in a wood, had the appearance of a man doomed to spend the rest of his life fighting for his homeland. Like the chief surgeon in Maoca, Commandant Hazim Fazlovic looked exhausted. Shells landed as we spoke. His battalion had one piece of equipment, which they proudly unveiled as the main defender of what was left of the village. It was a dull green Soviet T34 tank. It was really just a museum piece. The Serbs had later-generation T72s and T84s. But in this civil war, with the outside world refusing to donate arms, they had to fight with what they had, and the sight of the old tank was clearly reassuring for Commandant Fazlovic and his men. 'Every one of my men has been wounded at least once,' he told me. 'Some have been injured as many as seven times, and 133 of my men have been killed.'

That morning, about 150 shells had landed on the village. Someone should have told the Serbs they were wasting their time and their munitions. Since most of the houses were already in ruins, the impact was barely noticeable. The commandant said he had not had a single day off since the war began a year ago. His son had been killed and the rest of his family had moved farther south to seek refuge. 'We are very tired,' he said. Having suffered so much, he could find no sympathy for the western politicians who had tried to seek ways of bringing the slaughter to a close. Plans for safe havens for Muslim-dominated communities sounded fine, but Bosnia was far too complex to be resolved by well-meaning outsiders who seemed to underestimate the multiple strands of the civil war.

There were really three separate civil wars going on at the same time: the Serbs against the Bosnian Muslims and Croats, the Croats against the Muslims, and, in certain areas, Muslims and Croats fighting together against the Serbs. The racial antagonism between the Croats and Muslims in central and southern Bosnia was not going to go away if the West placed too much emphasis on punishing the Serbs and too little on resolving the hatreds between these two ethnic groups. So often, back in London, I would hear of the appalling shelling by the Serbs of the Muslim sector of Mostar in the south. But it was Croat gunners up in the hills around this city, not Serbs, who spent every day pounding the homes of the Muslims, which reduced the east side of Mostar where they lived to rubble. The residents of east Mostar lived like hermits in their cellars, escaping only for food and water if they could find any, and if they had the courage to dodge the artillery explosions.

I left Bosnia after a month of harrowing experiences, driving the Lada back over the mountains to the safety of Split. Before I left I had spoken to a female military media officer who had seen a Muslim woman with her breasts sliced off. Such experiences remain as dark memories for the rest of your life. Those seven white bodies wrapped in blankets and sheets, the surgeon bending over the bloodied and shattered leg of the young Muslim soldier, the sudden explosive sound of artillery fire, the fear of the unexpected as you drive through the Bosnian countryside… all these memories stuck in my mind as I tried to adapt to a different kind of normality back at home.

By the time I left central Bosnia for the journey to Split, all the elements of this war, from the most bizarre to the most savage, were present in one form or another around the British military camp in Vitez. Croats and Muslims were fighting each other right up to the perimeter fence, and the Serb frontline artillery positions had become menacingly in range. Sniping between the Croat and Muslim frontlines was so persistent one night that a British officer living in a house in the Muslim enclave at the side of the camp decided to do something about it. Major Roy Hunter, commanding officer of A Company of The Prince of Wales's Own Regiment of Yorkshire, a dashing figure with a moustache and dark, curly hair, climbed out of bed at 1.15am and fired a 1.5mm rocket illuminator on a parachute out of the window, like an SOS flare. The effect was to create daylight for sixty seconds. The snipers scuttled to their beds and left the angry major to sleep.

I returned to Britain in time to attend an aunt and uncle's golden wedding anniversary celebration in a house with an orchard in Sussex. It was a beautiful, sunny day. The orchard was full of people in summer clothes drinking champagne and eating buffet food. Forty-eight hours earlier I had been in Bosnia where it was normal to be scared, acceptable to be fired at and not unusual to see mutilated bodies. Here in the orchard, there was a different kind of normality, one that I was going to have to get used to as quickly as possible. But it was too early for me. I could feel tears squeezing into my eyes. My heart jumped for no reason. Above all, I couldn't talk in a normal way. I couldn't chat or laugh or be sociable. This was an afternoon of celebration for close relatives but I felt alone and strange and disorientated. I could speak to no one about it.

CHAPTER 10
THE MAN WHO CAME OUT OF THE SHADOWS WITH PIERCING EYES

An extraordinary event took place on the 24th of November 1993. For some time, the intelligence and security services in Britain had been gearing up for a new era of greater openness. MI5 led the way when Stella Rimington, a career intelligence officer, was appointed as Director-General of MI5, the first woman in that role and the first one to be officially outed as the head of Britain's domestic security service. She was a good choice because she liked publicity and flourished in the limelight, unlike her predecessors, who had remained buried in their burrows and were not required to make public appearances. When she appeared in public and posed for pictures in July 1993, Fleet Street went wild. John Bryant, deputy editor of *The Times* and a newsman to the core, spotted that she was wearing a huge ring on one finger. He asked me to find out whether the ring was a special communications device linked to GCHQ! Such was the excitement of having the head of MI5 appearing before the press.

MI5 was the first of the secret agencies to be put into the public limelight. But the Conservative Government wanted to put all the intelligence services on the statute books, which would mean announcing the names of the other agency chiefs and, if necessary, to put them on public display. MI6, the Secret Intelligence Service, had always relied on anonymity because it was in the business of running agents overseas; MI6 officers and their networks of agents needed to operate in the shadows.

However, in late 1993 it was to be the turn of MI6 and GCHQ to come out of their burrows. Douglas Hurd, the foreign secretary, had announced that the secret agencies under his wing were to be enshrined in legislation for the first time. On the 24th of November 1993, he invited about twenty of us to attend a press conference to discuss the proposed Intelligence Services Bill that would make MI6 and GCHQ officially legitimate organisations. We assembled in a basement room of the Foreign Office and waited for Mr Hurd to arrive. But, in a sensational move, because it was so totally unexpected, the foreign secretary entered the room followed by three startled-looking men.

Britain's top spooks were making their debut appearance. They sat down on the raised platform in front of us and stared at us as if we were aliens. Mr Hurd introduced them: Sir Colin McColl, Chief of the Secret Intelligence Service, Sir John Adye, Director of GCHQ, and Gerald Warner, Cabinet Office Security and Intelligence Coordinator.

It was impossible not to focus on Sir Colin McColl, not just because he was head of MI6, but because of his dark, piercing eyes which seemed entirely appropriate for a man with all those secrets in his head. When he spoke he had a soft, gentle voice. Spies, like librarians, are used to speaking in low tones! The other two were less impressive. Sir John looked like a fairly normal civil servant and Gerald Warner had a pugnacious appearance and spoke few words. He seemed rather stiff, and was probably content that the reporters in the room threw nearly all their questions at Sir Colin, who leant forward on the table in front of him to deliver his carefully modulated replies. The atmosphere was conspiratorial; we reporters were desperate to find out everything we could but were somewhat in awe of the man with the piercing eyes, and Sir Colin was determined to keep his answers within the bounds of what was permitted. He could tell us what we needed to know but not what we wanted to know. His performance was riveting.

We weren't allowed to publish his photograph, so *The Times* resorted to the best alternative which was to print a large picture of Sir Alec Guinness in his John Le Carré role as George Smiley, looking elegant in a dark overcoat with bowler hat and rolled umbrella in one hand, standing in Horse Guards Parade. Smiley, the central character in the legendary spy books, was a senior MI5 intelligence officer, hunting down traitors in the service. Fleet Street has often got its MI5s and MI6s muddled up; however, when MI6 moved premises to set up home in Vauxhall Cross, the modern building on the south bank of the Thames, it became easier for news editors and picture editors to remember who was what and where.

The appearance of Sir Colin McColl in public for the first time leant itself to a number of excited articles by the newspapers, including my own. Spies who reveal themselves always 'step out of the shadows'. It's a cliché but it works. It was a former head of BND, the German equivalent of MI6, who came up with the most memorable description of Britain's Secret Intelligence Service. He called it 'the service that still wears soft shoes'. Sir Colin recalled the phrase when he met the press at the Foreign Office.

This was a truly British occasion, the debut performance by the boss of the soft-shoe brigade. Sir Colin pleaded with us to be allowed to return to the shadows of his secret world because, he said, the agents who worked for his service needed total secrecy and had to be confident that their identity and their undercover work would always be protected. Because of the conspiratorial atmosphere in the Foreign Office basement room on that unprecedented day, everyone in the room appeared to sympathise with this plea. We would, in a way, be part of his agent-protection system, ensuring that our articles didn't breach the rules that ensured MI6 could carry out its covert work without the flash of a Fleet Street photographer's camera or the snooping of a reporter. We had Whitehall's D-Notice system, the Ministry of Defence's list of rules when writing about issues of national security, but Sir Colin's words, delivered in such a charming fashion, helped to remind us all that in our role as specialist defence reporters we had responsibilities.

On this unique occasion, writing about the unveiling of Sir Colin, I felt it was unlikely to breach national security by revealing a little bit about Century House. Everyone in the Foreign Office room knew that the Chief of the Secret Intelligence Service, known throughout Whitehall as 'C', wrote all his memos and letters in green ink. It was a tradition which Sir Colin was happy to confirm.

I was back in Bosnia in April 1994. The war had moved on, or, more accurately, the peace efforts had accelerated. A ceasefire of sorts between the Muslims and Croats was holding, but offensives were still underway against the Serbs and by the Serbs. Britain's involvement had proliferated, with a second battalion being sent to beef up the numbers in an attempt to prop up what was being optimistically seen as a creeping peace momentum. NATO had also swung into action, sending ground-attack aircraft to target and deter the Serbs. The threat of airstrikes had one dramatic result. With some neat persuasive diplomacy by the Russians, and NATO's bombers in the air waiting to strike after an ultimatum had been issued by the alliance, the Serbs pulled back their heavy artillery from the hills overlooking Sarajevo. Convoys of guns began moving off the hills in February 1994.

It was the most significant sign that even the Serbs were beginning to come to terms with the possibility of a diplomatic solution.

But it wasn't the end of the war. At the end of March, four Serb Galeb aircraft, returning from a bombing mission over the Muslim-held town of Bugojno and a munitions factory in Travnik, were intercepted by two pairs of US Air Force F16s and blown out of the sky. The Serbs had breached the UN no-fly-zone that NATO had been enforcing from April 1993. It was NATO's first offensive action in its forty-five-year history. The Cold War had been a dangerous and potentially cataclysmic period in history, but the western alliance was never called upon to fire its weapons in anger. The shooting-down of the four Serb light aircraft, possibly one of the easiest missions that could be devised for the F16s, heralded a new era in which NATO would be forced to turn more and more towards offensive action to resolve regional conflicts. Not even the smartest generals in the West would ever have predicted in 1994 that the alliance would within a few years be immersed in the biggest war of its life in a country where the enemy would fight with Kalashnikovs, wearing flip-flops on their feet. Afghanistan and the Taleban were still seven years away.

My priority during my third trip to Bosnia was to interview the new star running the show. Lieutenant-General Sir Michael Rose, the overall United Nations commander in Bosnia, had set himself up in a headquarters in Sarajevo. General Rose, like Sir Peter de La Billière, commander of the British force in the 1991 Gulf War, had a special pedigree. He had served with the SAS, commanded the famous regiment, and was appointed the first Director Special Forces. He was probably most famous for leading the SAS undercover units in the 1982 Falklands War. Unlike General de la Billière, General Rose was a man who understood the value of self-promotion as a way of encouraging respect from his potential enemies. He went everywhere in Bosnia with a heavily-gunned team of bodyguards, although he relied for his personal protection on a huge soldier nicknamed Goose. The touch of Hollywood did no harm. The Serbs, in particular, were led by hoodlums and they quickly learned that it was foolish to try and outwit the new UN commander. General Rose could get angry.

When I met him in his office at UN headquarters in Sarajevo, Tito's former palace, he was the very picture of a man satisfied with his job. He was also optimistic about Bosnia's future. He had some reason to be so. Just a few months earlier, the city had been hit by up to 1,200 shells every day, and anyone venturing out from their cellars was targeted by snipers. Sarajevo was where the world's finest ice-skating dancers, Jayne Torvill and Christopher Dean, had won a gold medal in the Winter Olympics of 1984. But in the 1990s it had become the most dangerous city in the world. Now, here was General Rose, his sleeves rolled up and his arms folded, masterminding what he believed would be a new and more positive future for Bosnia's capital.

Sarajevo was still a divided city, but from the open window of General Rose's office you could hear the sound of traffic and people – a truly dramatic transformation. However, the Serbs were still engaged in ethnic cleansing in parts of Bosnia and were not yet signed up for peace. General Rose was convinced they would sign a peace deal and was already looking ahead to the major challenge that would follow the end of the war. He had 15,000 UN troops under his command at that stage but envisioned a requirement of between 40,000 and 50,000 to help enforce a three-way peace deal between the Serbs, Croats and Muslims. There were an estimated 200,000 fighters among the three ethnic factions. The countries that had sent troops for the UN Protection Force (UNPROFOR) were a mixed bag of nations. About 800 Ukrainian soldiers were due to arrive within a few weeks and General Rose was going to dispatch them to Gorazde, a Muslim enclave south of Sarajevo which the Serbs had been shelling. The Ukrainians arrived in huge armoured troop-carrying vehicles. But some of the soldiers spent more time indulging in a rewarding petrol-scam operation than peacekeeping.

General Rose also had the difficult challenge of deciding where to deploy 2,700 Turkish soldiers who were due to arrive soon. Nothing was wrong with the Turks; they always looked highly professional and were acknowledged to be valuable members of NATO. But they were returning to a country where they were an occupying force for centuries and had been responsible for the slaughter of the Serb army at Kosovo, then part of Yugoslavia. People in Bosnia had long memories. Fitting the well-trained Turks into the peacekeeping mission was going to need political and military finesse. But General Rose was more than happy to have some professional reinforcements arriving, not least the promise of American troops. There was no question that the presence of US soldiers or Marines would provide that extra firepower ingredient for General Rose's plans for a post-peace deal operation. Having American military on board was always a bonus, even if their idea of peacekeeping was to travel around in heavy armour, dressed to kill as warriors with wrap-around sunglasses!

Gorazde, thirty-five miles southeast of Sarajevo, was to be General Rose's most painful experience. It was supposed to be a UN safe haven for Muslims, but despite all his attempts to persuade the Serb commanders, notably General Ratko Mladic, the rock-faced military chief, to back off, the strategic location of the town, close to the Serbian border, was too important for the Serbs. They kept on pounding away from their siege positions around Gorazde, knowing that time was running out for them. They clearly intended to seize Gorazde before the arrival of the 800 Ukrainians.

General Rose gambled by announcing that he intended to visit Gorazde. It was a typical act of bravado, daring the Serbs to stop him. But that's exactly what they did, much to the British general's fury. He got as far as Pale, the Serb stronghold just south of Sarajevo, before a Serb checkpoint barred his way. The Serbs then continued to attack Gorazde, driving out the civilian population, and at the same time thumbing their nose at General Rose. Gorazde appeared to be doomed. Frustrated by the Serb commander's obstruction and deceit, promising one thing and doing the opposite, General Rose finally resorted to seeking authority to bomb the Serb tanks shelling Gorazde. He had warned the Serbs that if they continued to advance against the UN enclave, there would be serious consequences. He had in mind a NATO precision-bombing raid. It would be the first time that the alliance had launched a ground-attack strike in the Bosnia conflict.

The wounding of an SAS trooper, one of seven from the special forces regiment who entered Gorazde secretly as part of a UN observer team, was the trigger for the airstrike. General Rose made a phone call to UN headquarters in New York and was told he had grounds for launching an airstrike. But the raid was to be as limited as possible. General Rose was at the head of a peacekeeping mission, not an all-combat arms occupying force. The aim was to stop the Serbs from firing shells into Gorazde but also to persuade them to sue for peace. Two US Air Force F16s dropped one 1,000lb bomb each on two Serb tanks. The bombings halted the shelling temporarily, but the Gorazde story was not yet over. The Serbs appeared to have no enthusiasm for peace – not at that stage, at least – and Gorazde became the focal point of an enduring tussle between General Mladic and the might of the United Nations, backed up by NATO. Gorazde was General Rose's personal nightmare. He had Sarajevo under his belt, which had significantly enhanced his reputation as a bold commander, but Gorazde remained a challenge.

Another place General Rose had yet to visit was the Muslim-populated eastern side of Mostar, for so long the target of Bosnian Croat artillery. Now there was peace between the Croats and Muslims, Mostar was trying to grasp a sense of a new future, without daily shellfire. I drove my Lada to Mostar to see for myself the devastation caused to this once beautiful city. The road I took seemed safe at the time, but only a few days later three Italian journalists travelling on the same route were killed by a hidden landmine.

Mostar was divided by the River Neretva, with the Croats on the western bank and the Muslims on the east side. Across the river was the famous Tito bridge, built by the Ottomans in the sixteenth century. But the bridge, like the Muslim section of the city, had been wiped off the map. I have never witnessed such destruction in any war I have covered. The Muslim side of Mostar reminded me of Oradour-sur-Glane, the town in France annihilated by the Nazis in the Second World War in revenge for attacks by the French Resistance, and left in ruins for future generations to remember what happened there. I walked around east Mostar, wondering if any human being could have survived such systematic shelling. But I spotted an old woman standing on the first floor of her home. The building was a crumbling wreck, totally open to the skies. She was a woman alone with her thoughts in the ruin of her home. But the shells had stopped falling.

The few people who did emerge onto the streets wandered aimlessly through the wreckage of their city, hoping perhaps to find something, anything that would help to improve their existence. Compared to Sarajevo, Gorazde and Maglaj (just three places which had been persistently shelled in the Bosnia war), east Mostar was in a category of its own. It was no longer one half of a city, it was just a pile of dusty bricks and twisted metal.

The occasional display of wisteria along a crumbling wall or the beat of a pop song bursting from a café which had partly survived the shelling provided the only reminder that this was once a city full of life and colour.

Yet, on the other side of the river, the Croat-dominated side, life could not have been more normal. All the cafés were full of people, laughing and chatting, and expensive, well-polished cars were driving around as if the war had never happened. Twice a day, following the ceasefire, Muslim families from east Mostar had the chance to meet the few relations who lived in west Mostar. They had not met for ten months, and in between the tears and the hugs they discovered how different life was in the divided city.

Mostar, Sarajevo and also Maglaj, three cities that had been shelled into submission, now faced a more optimistic, yet uncertain future. I went back to Maglaj, which was still living under the daily threat of snipers. But the siege of Maglaj was over. A company of British soldiers from the Coldstream Guards had arrived and had taken up residence at a school in the city. They had brought Warrior armoured vehicles with them, and one of them had been parked permanently in the school playground with its 30mm cannon aimed in the direction of the snipers up in the hills about 750 yards away. The most persistent sniper was firing from a bunker set between two other positions near a wood. On one occasion, the soldiers of 3 Company Coldstream Guards grew tired of being shot at and retaliated with ten rounds of 7.62mm machine gun fire to the left of the sniper's bunker, ten rounds to the right, another ten a few feet short of the position and then, for good measure, just in case the Serb gunman had failed to get the message, thirty rounds right through the middle.

The Serbs had already been forced to withdraw from their trenches south of Maglaj after a dazzling display of treachery by their former Croat allies. The Croats had colluded with the Serbs to target the population of 19,000 mainly Muslim inhabitants. But when the Croats and Muslims agreed a peace deal, the Croat fighters around Maglaj swapped sides and outflanked the Serbs. The withdrawal of the Serb forces south of the city was an extraordinary sight. Everyone was taken aback when they emerged from their trenches. There were hundreds of soldiers, T72 tanks and anti-aircraft guns, a favourite weapon of the Serbs, used like a howitzer, as well as artillery and heavy mortars. But the withdrawal did not mean the end of Maglaj's suffering; there were still Serb snipers and gun positions in the hills to the east and north of the city.

Maglaj remained a city unsure of itself. The bridge over the Bosna river, which linked the 500-year-old city to the mosque across the other side, was now used more freely by residents. However, the snipers who had claimed so many lives among the men and women dashing across to the mosque still had their sights set on the bridge.

Since the arrival of the British soldiers, however, only one mortar rocket had landed and only two civilians had been killed, both by sniper fire. Before the siege was lifted, Maglaj was being hit by an average of 500 shells a day, and once by 700. I'm not sure who did the counting but towns and cities throughout Bosnia had become statistical horror stories, 1,000-a-day shells here, 400 there. Maglaj was never as bad as Sarajevo, but it's a false comparison. For the people of Maglaj, the war had blighted their lives just as much as the shell-pounding had destroyed the lives of the residents of Sarajevo, and the merciless attacks on east Mostar had reduced that city's population to a Stone Age existence. It was estimated that the Croats launched 100,000 shells against east Mostar over ten months.

I left Bosnia with the fate of Gorazde and other so-called UN Muslim safe areas unresolved. The Serbs were still shelling Gorazde, ignoring the threat from NATO to launch airstrikes against them. The brutal attacks against Gorazde had reawakened fears in the five other bizarrely-named 'safe areas' – Sarajevo, Srebrenica, Tuzla, Bihac and Zepa – that they, too, would come under renewed artillery strikes. The fate of the Muslim men in Srebrenica has been well documented. Despite the presence of a Dutch battalion of about 500 soldiers in the town, Srebrenica was overrun by Serb forces in July 1995, and 8,000 Muslim men were slaughtered. The safe areas policy was never going to be respected by the Serbs, who were determined to seize as much territory as possible before the inevitable ceasefire and peace treaty were negotiated. The Dayton Accord, negotiated in the town in Ohio, was signed in November 1995. Yet, just four months before the war came to an end, the Serbs had committed the worst episode of genocide in Europe since the Nazi atrocities in the Second World War.

It was impossible to imagine how any of the cities in Bosnia could be rebuilt and returned to normal life. The challenge of reconstruction in east Mostar seemed almost beyond reach. But before returning home, I drove to Dubrovnik in Croatia to see how things had changed in the eighteen months since the end of the separate war in Croatia when the walled city was bombarded with shells from the guns of the Yugoslav army and by naval guns off the coast. For thirteen months, the inhabitants of this fine city, which had buildings dating back to the fourteenth century, had been under siege.

They had resisted and survived the artillery onslaught. On their worst day, 1,100 shells had landed in the city on the 6th of December 1991.

The world had watched and had done nothing. Croatia at that point had not been recognised as an independent state. The guns stopped firing in October 1992, and since then, the citizens of Dubrovnik, with help from a number of European countries, had been trying to return their city to its former glory. What I found when I visited the city was heartening. Dubrovnik had been extensively repaired, many of the roofs had been rebuilt, requiring 200,000 tiles. Dubrovnik no longer had the appearance of a city which had suffered months of shelling, proving that it was possible to push aside the horrors of war and rebuild the life of a community. Mortar rocket splatter marks on the polished stone paving in the main street were the only real sign of what had happened to the city during the siege, although wooden hoardings were still around a fifteenth century fountain which had been damaged. Miraculously, the cathedral escaped unscathed. One shell had hit the building but failed to detonate. The most encouraging change for Dubrovnik was that tourists were once again walking the streets. The Yugoslav army and navy had failed to learn the lessons of history: people under siege stay and survive. Although some women and children were allowed to leave, the majority of the city's inhabitants stayed, rebuilding their homes even while the shells were landing.

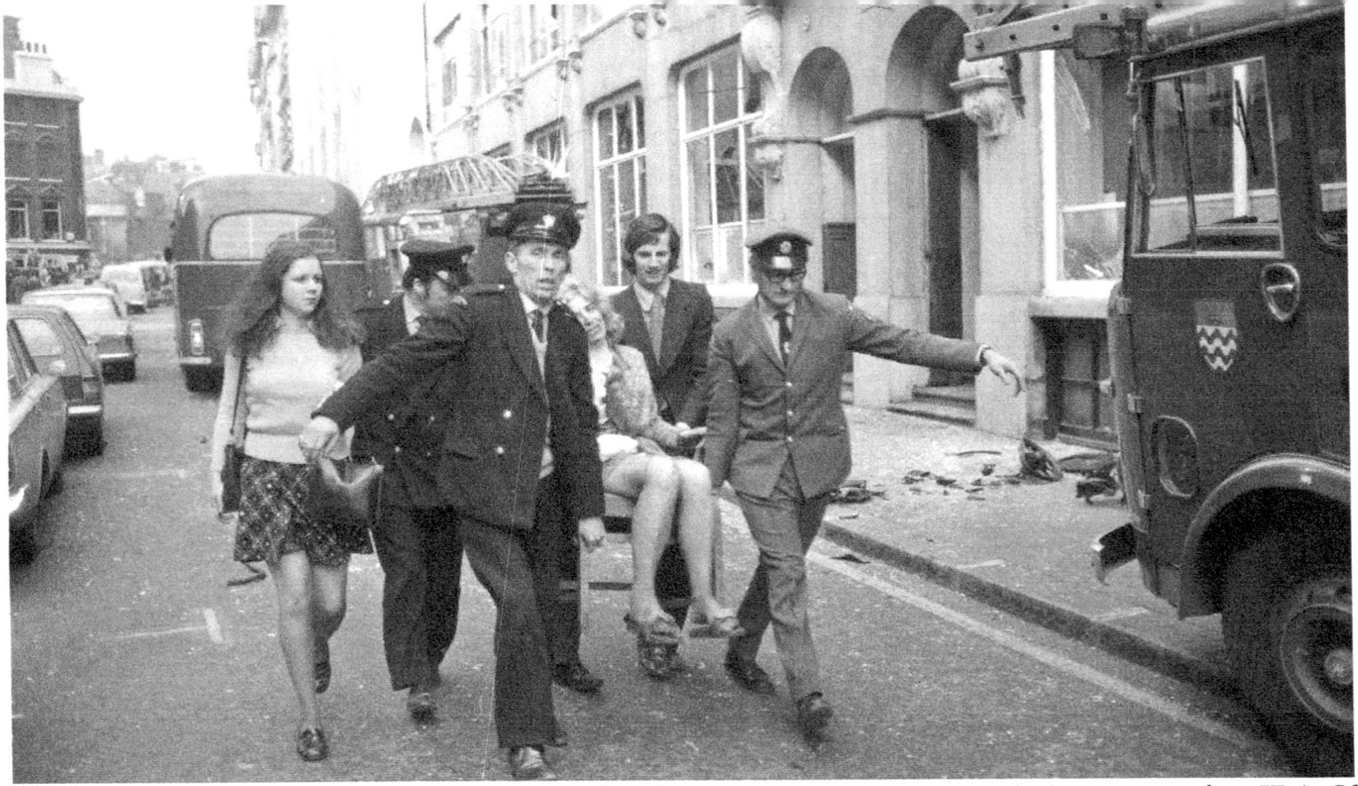

Caught by a Daily Telegraph photographer helping to carry a wounded woman after IRA Old Bailey bomb in 1973. (copyright Anthony Marshall, The Telegraph)

Man in velvet mufti: dapper Michael Evans of the Daily Express

Top-brass by-line: the Telegraph's Major-General Eddie Fursdon

nell says: 'I am very lucky that I don't have to strive to make things interesting. They just *are* interesting. The thing about this war is that so much about defence was theoretical – speculation about what weapons *might* do, and whether our ships *would* be vulnerable to enemy missiles. Now at least there is a practical application. I do, however, think that there's an irony in this little war. I believe that most of John Nott's decisions *are* right – that a surface fleet is too vulnerable and that planes and submarines are generally safer. Now, of course, we're going to see a huge lobby for a return to a more traditional navy, when it is almost impossible to imagine a similar situation arising ever again. Where else would we have to send a vast armada across thousands of miles to defend a tiny outpost?

'No, I didn't predict the invasion, not at all,' admitted Connell in the Kolossi Taverna, the workaday Greek köfta house monopolised by deadline-minded *ST* staffers. 'I think you could have asked everyone in this restaurant where they thought the next crisis would break, and I doubt a single person would even have mentioned the Falklands.'

Where, then, does Connell anticipate the next flashpoint? 'I wouldn't mind good odds on Albania.'

For Jon Connell, the crisis couldn't have come at a worse time. 'They invaded two days before I moved house to Brook Green; I hadn't even got the telephone connected. I had just flown back from the NATO summit at Colorado Springs with notebooks full of stories, all of which, of course, had to be jettisoned immediately. Since then it's been Falklands, Falklands, Falklands round the clock. I'm not complaining. Everything else in the paper seems irrelevant at the moment.'

He doesn't see his lack of first-hand military experience as a disadvantage. 'At least I don't suffer from any of the prejudices and preconceptions that a military man would have.' Moreover, he thinks that a civilian background has spared him an excessive interest in military hardware. 'Correspondents don't *personalise* defence enough. There is far too much speculation about whether the Exocet really can, say, travel across the sea at 600 miles an hour. There are so many fascinating characters involved in defence – people like Lawrence Freedman, the new professor of war studies at King's College – and I would like to put more emphasis on them.'

The most formidable defence correspondent is **Bridget Bloom**. Initially a shade brusque, she is well liked and highly regarded by her peers, which is usually a good sign. For thirteen years African correspondent of the *FT*, travelling on that continent for up to half the year, Bridget Bloom confesses that she had become increasingly disillusioned. 'I started reporting Africa in the late Sixties when the countries were first becoming independent and full of high hopes. Inevitably, with the passage of time, I saw the same sort of problems again and again.'

She became defence correspondent last November, lives in Notting Hill and operates from an office in the *FT* building covered with maps, defence reviews and silhouette charts of the fleet. 'I never played with toy soldiers and I never had a task force in my bath,' discloses Bridget Bloom, 'so I suppose I started this job at a disadvantage. I think it is indisputable, however, that the whole subject of defence has become so much *sexier* in the last three years.

'One thing I do think is that the defence lobby in Fleet Street had become really far too compliant. A cosy relationship had developed with the MoD and the defence industry, which probably wasn't a good thing. We had become too grateful and accepting of whatever they told us. I think once this crisis is over, we might all be a little less complacent.'

The two longest-serving correspondents are **Henry Stanhope** and **David Fairhall**. Stanhope took over his job at *The Times* from Charles Douglas-Home, now editor of the paper, who had in turn succeeded Lord Chalfont. Is defence, then, a short cut to the top? 'Not in my case,' says Stanhope, 'but I *have* had some distinguished predecessors.' A distinctly untidy man, with a shirt collar rucked half-way up his neck and the genial air of Mole from *Toad of Toad Hall*, Henry Stanhope rejects criticism that he has spent a decade hibernating in the MoD's pocket. 'That is a curious myth that goes round about us. I think it is put about by those people who invariably attack the press for being a tool of capitalism. They are also the sort of people who dislike defence anyway. So we are doubly vulnerable.'

'It is always a danger for any specialist correspondent, getting too cosy,' agrees David Fairhall. 'I wouldn't dream of relying purely on the Ministry.'

A Russian interpreter during his National Service, Fairhall has been pleasantly surprised by his dealings with the army. 'I didn't expect to get on with them, but I do. They're very straight, and generally less concerned about what's in it for them than commercial people.' Highly praised by his peers for his background articles on naval strategy (they were widely plagiarised at the start of the crisis), Fairhall is a great believer in the value of attending military exercises. 'One of the best pieces I've done lately was on the people who actually *handle* the Lance short-range nuclear weapons. I landed in a helicopter in the middle of a wood in Germany and saw the thing at close quarters.'

The nattiest dresser in the briefings room is **Michael Evans**, who unscrambles his shorthand in a brown velvet jacket and sharp worsted trousers. He was only promoted to his present job at the *Express* in January, so reckons he has faced 'the original baptism of fire.' Doubling as the paper's diplomatic correspondent, he was in Israel with Lord Carrington immediately before the invasion. 'We flew back on the Thursday night and landed at the VIP runway at Heathrow. Carrington was greeted by a reception committee of foreign office officials who said "The UN

Appearing in a fashion magazine article on defence correspondents during the Falklands War. (copyright Harpers & Queen)

On a Royal Fleet Auxiliary ship in the Gulf.

Driving my Lada Niva in Bosnia war.

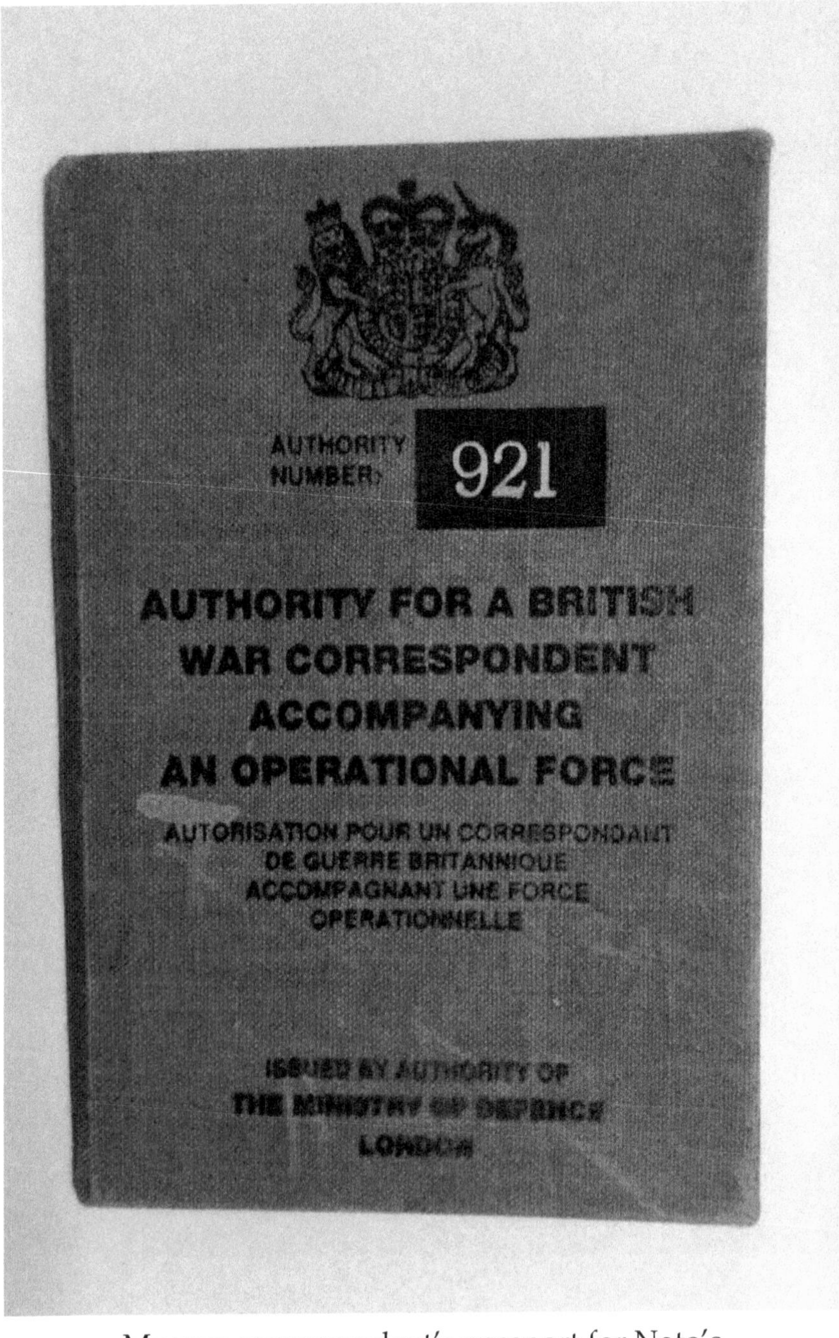

My war correspondent's passport for Nato's Kosovo intervention.

Travelling with a UK defence minister to Sierra Leone in 2000.

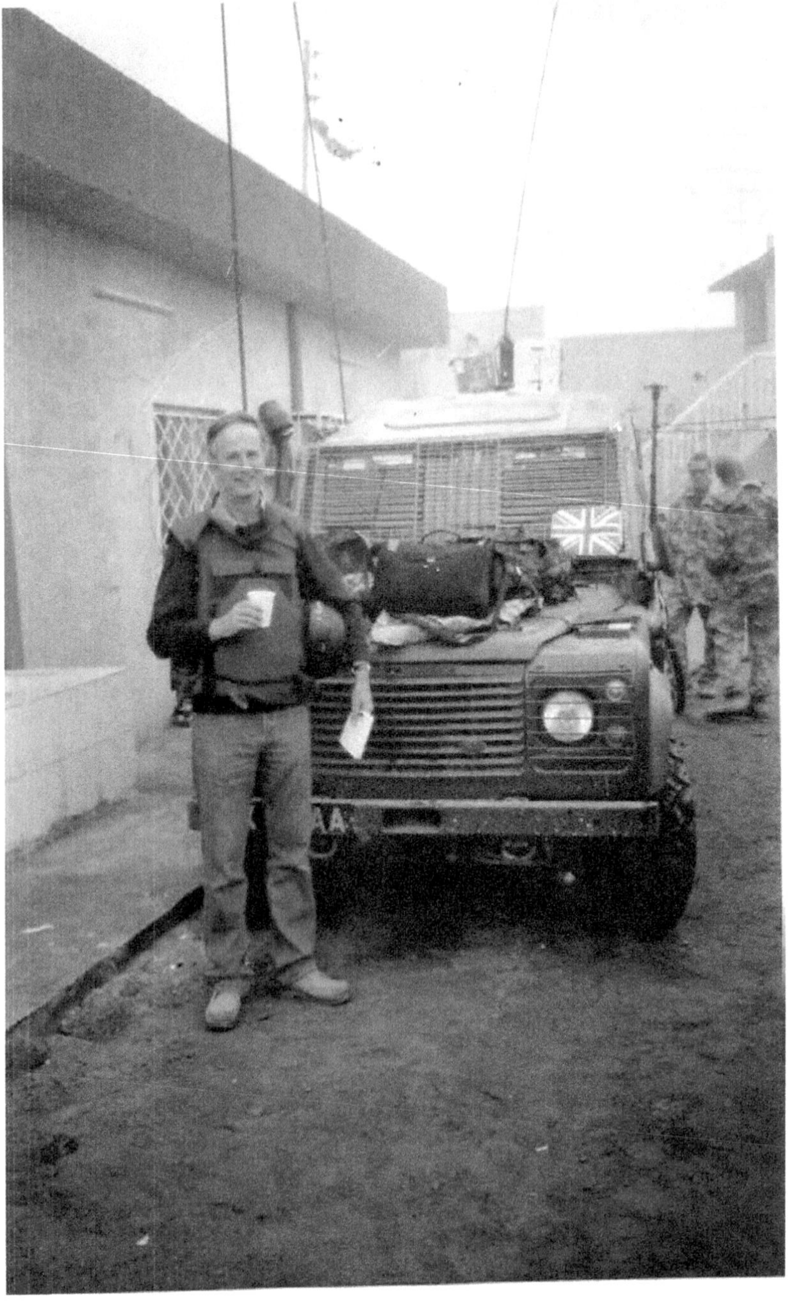

Covering elections in Az Zubayr, southern Iraq, in 2005.

Arriving at Basra military airport in southern Iraq.

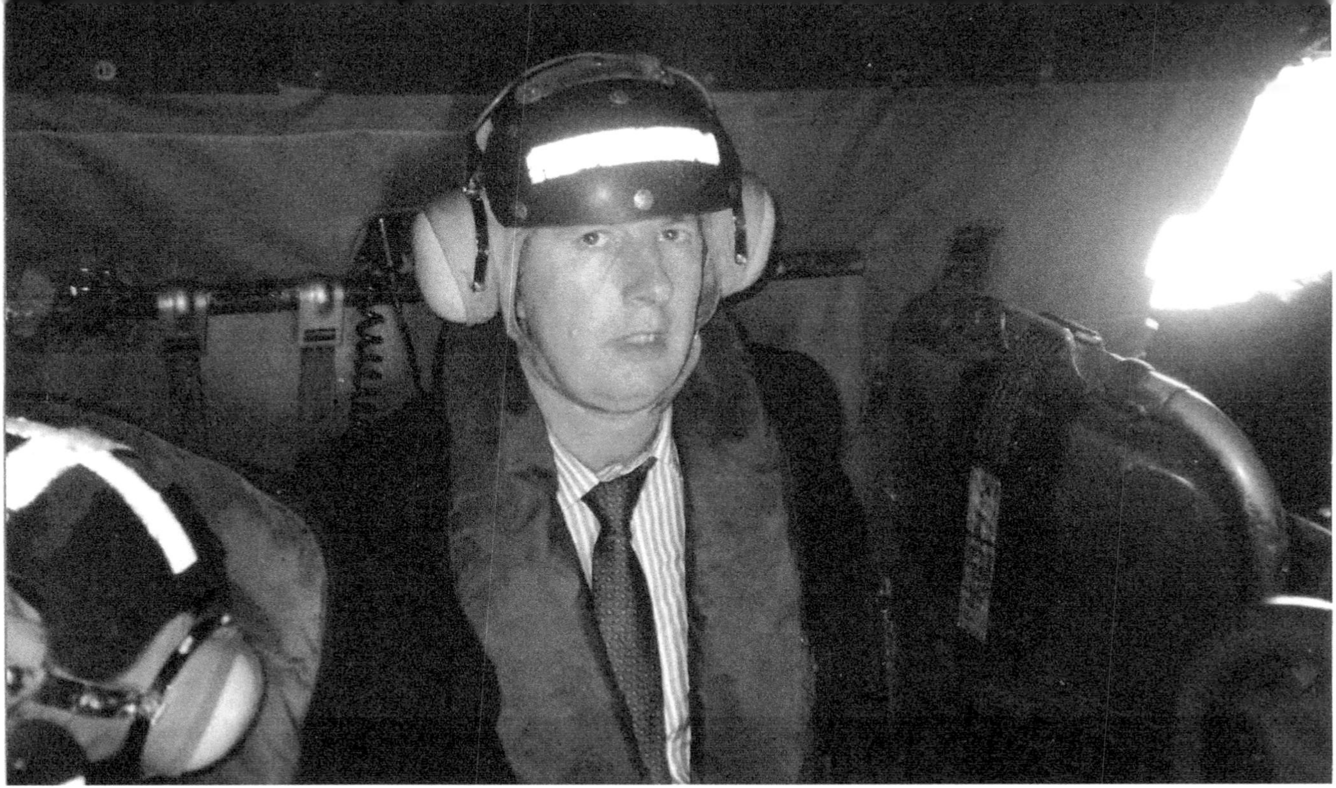

Exhausted on a helicopter ride in Iraq.

Blacked-up for a night mission against the Taleban in Kajaki, Helmand province.
(Chris Harris, The Times)

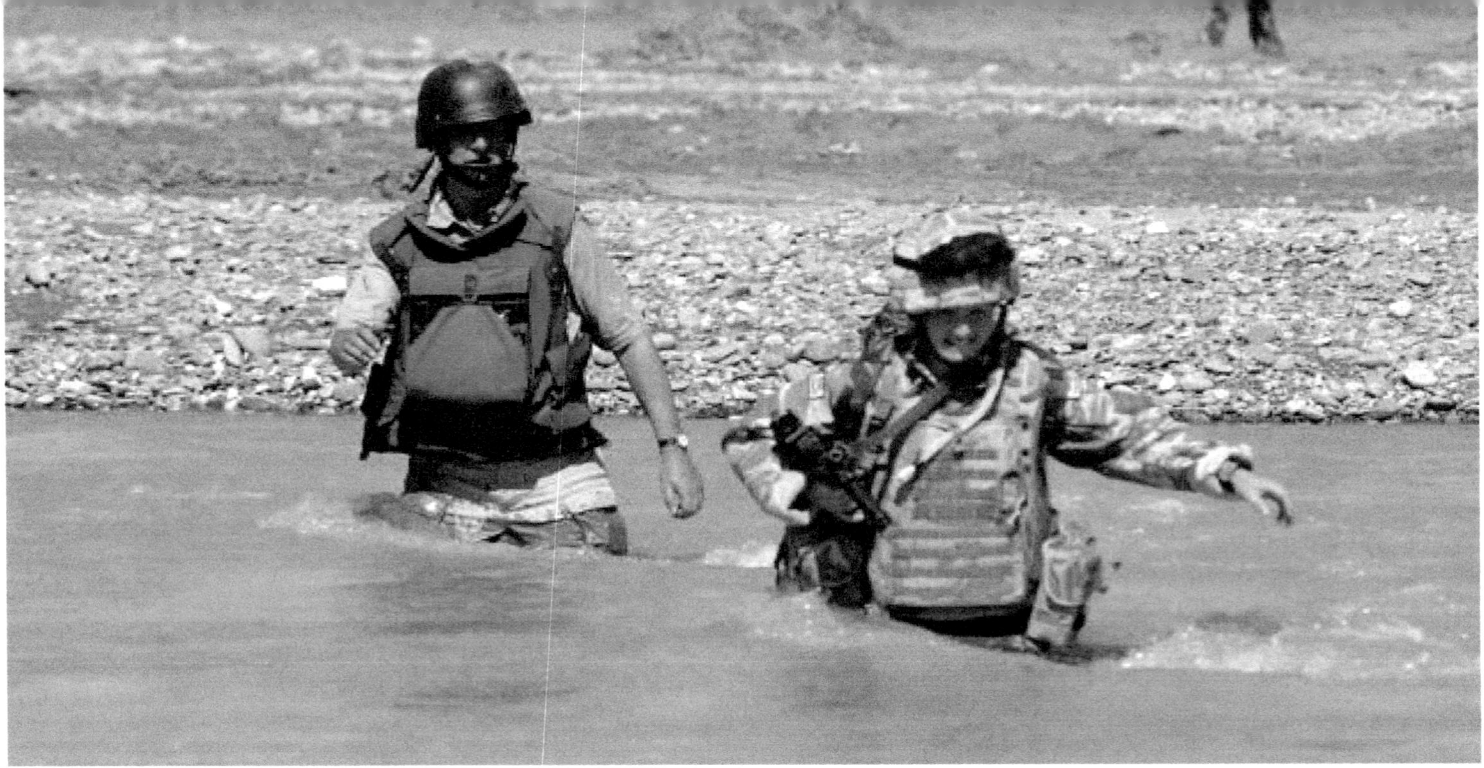

Wading though a fast-moving river in Helmand. (Richard Pohle, The Times)

Grabbing a moment to write my story in Afghanistan. (Richard Pohle, The Times)

CHAPTER 11
STANDING IN A CORNFIELD CONTEMPLATING WORLD WAR III

The young Parachute Regiment officer walked across the cornfield and delivered the following message to me and a small group of other journalists. 'You have to make a decision: you go with us or you say now that you want to stay behind. But I must warn you that it's going to be dangerous, there's going to be a lot of shooting, bullets flying everywhere. When the helicopters land, you'll have to jump out with the rest of us and duck your head and hope for the best.'

The twin rotor blades of the Chinooks were already whirring, and the pilots were signalling thumbs up. We were given no time to make up our minds. It was go or stay. Joining the paratroopers was the life-risking option. Staying behind was no option at all. I agreed to take my place on one of the helicopters. The others nodded their heads.

We were standing in the hot sun in a large cornfield not far from Skopje in the Former Yugoslav Republic of Macedonia, close to the border with Kosovo. It was the 11th of June 1999. The British paratroopers were part of a NATO peacekeeping force mandated by the UN to enter Kosovo, as Serbian troops, who had been illegally occupying the former Yugoslav province, retreated to Belgrade. Everything appeared to be in place for a classic heavy-handed peacekeeping mission. It was to be a show of force by NATO to encourage the Serbian army to withdraw, as agreed in lengthy negotiations held between its senior commanders and Lieutenant-General Sir Mike Jackson. He was the British officer selected to head the ground operation in his capacity as commander of the alliance's Rapid Reaction Corps, based in Germany.

However, mid afternoon, the day before General Jackson and his advance troops were due to cross the southern border into Kosovo, there came word that a convoy of Russian BMP troop-carriers, on peacekeeping duty in Bosnia, had crossed into Kosovo and was heading for Pristina, the capital of the former Yugoslav province. Moscow, it seemed, had decided to pre-empt the NATO mission and send its armoured vehicles to seize the airport at Pristina. If successful, Moscow, which supported President Milosevic, the Serbian leader, would then be in a position to dictate the future running of Kosovo. There were strong rumours that the Russians were also planning to fly in 4,000 Marines to secure Pristina airport, thus undermining General Jackson's carefully choreographed peacekeeping strategy.

I was lucky to be embedded with the 1st Battalion Parachute Regiment, which meant that I would be part of the first NATO troops to enter Kosovo. However, on Friday the 11th of June, a totally different prospect had emerged. General Jackson had been ordered to send British and French paratroopers by Chinook to Pristina to grab the airport before the Russians arrived, or to seize it back from them if the Russian convoy got there first. The order had come from NATO's Supreme Allied Commander Europe (SACEUR), General Wesley Clarke, a tough American with political ambitions.

General Jackson famously warned his superior that he was not prepared to start World War III by attacking the Russians, who had made it clear they wanted to be part of the peacekeeping mission but to have their own sector, independent of NATO. This had set off alarm bells because it seemed Moscow was plotting to take control of the north of Kosovo occupied by Serbs, leaving the south for NATO and the majority ethnic Albanian population. Partition, in other words.

But, standing in that cornfield, none of us knew what was going on between General Jackson and General Clarke. All we had been told was that we were to fly to Pristina and take on the Russians. General Jackson may not have wanted to start World War III, but the paratroopers and journalists waiting for the Chinooks to gear up for action were convinced that in a very short time there was going to be an explosion of firepower between British and French soldiers and the Russian troops, and the potential consequences were dangerously unpredictable.

I had a satellite phone with me and made a call

to the office to warn them what was happening. I also rang my wife to tell her there was a chance I might be heading for some excitement in Kosovo. I didn't want to alarm her. She had no idea that I would be flying into a hail of bullets. Several members of the Parachute Regiment came over when they saw me on the phone and asked if they could borrow it to ring their wives or girlfriends. I overheard one soldier spelling out precisely what lay ahead. He warned his partner that she might not see him again. The paratroopers seemed as nervous as we were. We stood around in groups and wondered how we would react when the Chinooks landed at Pristina airport. The BBC's Kate Adie was there, and she had a fixer with an SAS background who was unbelievably calm and reassuring.

Two hours went by. The Chinooks were by now hot and more than ready to go, the rotors were thump-thump-thumping, but still there was no order to take off. Then a vehicle was spotted travelling towards us. It stopped and out stepped a US Navy officer, Admiral James Ellis, NATO commander for southern Europe. He spoke with the commanding officer of the Parachute battalion, and within ten minutes we all got the same message. War with the Russians was off, or at least it was postponed. We were told to stand down.

The convoy of about thirty BMP armoured personnel carriers, carrying 250 Russian troops, had arrived at Pristina airport. If there was to be a confrontation with the Russians, it would take place the following day after the

NATO ground force had crossed the southern border of Kosovo as planned. I felt a turmoil of emotions: relief, certainly, but also frustration and disappointment. I had prepared myself for leaping out of a helicopter under fire, and now there was to be no dramatic story to write. The following day was also Saturday, a non-publishing day for *The Times*. So, all the drama I had written into my notebook and the likely face-off with the Russian troops at Pristina when the British paratroopers eventually arrived would have to be filed to *The Sunday Times*, and I would be competing for space with all their own correspondents. But none of them were present in that cornfield. It had been a unique experience. I can remember actually thinking, without any sense of melodrama, that I could be injured or killed. But I never seriously contemplated staying behind. It was too big a story to miss.

The war drums over Kosovo had been going on for a year. The ferocious ethnic cleansing attacks by Belgrade's troops in the province dominated by Albanian Muslims forced the West to take action. The growing thought was that 'something had to be done'. This was always a dangerous way of thinking because wrong judgments can be made when there's a political momentum for action. But the Western nations had acquired a taste for military intervention. The Bosnia civil war was under its belt and Iraqi troops had been driven out of Kuwait. President Clinton and Tony Blair had also launched Operation Desert Fox in December 1998 with a flurry of Tomahawk cruise missile strikes and bombing raids on Iraq to punish Saddam Hussein for obstructing UN inspectors who had been hunting for weapons of mass destruction. There was a growing sense that the big military powers in the West had demonstrated they had the will, as well as the capability, to end conflicts, with massive force if necessary.

President Milosevic was an old-fashioned dictator with a simple but brutal vision, which was to grab what he could when he could, hoping that the West would have neither the enthusiasm nor the consensus to stop him. However, as the end of the 1990s approached, he seriously miscalculated what the West was prepared to do, and he misjudged the mood of NATO's leaders, especially Bill Clinton and Tony Blair, who were of like mind about most things. Western leaders started speaking of the growing humanitarian disaster in Kosovo, and, on that pretext, they decided there was sufficient international legal justification under the UN Charter for military intervention. Bombing the Serbs into submission became the buzz phrase, and NATO was given the role of masterminding an air campaign which would persuade Milosevic to call back his soldiers and leave Kosovo to decide its own future without having Belgrade's storm troopers careering around the countryside, killing and maiming and driving tens of thousands of Muslims out of their homes.

The bombing campaign in early 1999 took

Milosevic and pretty well everyone else by surprise. Far from launching a precision-strike attack, knocking out air defence systems and the odd Serbian tank as an inducement to get Belgrade to back off, NATO's strategy was unexpectedly ambitious. Instead of just focusing on targets in Kosovo, NATO air commanders put the whole of Yugoslavia into their gun sights, and suddenly bombs were falling on Belgrade, on power stations and military barracks. Eleven NATO countries were involved, but America, in the lead, drew on its full inventory of military aircraft to frighten Milosevic, including the ever-faithful B52 bomber.

The bombing of Belgrade and the shattering of Yugoslavia's infrastructure eventually did the trick, and Milosevic caved in. Defeat for Milosevic was followed by an agreement for a NATO peacekeeping force to enter Kosovo and stand guard as Belgrade's troops withdrew, and to prevent outbreaks of violence between the remaining Serbs and the ethnic Albanians.

With World War III put on hold, I returned to my hotel in Skopje and got up in the early hours the following morning to be ready to fly by helicopter into Kosovo for NATO's new mission. Waiting in the dark beside a road for my helicopter ride, I peered through the pre-dawn gloom and saw a long line of British paratroopers, many of them quite short and very young, and weighed down with enormous bergens, marching past. These were to be my companions for the next few hours. The plan was for me to fly with the Paras and be dropped off the other side of the border, before meeting up with a colleague from the *Daily Telegraph,* Tim Butcher, who was driving across in a Land Rover. He was the paper's defence correspondent and we had always got on well. So a deal had been done in London, through the Newspaper Publishers Association, for me and Tim to travel together and cover the initial stages of the peacekeeping mission as pool reporters for the rest of Fleet Street. So, whatever we wrote each day would be provided for all the newspapers that had failed to win a slot with the NATO force as embedded reporters.

As Tim had an armoured Land Rover, the same one his newspaper had deployed to Bosnia, the Fleet Street editors had agreed that we should go in as a team. There had been a bit of backdoor negotiations before names were put in the hat under the Newspaper Publishers Association scheme for pool reporting, so it was a somewhat fixed lottery. My name and Tim's name came out of the hat. Both newspapers were guaranteed to be represented, which may have been unfair for the rest of Fleet Street but suited Tim and me. Other names came out of the hat, without any previous arrangement. Papers that failed to win a place in the pool team thought it was just luck that my name and Tim Butcher's name had been drawn in the lottery.

Anthony Loyd, my old colleague from the Bosnia war, had already been filing dramatic tales from Kosovo after he joined up with the ethnic Albanian Kosovo Liberation Army, the resistance force fighting the Serbs, and it was clear there were going to be some stirring stories to write as the Serb soldiers started to withdraw.

Flying in a Chinook as the sun begins to emerge on the horizon, packed in with paratroopers with grim, camouflaged faces, is what being a national newspaper defence correspondent is all about. Exciting, thrilling and stomach-churning. We landed in the middle of a road. As the paratroopers spread out, I waited for the arrival of Tim Butcher in his Land Rover. The one-hundred-member advance party from the 1st Battalion Parachute Regiment were the first British soldiers to enter Kosovo, and, although we were to part company, I knew I would see them and their commanding officer, Lieutenant-Colonel Paul Gibson, at some stage later when they entered Pristina to liberate the capital from the withdrawing Serbian occupying force.

When Tim crossed the border in his Land Rover, we set off immediately, heading for Pristina, looking out for Serb troops as we went. We had little idea how the withdrawals were going. We had to take into account the possibility that some Serb units might feel aggrieved about the order to retreat to Belgrade and could take revenge on Albanian families as they drove north. There were also risks for two British defence correspondents travelling on their own without the protection of the British Army. But we kept driving towards Pristina. The route was remarkably quiet. There was no sign of anyone in uniform, friend or potential foe. After an hour or so, we came across a British Army Land Rover, belonging to a reconnaissance unit which had been checking out the area. The young officer with a couple of soldiers warned us that there were no NATO troops in Pristina and that it might be dangerous to carry on into the city.

We decided to take their advice and drive, instead, to Pristina airport or as close as possible to await the arrival of General Jackson, who planned to confront the Russians, who were then in control of the airfield. Not a confrontation with guns firing but with military diplomacy. The Russians could not be allowed to retain control of Pristina airport, because General Jackson's whole peacekeeping mission depended on having the airport as the base for flying supplies and ammunition into the province for the duration of the campaign.

All the way from the southern Kosovo border, neither Tim nor I could get a signal for our satellite phones. Kosovo had been in a state of war for about a year and communications were in disarray. For a reporter covering a major international story, this was potentially disastrous. We had a great tale to tell but no way of filing it back to London! Then a miracle happened. As we drove round a corner close to the entrance of Pristina airport, our phones went PING! A satellite was overhead. We both laughed. After a day of tension there was such a sense of relief. From then on, we thought nothing could go wrong. We would have a terrific story to write and satellite signal to transfer the words all the way back to Blighty.

But when we arrived at the front entrance of the airport, it was blocked by two Russian BMP armoured personnel carriers, with soldiers who waved their guns at us. We turned round and headed back a few hundred yards and spotted a group of other journalists at a house set back off the road. It was my old friend Kate Adie and her television crew. We joined them. She had persuaded the owner of the house to let them use the premises as their headquarters for filing, and for sleeping for at least one night, while the airport impasse was resolved.

Eventually, the Russians allowed us into the airport because by then their commanding officer had been contacted by General Jackson's staff and it had been agreed that the British officer would be allowed to fly in by helicopter and hold a press conference. We all drove into the airport in the late afternoon and assembled on the runway, waiting for the arrival of General Jackson. I rang the *Sunday Times* to tell them I was on the spot and that I was happy to file to them.

Suddenly, the heavens opened and it began to pour with monsoon-style rain. At the same time, the Russians started to play heavy. A BMP vehicle which had been patrolling the perimeter of the airfield turned inwards and headed straight for us, accelerating. It was clear the driver had no intention of stopping but wanted either to drive a wedge through the middle of us or run us down. Those of us directly in his way, including me, had to leap for our lives, and as the BMP swept through, the puddles which had collected from the downpour sprayed us with dirty rainwater. Several of us waved fists at the Russians and called them names that, even if lost in translation, would have been easily decipherable as angry swear words, had the roar of the BMP not drowned out our protests.

The Russians were playing a dangerous taunting game, reminding the assembled international media that they had got to the airport first and were in charge. The majority of reporters were now soaked to the skin. General Jackson's helicopter was delayed because of the appalling weather. The rain was still falling when the helicopter arrived. The general, wearing his Parachute Regiment maroon beret, stood on a makeshift platform in front of the TV crews' microphones and reached inside his combat jacket pocket for the speech he had hastily put together on his flight to Pristina. After speaking for less than a minute, the written words on the piece of paper were a mass of rain-soaked smudges, so he screwed it up, and just told us it was an historic day and said he planned to go and see the Russian general to sort out the airport dilemma.

I rang the foreign desk of *The Sunday Times* and dictated over the phone the dramatic events of the previous hour. There was no time to write an elegant piece. They needed some drama from Pristina to add to the files already sent from their correspondents in Moscow, Belgrade and London, and I was the man on the spot. Having filed, Tim and I drove back to the

BBC 'house' round the corner and settled down for the night. Liberating Pristina would have to wait until the following day. Tim turned out to be an extraordinarily inventive cook. He took all our rations and anything else he could lay his hands on and put the lot in a pot. He produced a wonderful stew, hot and tasty, and everyone tucked in before collapsing in sleeping bags on the floor or wherever they could find a more comfortable resting-place. By the morning, it had stopped raining.

We later discovered that General Jackson had played a blinder. He spoke Russian, as a consequence of his time as an officer in the British Army Intelligence Corps, and he soon struck up a good working relationship with his Russian counterpart. A bottle of whiskey and two tumblers also helped to smooth relations. By the time they had finished talking, a deal was fixed. General Jackson discovered early on that the Russian convoy had set off from Bosnia at short notice and had arrived at Pristina airport with a minimum of supplies. They had no water and little food. General Jackson promised to supply him and his men with whatever they needed, and after another tumbler of whiskey or two, the potential crisis was over.

General Jackson had had the courage to disobey the order from his NATO superior, General Wesley Clark, to send British and French paratroopers to seize the airport from the Russians. Now, with the offer of food and water and the generous intake of good whiskey, the Russian-speaking British general had calmed what could have been a dangerous confrontation. The 4,000 Russian Marines reportedly waiting to take off for Pristina had obviously been sent home. The Russian general agreed to split control of the airport for the time being. It was an amicable compromise. General Jackson could now get on with his peacekeeping mission. It was a triumph of whiskey diplomacy.

The successful negotiations between General Jackson and Serbian commanders on the border of Kosovo and the Former Yugoslav Republic of Macedonia, which fine-tuned the timetable for the entry of NATO troops and the withdrawal of Belgrade's forces, had been driven by a tough message from the alliance's heads of government summit in Washington two months earlier. Tony Blair, who had become prime minister in 1997, was a keen advocate of the 'stick' approach to diplomacy: push for a diplomatic solution to a crisis but wave the big stick of military action if all else fails. In this case, he felt Belgrade should be told that NATO would launch a land invasion of Kosovo to drive out the Serbian troops by force. President Bill Clinton was not so keen, but there was land-invasion mood music at the Washington summit which would have reached the ears of President Milosevic. He was already suffering day and night air raids, and now he had the prospect of NATO troops, tanks, artillery and armoured personnel carriers advancing into Kosovo, defeating his army and delivering his final humiliation. The game was up.

I had travelled to Washington in Tony Blair's chartered plane to cover the summit. I was the only reporter on board to have a photographer with me. *The Times* was determined to have a photograph of Prime Minister Blair sitting in the plane, contemplating the summit ahead. Travelling with the prime minister of the day is always fun, especially one as charismatic as Tony Blair, who had an easy smile and a good sense of how to use the media to his own advantage. There seemed little doubt in my mind that he would agree to have his picture taken. However, when the photographer, Chris Harris, asked the Downing Street staff to fix a time for when he could go forward in the plane and take a picture, halfway across the Atlantic, he was rebuffed. There would be no photographs of the prime minister on board. Chris Harris came to me in dismay and asked if I could intervene. I went to see Alastair Campbell and told him that the main reason why Chris Harris was coming with me to Washington was to photograph his boss en route to the US, and that if he failed in his mission, there would be all hell to pay back at *The Times*. He promised to put my case to Blair.

A few minutes later, he came back to my seat and said: 'OK, it's on.' Chris got his picture, which was duly published in *The Times*. It was good for us and good for the PM. It was a softly-focused picture of Blair looking out of the window in contemplative mood.

Later on in the flight, Blair came through to see all the reporters for a quick chat before we landed in the United States. We grouped around in a semi-circle. I stood at the back, Alastair Campbell stood to the right, with his arms folded, looking pensive. He's very tall, so he could see over the heads of everyone in the reporters' group and was in eye contact with Blair. Most of the reporters were political correspondents, members of the parliamentary lobby, and were well known to Blair. He knew how to deal with their tricky questions, many of which were about domestic issues, not about the upcoming summit and the prospects of a land war in Kosovo. One political correspondent asked a particularly cunning leading question and I spotted Alastair standing bolt upright and gently shaking his head. Blair glanced at Campbell and also spotted the movement of his head, and gave a harmless reply which didn't answer the question.

I smiled to myself. One shake of the head from his press secretary, and Blair dutifully responded. I had never underestimated Alastair Campbell, but that vignette of power was an eye-opener. I was impressed. He was just doing his job, of course, but from his lofty position he had seen through the political reporter's masterful question and knew that a wrong answer could be disastrous.

We were not heading for Washington but for Chicago. Blair had a speech to give before flying up to DC. It was to be a special speech, not about Kosovo as such, not about NATO, nor the role of the special relationship between the US and Britain, but Blair's own personal vision about the morality of military intervention. Alastair had gone around emphasising the importance of the speech, and when we saw an embargoed copy, it was certainly extraordinary stuff. He was envisaging Britain playing a world role in the future that would encompass sending troops anywhere around the globe where people desperately needed help against tyrants or humanitarian disasters.

Blair was in an evangelistic mood. He felt that Kosovo had set a precedent and as prime minister of Britain he wanted to spread the word around the world that under his leadership, the British armed forces would be ready to respond to appeals for help. It was bold stuff.

As soon as he had finished his speech, the reporters travelling with him were ushered out and told to get on the bus for the airport. The plane was due to leave for Washington in a short time and we had to be on board before Blair arrived. I was frantically writing my story on the speech. I wanted to do the speech justice and, above all, I wanted a Chicago dateline! By the time we reached the airport, I had written three-quarters of the story but needed another fifteen minutes to finish it and file it to London, using my satellite phone as the data link. The Downing Street minders were rushing everyone to the steps of the plane, but I said I had to finish my story. I refused to join them. I sat on some steps about a hundred yards from the plane and typed away furiously, glancing every few seconds at the copy of the speech to make sure I was getting the quotes right.

A Downing Street official was beckoning to me, waving his arms from the entrance of the plane. He was probably mouthing obscenities at me, but I kept going. The story was finished. I attached the satellite phone connection into the laptop socket and pressed 'send'. The job was done. Pre-satellite phone days, my story could have been written but not filed! I grabbed my bag and ran to the plane, leaping up the stairs just as Blair and his entourage arrived in their motorcade. I wondered why I was the only reporter who had felt the need to file before we arrived in Washington. The news agencies would have filed but they had local correspondents in Chicago who had the time to write composite pieces. I don't know what the gaggle of political correspondents planned to do, but they must have risked waiting to write their stories after arriving in Washington. But the five-hour time difference with London would have made it a challenge to meet their deadlines.

The lesson I had learned so many times over the years was, if practical, never to board a plane or any other form of transport until the story had been written. First of all, it meant that you could enjoy the trip without having the stress of writing a piece the other end, and second, if anything goes wrong, like the plane is diverted in a storm, the boat sinks or the train breaks down, the story never gets to be written. The third lesson was that you should never rely on anyone else to file your story for you.

Once, as a reporter on the *Daily Express*, I

was sent to French Guiana for the launch of a European satellite from a rocket station in the middle of the jungle near the town of Kourou. I was commissioned to write a feature about the business prospects for Britain arising from the European space programme. I attended all the briefings, I went to the site of the imminent rocket launch, I interviewed everyone worth interviewing and then went back to the media centre to write my piece. I wrote 800 words, but was then informed I had to leave immediately to go back to the rocket launch site for lunch with all the visiting delegates from Europe who were there to witness the great moment when the fabulously expensive satellite was to be hurled into space early the following morning.

It was the 1980s. There was no laptop or attachable satellite phone. It had to be sent by telex. I was perfectly capable of telexing. I had telexed my stories the first time I went to the Falklands. But it takes time. It's a laborious process. I took my typed story to the telex operator at the media centre and asked him if he would be kind enough to file it for me, and gave him the details of the *Daily Express* link. He promised to do as I asked, and started telexing immediately. I turned round at the door and watched him for a moment, his fingers flying over the telex machine. I was confident he would finish in ten or fifteen minutes, and left for the coach to the jungle site to enjoy lunch, knowing that my feature would soon be arriving at the foreign desk of the *Daily Express*.

I returned mid afternoon and immediately

rang the foreign desk. 'Everything OK?' I asked. 'Have you got the feature all right?'

'No,' came the reply. They said they had never received it and now it was too late – something else was being used. It was devastating. What had gone wrong? I went to the media centre and found the man who had promised to telex my story.

'What happened? My paper never got my story. Did you send it?' I asked in a rush of words.

He looked shocked. 'Oh, yes, I'm sorry. I'd nearly finished the telex, then an urgent phone call came through from Paris. When I'd finished with that, it was lunchtime. After lunch, I was very busy. I'm afraid I forgot about your telex. But I can send it now.'

There was no point in being angry. The man was an incompetent, useless, lunch-eating, totally unreliable bureaucrat. But I should have telexed the story myself, or at least stood over him as he sent it to know for sure that it had gone before he left for his lunch. I should have skipped my own lunch. A big mistake. I vowed never to rely ever again on anyone as far as sending my stories was concerned. No one else has the same sense of what a Fleet Street deadline means. Why should they?

In the end, my disastrous trip was matched by disaster in the jungle. The European Space Agency rocket with the bright, shiny satellite attached took off successfully to great cheers and back-slapping among the scientists and VIPs. However, after fifteen minutes, the rocket stopped going upwards, faltered briefly, then turned upside down and headed for a permanent resting-place in the ocean. There was nothing left but to go home, dispirited and downcast.

CHAPTER 12
A DRIPPING TAP TELLS ITS OWN STORY

I had never been part of a liberation force. As British troops entered Pristina from the east and west of the city, the ethnic Albanian population crowded the streets and greeted them with roses and chocolates. The first to enter the city were the Irish Guards in their Warrior armoured vehicles that were soon covered in flowers. Then, in a spectacular demonstration of military exhibitionism, 800 British paratroopers landed in Pristina in a flurry of Chinook and Puma helicopters in the eastern part of the city and started spreading out, alert for angry Serbs. Going on patrol with them was like taking part in a Hollywood war film with every soldier being surrounded by laughing and happy locals. After months of suffering an oppressive occupation by Milosevic's bully boys, the presence of British soldiers walking around with their rifles at the ready gave the citizens their first glimpse of freedom.

Pristina was full of journalists. This was *the* big foreign story, and everyone in Fleet Street and from other European newspapers and television companies competed for space in the only hotel in town. The Grand Hotel was a shambles: it had suffered repeated bombing, and the entrance, foyer and half of the rooms were blackened shells. But, amazingly, it was open for business. Not all of the waiters and chefs had run off, and the dining room was functioning. The first person I saw when I arrived at the hotel to grab one of the rooms was my lovely colleague, Janine di Giovanni, a war veteran who always looked glamorous whatever the circumstances. We hugged and exchanged experiences. *The Times* had come mob-handed. Danny McGrory, former colleague from the *Daily Express* who was now with *The Times*, and Stephen Farrell, an up-and-coming reporter with a liking for communication gadgets, were also in Kosovo. We would need to meet and decide how to carve up the job between us. My role was a designated assignment because I had come in as part of the 1st Battalion Parachute Regiment, so I had access to one of the key liberating military units. Janine, Danny and Steve, who had driven across the Kosovo border in a gold-coloured Jeep, would do their own thing, hunting for stories, leaving me to report on the mission of the British troops.

Every day was an eye-opener. This was a country which had suffered a brutal occupation, and there were still areas of acute tension between Serb citizens and ethnic Albanians. There was also a growing awareness that, hidden in the countryside, there would be evidence of massacres, freshly dug graves or suspicious earth mounds containing slaughtered Albanians. The first few days were spent chasing rumours. The first suspected mass grave was found at Kacanik, which was on the main ethnic-cleansing route used by the Serbs. Local people spoke of horrifying experiences, relaying stories of men and women being mown down by Serb machine gun fire as they tried to scrabble up the hills around their homes to escape. Some of the witnesses were too frightened to speak, even though they knew the Serb troops had left the area and were heading for Belgrade.

Mejsere Krironjeva, a twenty-six-year-old woman with eyes that never stopped flicking from one side to the other, told me she was in the town when the Serbs arrived at about eleven o'clock in the morning on the 9th of April. Seventy people were killed, she said. 'It went on for twelve hours. People started to flee, but the Serbs shot them down and threw grenades,' she recalled. The local cemetery was filled with fresh graves, marked by numbered stakes. War crimes investigators were called in.

The most chilling discovery was a torture chamber in the basement of the main Serb police station in Pristina. It was found by British soldiers, and I was allowed to go down the seventeen concrete steps into the foul-smelling room to see for myself what must have taken place during the Serb military occupation. There was nothing sophisticated about the torture implements: knuckle-dusters with sharp edges, truncheons, one split in half by the force of the blows, cudgels, a long knife with a two-foot blade, a baseball bat, heavy metal chains, a pickaxe, a large brown leather belt, a car battery for electrode treatment and a black hood. Round one corner, in a separate room, there was a bed with a leather strap at the head for restraining the victims. A bullet-riddled mattress lay on the floor next to the bed.

In the main torture chamber, there was a pile of sodden clothes in a corner. On a ledge, there was a single blue baby shoe. Little was left to the imagination. When I spotted a chair without a seat, with a dripping pipe directly overhead, it was too easy to visualise another torture tactic. The atmosphere in the empty chamber was claustrophobic. The air was damp and cold. Piled on one side of the chamber was an assortment of medical paraphernalia, including swabs, pills, field dressings – some covered in dried blood – and bandages.

The victims were brought here to confess, yet inscribed in Serbo-Croat on a baseball bat used for beatings were the words 'shut your mouth'.

British officials estimated that the Serbs had killed 10,000 people in just three months, which would make their rampage through Kosovo one of the bloodiest episodes in recent memory. How many died in that torture chamber? No one knew. But it was an experience that stayed with me for a long time.

During the NATO bombing campaign, military spokesmen had made many grandiose claims about knocking out up to sixty percent of Serb tanks and artillery in Kosovo. But sitting at the side of the road on the northern outskirts of Pristina on the day the Serb forces drove a convoy of low-loader transport vehicles up the hill out of the city told a different story. The transporters were carrying tanks. The convoy consisted of hundreds of vehicles, and I lost count of the number of T72, T55 and T54 tanks being transported. Undamaged tanks – not a mark on them. In addition, there were D90 self-propelled howitzers and tracked, armoured personnel carriers. It was an impressive display of firepower.

So what was the explanation? Had NATO been lying, or was the alliance just fooling itself? The answer became clear after I began to drive around Kosovo. Every field had cardboard tanks under camouflage. The Serbs had gone out of their way to deceive NATO's bombers, creating a force of fake tanks. From 15,000 feet, they must have looked pretty genuine. It was classic Soviet-style 'maskirovka' deception tactics. Many of the cardboard models had also survived the 'pinpoint' airstrikes. Undoubtedly, the persistent cloud cover over the province during the bombing raids had played havoc with accuracy.

Nevertheless, for once, the international community which had been horrified by the mass slaughter of civilians in Kosovo was justified in feeling the air campaign and the peacekeeping intervention had been a success. By the deadline of midnight on the 20th of June 1999, every Serb soldier and Ministry of Interior policeman had exited the province. About 41,000 men in uniform, some of whom had committed war crimes, had crossed the border, leaving behind about 60,000 Serb civilians to continue living resentfully with their Albanian neighbours. Keeping them apart and preventing further bloodshed would be the responsibility of General Jackson and the 50,000 troops under his command.

For reporters covering the peacekeeping mission, it was an assignment without luxuries. Even the war reporters who liked to cover conflicts from the comfort of a nice hotel had to put up with pretty primitive conditions. It was hard to find a tap that produced water, let alone water clean enough to drink. I, Tim Butcher of the *Daily Telegraph,* James Dalrymple of *The Independent,* Nick Parker of *The Sun* and the redoubtable, charming Ross Benson of the *Daily Mail* were known by the assembled gathering of correspondents as 'the rufty tufties', because we were supposed to travel with the British Army units to which we had each been assigned. We had to sleep wherever the units stopped for the night, often out in the open and usually in a sleeping bag at the side of the road or on a wall. We had to eat cooked but cold army rations out of tear-off bags. The rest of the reporting fraternity relied on the Grand Hotel staff to provide meals from the limited supplies. These reporters and TV crews had arrived in Kosovo in an assortment of fancy Jeeps that cluttered the road outside the hotel. If it wasn't for the blackened windows, bombed-out foyer and dangerously uneven staircase leading to the blasted rooms, one might have imagined that some sort of Jeep convention was underway.

The journalists themselves had flocked to Kosovo from all over Europe and beyond, but not all of them were up for taking risks. Some journalists were first-time war reporters who refused to go in search of stories that hinted at risk. Others were veterans who had covered the Vietnam War and numerous other hellspots, and their experience was awe-inspiring. Seeing so many reporters, photographers and cameramen milling around reminded me of the early days of the Bosnian War, when the novelty of having a conflict within such easy reach attracted hordes of members of the Fourth Estate.

Pristina was the only spot in Kosovo where mobile phones worked, which was why so many of the assembled journalists had set up shop in the capital, venturing out during the day and then returning to the Grand Hotel to send their stories back to their news desks. The broadcasters had arrived with their satellite dishes attached to vans, and Pristina was swamped with the television boys walking around with earphones and muttering darkly into mobiles to fix one-on-ones between HQ back in London, or wherever, and the anchors who had flown into Kosovo to mastermind the news shows. When Fleet Street and the broadcasters gather together in such large numbers, it is probably akin to being occupied all over again in the eyes of the suffering locals.

One shocking night ruined the general atmosphere of bonhomie and mild drunkenness. Two German journalists had decided foolishly to stay out after dark and were still in the old city of Prizren in southern Kosovo when the rest of the reporters were tucking into their first proper meal of the day, courtesy of the ever-patient Grand Hotel kitchen staff. The German reporters were stopped at a Serb police checkpoint and shot dead. It was a reminder to all of us that even in an *après*-war period, there could be dangers around every corner. The jollity that night faded fast.

General Jackson stayed as commander of the Kosovo peacekeeping force until October 1999, and few doubted that his tough leadership had been the key ingredient in NATO's successful mission. He had become almost a cult figure with his deep gravelly voice, his slightly stooped figure and the prominent bags under his eyes. He knew how to relax at the end of a long day. I was once summoned to his headquarters in Pristina for a chat and was greeted with a large tumbler of whiskey filled nearly to the top. I wasn't a whiskey drinker, but I had little choice but to sip the liquor as he downed his glass and helped himself to a second. He was, as ever, great company, but by the time I emerged into the darkness and staggered towards the Grand Hotel I vowed that I would never touch whiskey again – not unless, of course, it was thrust into my hand by the dear general. I had no doubt that I would be seeing him again in his next jobs as he worked his way up the promotion ladder to British Army chief.

My most treasured possession from the Kosovo operation was a brown war correspondent's passport, issued to me by the Ministry of Defence in my capacity as an officially-assigned embedded reporter with the British troops. It was the first and only time that the Ministry of Defence had decided to produce a formal document to be carried by reporters. Unfortunately, it was a time-limited passport, and during my weeks covering the peacekeeping mission in Kosovo I was never asked to show it to anyone. It remained fresh-smelling and virgin for at least two weeks, tucked safely away inside my jacket. Only when I got caught in a downpour while I was holding it in my hand did its pristine newness get slightly tainted by raindrops. It still looked too unused and unwanted, so I dropped it in a large puddle and rubbed it dry. Now my war correspondent's passport looked as if it had been somewhere, perhaps somewhere dangerous… and wet.

In May 2000, I was caught up in another war in another part of the world. I was driving my 1984 Jaguar Sovereign to the office when my mobile phone rang. It wasn't yet illegal to talk on the phone while driving, so I picked it up. It was the foreign desk.

'Have you got your passport?'

I always had my passport with me.

'We want you to get to Sierra Leone as fast as possible.'

I turned round and drove home to pack. Sierra Leone over the last few weeks had become a big story. The former British colony was being overrun by a wild revolutionary militia force. An expanded British Army battalion of about 1,000 Parachute Regiment soldiers had been sent to Freetown, the capital, to help evacuate hundreds of British nationals. But the role of the Paras suddenly changed. They were the only military available to defend Freetown from being seized by the rebels. The Revolutionary United Front (RUF), a fearsome group of fighters high on drugs with scores of dragooned child soldiers among their numbers, was at the gates of the capital. The British Government spoke calmly of the paratroopers playing a non-combat role, evacuating 500 British nationals to safety and leaving the United Nations force already in Sierra Leone to deal with the rebels. But this was wishful thinking. The intelligence from the frontline was far scarier. A total of 500 UN African peacekeepers had been held hostage by the rebels, and the blue-beret brigade didn't seem up to fighting off the RUF. That wasn't their role. With the dispatching of about 800 Royal Marines on board *HMS Ocean*, the Royal Navy's helicopter carrier, Britain's military presence in the region was building up rapidly. It looked like war, or, at the very least, a dangerous and potentially explosive stand-off between the wild rebels and the British paratroopers. But there was no Ministry of Defence plan for a war. What was later to happen was all ad hoc, driven by the British military commander in Freetown who improvised, against his superiors' orders, to save the capital.

I flew into Freetown and was greeted by

British paratroopers who had sealed off the airport and were perched tense and ready around the runway. Even as the government in London struggled to come to terms with what was going on in Sierra Leone, Fleet Street had once again gathered for a new war. The majority were holed up in the Mammy Yoko Hotel where the UN also had its headquarters. When I arrived there were no rooms left, but before I departed to find accommodation farther up the coast, I wandered down to the beach to see if I could spot any colleagues. There might have been a war on, but if there's a beach and warm weather, and the story has been filed, most journalists would grab the chance of a swim to relax. Sure enough, there emerging from the sea wrapped in a sarong-type swimsuit was my colleague, Janine di Giovanni. What a contrast to the last time we met, in the burnt-out hulk of the Grand Hotel in Pristina. Janine had been filing from Sierra Leone for some weeks as the civil war raged. She had already experienced frightening moments surrounded by mobs, but right now she was walking up the beach looking serenely calm. I grinned and waved.

I took to Sierra Leone immediately. The country had suffered endless civil war, and the wild bunch at the gates of Freetown was ready to murder and rape if given the chance. But with the British paratroopers present and Royal Marines offshore, life could go on in Freetown with a reasonable degree of safety. Being a former part of the once great British Empire, and thus pink on the world map, Sierra

Leoneans loved anyone from their mother country; to prove it, the schoolchildren, dressed immaculately in British-style uniforms that could have come from Harrods, walked down the streets crocodile-fashion, cheerily waving and chatting, as if they knew that the Queen of England had sent her soldiers to protect them.

Our job as reporters was to leave the comfort zone of Freetown and venture out into the potentially dangerous areas outside the capital where the rebels were hiding. But in the evening, we all had one thing in mind which was to sit down in one of the many relatively primitive restaurants and eat garlic prawns, an absolutely delicious speciality of Freetown's chefs.

One of the hardest-working and determined reporters was Kurt Schork of Reuters, having switched careers late in his life. He had always wanted to be a war correspondent, but before he made his name reporting from Sarajevo in the Bosnia conflict, he had worked for an estate agency business in America, run the New York transport authority, and become a senior staff member for Michael Dukakis who failed disastrously as the Democratic presidential candidate in 1988.

Suddenly, he was dead. He got up early one morning to carry out what was known as the 'milk run', driving down a stretch of road towards the town of Lunsar, which lay about sixty miles northeast of Freetown, where the RUF rebels were known to be operating. Travelling with him were Miguel Gil Moreno de

Mora, a Spanish Associated Press cameraman, Yannis Behrakis, a Greek photographer, and Mark Chisholm, a South African television cameraman. The latter two also worked for Reuters. They had been told the road was safe. But, as they drove down it, ten RUF fighters dressed in T-shirts leapt from hiding places at the side of the road and opened fire with automatic rifles. Kurt was shot fatally in the head. Miguel also died as the spray of bullets hurtled into the vehicles indiscriminately.

Back in Freetown, we heard nothing of this disaster for some time. Then rumours started to fly around that journalists, unidentified at that stage, had been attacked in an ambush. There were reports that two had been killed. We all rushed to the Mammy Yoko Hotel, but no one from the UN headquarters could tell us the one thing we needed to know. Who had been killed? It was shortly before midnight that day – the 24th of May 2000 – that the names emerged. By then, we had all guessed. Kurt and Miguel were not among us, and we had been told that the two dead were an American and a Spaniard. It was a massive blow. Kurt had taken risks throughout his war corresponding career, but he seemed so tough and capable that for him to be mown down by rebel fighters on a road he had been assured was safe was almost beyond comprehension.

There were demands for background stories from London and, as I was the reporter on the spot, even though I had not known Kurt as well as some other colleagues, I made several calls and wrote a eulogy of Kurt's extraordinary career. One urgent matter had to be dealt with before anything else: Anthony Loyd was one of Kurt's greatest friends and had to be told. I discovered from the foreign desk that he was in Addis Ababa in Ethiopia. It was two in the morning there, but I phoned his hotel room. He answered immediately. I told him I had terrible news, but he knew already; another friend had phoned him shortly before my call. Anthony provided me with some snippets of Kurt's life, which helped to add some colour to the piece I wrote. The next day, I interviewed the Greek photographer who had been wounded in the leg during the ambush. He was due to fly out of the country for treatment but I managed to get to him before he left. He looked stunned but recounted the moments of terror he faced as he tried to escape through the bush while the wild men of the RUF hunted him down.

The issue of child soldiers was one of the biggest scandals of the Sierra Leone civil war. Both sides in the war, the rebels and the Sierra Leone army, had child gunmen among their ranks, but the scariest were serving under the RUF. I came across one child soldier whose affiliation was unclear, but he had the look of a rebel. His eyes were dulled by constant drinking of a strong cough mixture which seemed to be the favourite drug to keep them under control. Well, cough mixture and some other substance – probably cocaine. The kid was no more than ten, and as soon as I started to approach him he produced the longest knife I'd ever seen, a big, brutal curving blade with a thick handle. He proudly held it up and made a jerky move. His glazed eyes registered no emotion. Children, as ever, were the tragic victims of war.

But the most gruesome sight around Freetown and in the areas around the capital were the machete victims. The rebels used butcher's machetes to chop off people's limbs, and they were brought into Freetown for emergency surgery. There were so many locals with missing arms and legs that a special recuperation centre was set up for them, overlooking the sea.

Freetown was saved from an RUF takeover by the British paratroopers and Royal Marines, and by daily low-flying Royal Navy Harriers off the carrier, *HMS Illustrious,* whose thunderous jet engines were intended to frighten the rebels. But the multitude of machete victims was a constant reminder of the sheer brutality lurking in the bush not far from the capital. The British military was going to have to stay longer than had been planned. The UN peacekeeping force, despite its size, could not be relied on to beat off the rebels, and the locals liked having the British around.

The officer in charge, Brigadier David Richards, had shown a natural talent for the job that consisted of a number of diverse elements: toughness in dealing with the rebel threat, diplomatic skills in advising the country's leader, President Ahmad Kabbah, a gentle soul who wore fancy slipper-like shoes, and expertise in dealing with the local population, in particular the radio stations. He had an intuitive understanding about the need to spread information to the people of the country he had been sent to protect. It wasn't propaganda, it was just keeping them informed of what was happening and how the British military was handling it. Brigadier Richards – who was, in due course, to rise to the most prestigious job in Britain's armed forces, chief of the defence staff – also liked the media. I spent time with him in his hilltop chalet headquarters in Freetown, and he loved to talk about how important a role we were all playing in disseminating the story of Sierra Leone. Positive stories, where they were possible, helped his cause and assisted in maintaining support for the mission back home.

A military command job overseas is partly about politics, and Brigadier Richards was particularly adroit at keeping all the components of his role in Sierra Leone under control, and doing so in a relaxed and friendly fashion that helped to spread the message that Operation Palliser, as the campaign was codenamed, was going to be slotted into the history books as a successful mission. After the Falklands victory in 1982 and the perceived success of Kosovo in 1999, the reputation of the British military was running pretty high. However, the victory in Sierra Leone would never have been achieved had Brigadier Richards stuck to his initial orders, which were to carry out a 'non-combatant evacuation' of British nationals and then swiftly depart. He saw that more could be done with the military assets he had under his command and decided to ignore his bosses back in London. Freetown was saved as a result.

The RUF never entered the capital. But, in September that year, something went seriously wrong. A group of soldiers from the Royal Irish Regiment, travelling in a convoy of Land Rovers, turned left instead of right on their way back to camp and found themselves surrounded by probably the most extreme rebel militia of the lot, the West End Boys, a jungle-based group on the fringe of the anti-government forces. They were potent, well-armed and murderous. After frantic negotiations, six of the kidnapped soldiers were released, but the remainder, five British and one Sierra Leonean liaison officer, disappeared into the jungle, and their lives were considered to be at high risk. The circumstances behind their bizarre map-reading error were put to one side for a later investigation. Clearly, it was highly embarrassing that well-trained soldiers of the British Army had been captured by drug-fuelled jungle fighters. But the only issue at stake was how to find them and rescue them before they were butchered. This was clearly a job for the SAS, but the Ministry of Defence in London was giving nothing away. In the end, it was a combination of SAS, SBS (Special Boat Service) and 1st Battalion Parachute Regiment.

I had returned from Sierra Leone by that stage and was on a week's holiday with my family down in Cornwall. By chance, I switched on the TV in the morning on the first Sunday of the holiday. It was the *David Frost Show*.

His interviewee was none other than General Sir Charles Guthrie, Chief of the Defence Staff and a former SAS squadron commander. Frost asked him about the Royal Irish Regiment soldiers still being held captive and, to my astonishment, he announced that there had been a dramatic development. The soldiers had been freed unharmed after a special rescue operation, although a young SAS trooper, one of the soldiers involved in the dangerous mission, had been fatally shot as he jumped out of a Chinook helicopter. It was a spectacular announcement. Normally these sorts of statements are made to the House of Commons by the prime minister or the defence secretary, but it was a Sunday, so here was the military's top man seizing his moment. He could hardly contain his excitement.

I rang *The Times* and told them I would find out what I could and send them a story from Cornwall. I couldn't bear the thought that some other reporter would be sent off to the Ministry of Defence to write the story because I was on holiday. I rang everyone I could, listed in my contacts book, and over a period of about an hour gleaned such a huge amount of detail, including which squadron of the SAS was used in the rescue, that I was able to sit down at my laptop and write a 1,000-word piece while the rest of the family were down on the beach. My story was on the computer screens in the office before Alan Hamilton, the reporter sent to the MoD, returned from the press conference that gave out the basic facts of the rescue operation.

Alan, a man who could turn the most ordinary story into glowing prose, was told that unless he had something to add, the desk was very sorry but the defence editor in Cornwall – I had been promoted from defence correspondent to defence editor in 1998 – had already written an account. Alan read my story, checked his notes from the press conference, and declared that I had far more detail than he had been given by the MoD officials, and felt he had no reason to add, rewrite or insert a single word. He told me later he had laughed when the desk had warned him that I had already written the story.

'I wasn't in the least surprised,' he said.

Best of all, he didn't bear a grudge at all; he just accepted it good-naturedly. I went down to the beach and joined the rest of the family just as the sun began to dip towards the horizon. Another holiday ruined – but by a cracking story.

CHAPTER 13
ROCKETS AWAY

News never stops. You go home after a long day and settle down for the evening when the phone rings. On the 20th of September 2000, the night news desk rang to say that there seemed to have been some sort of explosion near MI6. First reports on the agency wires indicated it was a small explosive device hidden inside a bin outside the headquarters of the Secret Intelligence Service. Not necessarily a major story, but intriguing.

It was now ten o'clock at night. The first edition had already gone, so I had about half an hour to check it out with my intelligence sources to see if the incident was more interesting than it seemed.

I rang a special contact on his mobile. He told me he was in the back of a taxi. He then uttered the words which dramatically changed the story and my next sixty minutes: 'No it wasn't a bomb in a bin, it was a rocket. MI6 has been hit by a rocket.'

Someone had fired Soviet-made rocket-propelled grenades at the front of the building and had struck a window construction on the seventh floor. My contact said the rocket had been launched from a small public park the other side of Vauxhall railway station, which is located alongside the south embankment road that runs in front of MI6. The rockets had caused damage, but nothing of great significance. No one had been injured.

It was a massive story. The IRA – it was assumed to be the Irish terrorists – had brazenly attacked one of the most symbolic targets in London. I thanked my contact and, with huge excitement, rang the night news desk to give them the news.

'IT WAS A ROCKET!'

I had thirty minutes or so to write the late edition splash, but the story was so dramatic it almost wrote itself. When I finished it and pressed 'send', the Press Association, the main UK news agency, was still speculating about a bomb in a waste bin. All the late editions of the rival newspapers also told of a bomb exploding outside MI6 headquarters and quoted police sources suggesting it was some form of explosive device which had been concealed in a bin. The late edition of *The Times* had the real story: 'MI6 hit by rocket-launched grenades'.

My faded blue contacts book, a bulging, somewhat disfigured and disorganised accumulation of names and telephone numbers, had, once again, proved invaluable. Ben Preston, the home news editor for *The Times*, passed on his congratulations the following morning. John Wellman, his deputy, the sort of newsman every reporter needs on a desk, always enthusiastic and excited by scoops, was equally appreciative. There's nothing like comparing your own paper with all the rivals and seeing that on this occasion we had beaten everyone to the best story. It made the morning editorial conference for the editor and his top executives a time of smiling faces, instead of harsh comments and inquests about why we had missed some story that a rival had published on its front page.

The same sense of excitement and drama happened only four weeks later. A Royal Navy nuclear-powered submarine, *HMS Tireless,* had limped into Gibraltar in May with what was feared to be a crack in the pipes leading to the water-cooling system around the nuclear reactor. Nuclear-powered subs are among the most treasured of warfighting platforms because they can operate unseen and unheard under the oceans for five or six months without needing to come up for air. The length of their patrols is governed not by the amount of fuel in the tanks but by the food stocks in the fridge. When the sausages are finished, the crew needs to get back home to restock, but the fuel never runs out. However, with nuclear fuel rods generating the heat to drive the steam turbines, there have to be excessive precautions taken to ensure that everything is properly sealed. The dreaded scenario with anything nuclear-powered is the 'meltdown' situation in which the reactor becomes so uncontrollably overheated that it literally explodes downwards and spreads radioactivity around. In the confined space of a submarine, it leaves little to the imagination. So when the first crack appeared in the piping on *HMS Tireless*, the Royal Navy ordered the commanding officer to steam slowly to the nearest port, Gibraltar.

For defence correspondents, the first question was: what about all the other nuclear subs? Was there a danger that they, too, would need to be checked for cracked pipes? The Royal Navy was circumspect, insisting that an investigation into the suspected crack found on *HMS Tireless* had to be completed before any decision was made about the other boats. They claimed there was no reason to suppose that other submarines out on patrol were suffering from the same defect. This went on for weeks. I asked the same question again and again and again, just in case one day the answer might be different. I knew my rivals would be doing likewise. The Royal Navy and Ministry of Defence stuck to the same line. There was no change, and *HMS Tireless* was still being checked. Months went by.

Shortly before 4pm on the 20th of October 2000, I received a phone call from the MoD, in reply to my routine question about possible implications for the rest of the fleet of nuclear-powered submarines. The answer this time was sensationally different. A decision had been taken to recall all of the Royal Navy's twelve nuclear-powered submarines so that each one could be checked for cracks. Not all the subs were out on patrol, of course; some were in dock, some were in training and others were going through routine, mid-term, or long-term maintenance cycles. So the checks could be handled in a systematic way without having to bring every boat back to base immediately.

However, the fact was the decision had been made to recall all of them in due order because of concerns that the crack found on *HMS Tireless* might also be present in other boats. I asked so many questions that the MoD official the other end of the line told me he would try to put me in touch with the head of the Royal Navy's strategic systems, an admiral, who could answer my questions more authoritatively. He promised to ring me back within half an hour.

I ran to the news desk and rather melodramatically announced to Ben Preston: 'Have I got a good story for you!'

It was now 4pm, the moment when the news editor had to attend the afternoon editorial conference. There was no time to add my story to his news schedule list. But he walked off, clutching his list, with my breaking story in his head.

The admiral got in touch with me, as promised; a smart move by the MoD, because it meant I had the most senior in-house nuclear submarine expert at my disposal, and he answered my questions with total clarity and honesty while attempting to put the recall decision into context. The MoD was worried that I might write a story saying every Royal Navy nuclear sub was on the brink of an atomic explosion. There was no question of me writing such a story, but I still needed to know all the facts before I could properly report on what was a dramatically significant move by the Navy chiefs.

We splashed the story the next day, and after the first edition every other Fleet Street newspaper followed it up. The MoD clearly knew that, once the decision to recall the submarines had been taken, it would be impossible to keep it a secret for long. There were people out there who monitored the comings and goings of nuclear submarines, in and out of their home port, and the return of so many boats over a relatively short period would have raised questions. Then the MoD would have been accused of a cover-up, and the very headlines ministers and officials were anxious to avoid about submarines in 'meltdown nightmare' would have appeared on every front page.

It was the first and only time I had the head of the Royal Navy's strategic systems on the other end of the line answering all my questions. The only other occasion an admiral in the MoD was so forthcoming was when I had asked to see someone who could talk to me about the sinking of the Argentine cruiser, the *Belgrano,* during the 1982 Falklands War. But for that interview I went to the MoD and sat down with him for an hour or two before writing my piece across two pages in the *Daily Express*. For the nuclear sub recall story, there was no time for a sit-down in front of an admiral. It had to be a phone call, which must have been pretty tough, even nerve-wracking, for the admiral, who would not have been used to discussing with a Fleet Street reporter matters that, under normal circumstances, would have been highly classified.

At that time, Balkans news never stopped either. After Bosnia and Kosovo, it was the turn of the Former Yugoslav Republic of Macedonia. It had to be called that because Greece claimed ownership of the name Macedonia, and there couldn't be two Macedonias. In 2001, after a six-month civil war in the Former Yugoslav Republic of Macedonia, involving government forces and ethnic Albanian rebels, the international community decided that some form of intervention was required, and NATO was mandated to send troops into the country to oversee a handover of weapons by the rebel factions as part of an overall peace agreement. It sounded like one of those symbolic gestures which would mean little in the grand scheme of things. How could anyone be sure that every rifle, every mortar rocket, every artillery piece and, most importantly, every man-portable surface-to-air missile-launcher was going to be handed over voluntarily? NATO was confident it could do the job and a senior British officer called Brigadier Barney White-Spunner, a jovial chap with an easy manner, was selected to command a 3,500-man alliance force to mastermind the arms handover show.

It was too good a story to miss, so I flew out to Skopje in late August to witness the rebels coming out of the hills to dispose of their weapons. Britain was called upon to provide the bulk of the force – about 2,000 troops – for the operation, which was rather quaintly codenamed Essential Harvest.

A lot of preparation work had to be carried out before the weapon-handover queues could start forming up, so there was time to travel around the country to discover how the civil war had affected the population of this small Balkan nation. One morning, several of us set off by car out of Skopje, but we had just reached the outskirts of the city when word reached us that there had been an incident at a bridge and a British soldier had been killed. We headed back to the city and found the bridge. The incident itself was over and there were no police around. But, by chatting to the nearest locals who lived close to the bridge, we learnt that a group of youths had thrown a concrete slab over the edge as a British Army Land Rover was passing beneath. Sapper Ian Collins, who was only twenty-two, was struck in the head and died. He had arrived in Skopje just a few days earlier. His mission was supposed to have been relatively danger-free, but his short army career had come to a shocking end. It was a pointless protest by a group of mindless teenage thugs. The police turned up at least half an hour after we had finished interviewing every local resident, all of whom seemed to know who was responsible for the attack. But the police were more interested in getting rid of us than doing their job. The story was the splash the next day, and the tragic death of a young soldier trying to play his part in a peacekeeping mission provoked many questions. Why were British soldiers once again putting their lives at risk in the Balkans? Well, the incident had little – if anything – to do with the arms handover. It was just a tragic case of a British soldier being in the wrong place.

Elsewhere in the country, there were still

rebel commanders strutting around like barons in charge of their fiefdoms. I came across one in a small village called Poroj about an hour's drive from Skopje. I was with David Williams, chief reporter of the *Daily Mail,* and David Crump, a photographer on the paper. They were a good team. Dave Williams was a sleuth reporter who never gave up on a story, and Crumpy, as he was known, was the best possible companion to have in a tough spot, always cheerful and seldom without a smile on his face. On this occasion I had been assigned to the story without a photographer.

We went in search of the rebel commander and found him sitting in a café. He looked exactly how I had imagined a rebel commander in the Balkans: about six feet tall with thick, wavy dark hair, a large beard, black eyes, a bandana strapped round his head, a full combat outfit and pistols tucked into holsters. He was a brigand, and he certainly looked the part. We approached him tentatively. Our first question produced a grunt and a swivel of the head; he wasn't interested in talking to us. But sitting with him was another rebel who spoke a little English. As a result, we got a few usable quotes about his view of the peacekeeping effort. Crumpy then asked if he could take a photograph. The rebel commander was adamant – no pictures.

I turned to the other fighter and said: 'Can you tell him that he looks fantastic in all his gear and that it would be really great to take his photograph?'

There was a long exchange of words between

the two men. The rebel commander spoke most of them, and after what seemed to be a tirade from him, making us think that we would be strung up on the nearest tree branch if we didn't get the hell out of his domain, the interpreter replied: 'He says, where do you want him to stand?'

Appealing to his vanity had done the trick. He ended up standing with one leg up on a rock against the background of a wall pockmarked with bullet holes, holding his AK47 assault rifle in both hands. Crumpy took a classic picture. Typical of the man, he sent a copy of his photograph free gratis to the picture desk at *The Times*. We ran it the next day with my story about the day's events, including the quotes from the rebel commander. The *Daily Mail* ran neither the story nor the picture.

One evening, at the hotel in Skopje, a British Army sergeant was asking for me. I introduced myself to him and he said his unit wanted me to witness the first handover of rebel arms planned for the following morning. I jumped at the chance, and early the next day I was picked up and taken to a remote site in a valley, surrounded by hills and forests, where rebels were supposed to turn up and start surrendering their weapons. Brigadier Barney White-Spunner had arranged for snipers to hide in the hills with their sights trained on the rebels as they arrived for the ceremony, just in case one of them changed their mind and looked set to open fire. The British unit I was with had set up a table and chairs, and when rebels started to emerge carrying an assortment of weapons they were told to form a queue. Amazingly, they obeyed. It was a bizarre situation. Rebels who had fought for six months against government forces now stood a little nervously in a relatively straight line, waiting their turn to be formally disarmed and have the whole process chronicled in a large notebook by a couple of British officers. Armed soldiers stood around to keep the peace, if peace had to be kept. I watched from a few yards away.

I noticed that one of the rebels was carrying a long cardboard box. It contained a shoulder-launched surface-to-air missile. A British officer said it was in pristine condition. In other words, it was unused and still in its production-line wrapping. The vast majority handed over their AK47s, but a few were carrying rocket-propelled grenades and pistols. The pile of weapons was beginning to look impressive. But, of course, this was the Balkans; no doubt every rebel who delivered an AK47 had another four hidden in his attic or shed or under his bed. AK47s in the Balkans were as common as walking sticks in Britain. Nevertheless, the surrendering of arms was an acknowledgment that the civil war in the Former Yugoslav Republic of Macedonia was over, and the British brigadier could return home with his men, satisfied that the mission had been successfully completed.

The year 2001 was all about one event, and its implications had repercussions for the future of many of the world's nations. It dictated the direction of my career on *The Times* and it ruined an important family occasion. The hijacking of four airliners by nineteen al-Qaeda terrorists, and the path of destruction they took once they had taken over the pilots' seats, began just as I was wandering back from a local sandwich bar with a number of colleagues. We were walking across the car park towards *The Times* office when a colleague from production hailed us: 'You should see what's going on! A plane has just crashed into the Twin Towers!'

We started to run, and joined the gathering of reporters, subeditors and others in front of the main television, hung from the ceiling above the news desk. Ten minutes went by and suddenly we all spotted the same thing. Another plane was heading for the Twin Towers and, as we watched, there was a brilliant splash of white heat on the television screen, followed by black smoke. We all knew that we were witnessing the most outrageous terrorist attack ever devised. The full impact was hard to grasp, but when the third hijacked plane crashed into the Pentagon and a fourth was reported to be heading for the White House or the Capitol, it was like some extraterrestrial force was taking over the world. Above all, we felt helpless. The only thing we could do was to start writing the paper for the next day.

The editor ordered a separate supplement, to be filled with photographs that would tell the story more graphically than any words, however elegantly constructed. My role that day was to predict the immensity of the investigation that would have to be held, the tracking down of the terrorist masterminds behind the hijack plot and the questions that would be raised about the failure of America's vast intelligence community to prevent such a monstrous attack.

I felt – we all felt – that the world had irretrievably changed. There were braver, or perhaps more foolish, commentators spouting on the television who insisted that, while the terrorist attack was a catastrophic event, the world would carry on as before. According to them, the world's economies would not be shaken; people would not have to transform their lives because of al-Qaeda; no governments would fall. It was not like the planet had been damaged by a nuclear strike. To an extent, these commentators were right. I went home after writing my story, ate my supper, watched some television and went to bed. The next day, I got up at my normal time and travelled to work. The trains were running as usual. Yet, there was unquestionably a sense of foreboding, a feeling of vulnerability that hadn't been there before 9/11. The duration of this feeling depended on the world's reaction to the terrorists who had succeeded in orchestrating the biggest surprise attack on the United States of America since the Japanese air raids on Pearl Harbour in 1941.

Osama bin Laden's plane plot had been designed not just to destroy iconic landmarks and kill thousands of people but also to undermine America's confidence in itself and bring down the economy. Bin Laden's wider aims failed. America survived, the economy was strong enough to withstand the huge pressures on the dollar and President George W. Bush delivered arguably one of the finest speeches of any US president. It lifted the hopes of the average American citizen and reminded the rest of the world that America was not going to be cowed by a group of fanatical terrorists plotting and planning from their hideouts in Afghanistan and Pakistan. Whatever anyone thought of President Bush subsequently, the speech in which he pledged that America would face up to its enemies was as good as any of the more famous addresses given by his predecessors. And that includes President John F. Kennedy's speech at his inauguration ceremony in which he called upon the people to think what they could do for their country, and his address in Germany beginning '*Ich bin ein Berliner*'.

War drums began to sound all over again. It was clear President Bush wanted to exact punishment and revenge, and the man in his sights was Osama bin Laden, who was known to be hiding in the mountains in Afghanistan. As the tempo for a US-led war against al-Qaeda in Afghanistan steadily rose, I had to break the news to *The Times* that my oldest son, Sam, was getting married on the 6th of October, in a ceremony overlooking a beach at Lindos on the Greek island of Rhodes, and that I planned to be away for a week, a few days either side of the wedding. Ben Preston, the news editor, said it was 'sod's law' that I should have a family wedding just when a war was about to break out. I told him that, if necessary, I could attend the wedding on the Saturday and return the following day, leaving the rest of the family to enjoy the week's holiday. He thought that was a good option to keep in mind.

We all flew out on the 3rd of October and spent an idyllic few days swimming and sunbathing, and then dressed up for the wedding on the Saturday. Chris, our middle son, had forgotten to bring shoes to go with his wedding suit and stood throughout the ceremony in black socks. The service was short and in Greek. It was perfect. The imminent war was forgotten. We ate on the rooftop of a restaurant in the middle of Lindos and toasted Sam and his bride, Mel.

Later that day, I rang one of my best contacts at the MoD in London. The conversation went like this:

'I'm currently in Rhodes at my son's wedding. If you were me, would you stay here for another four days?'

His reply: 'If I was you, I wouldn't stay.'

The following morning, I said goodbye to Sam and the rest of the family and took a taxi to Rhodes airport. As I queued up for the first flight back to London, I looked nervously at a couple of fellow passengers. That was the way it was, even a month after the 9/11 terrorist attacks. Every airline passenger was a potential terrorist hijacker. I thought the chances of a terrorist plot originating from the island of Rhodes was a little far-fetched, so I boarded the plane and it took off at 10am.

After landing at Heathrow, I took a taxi to my home in southwest London, changed, and then drove my Jag to *The Times* office in Wapping. I parked in the car park and ran to the office. It was 7pm. When I arrived on the editorial floor, everyone in the office was grouped around the television above the news desk. They were watching breaking news. Simon Pearson, the chief night editor, turned round at that moment and spotted me.

'Is this the real thing – is this it?' he asked.

I took one look at the scenes of explosions in the night sky running live on CNN and replied, 'Yes, this is real; it has begun.'

I had arrived in the office at precisely the moment when the first US airstrikes had begun in Afghanistan, and walked quickly to my desk to start writing my contribution towards the splash. Twenty-four hours earlier, I had been celebrating my son's wedding with champagne and lamb kebabs. I had, again, let my family down, putting work before anything else. But the news desk expressed huge relief that the defence editor was back in the office. No one asked me how the wedding had gone.

While the bombings in Afghanistan continued and US special forces, backed by CIA paramilitary officers, started to try and flush out Osama bin Laden from his mountain stronghold, there was much discussion about the role Britain could play. The SAS were in demand, but Tony Blair was keen to offer a substantial package to back Britain's main ally.

As it happened, Britain had planned one

of the biggest exercises for years, in the Gulf state of Oman, and I was accredited, along with numerous other reporters, to witness the training. Normally, military exercises were boring because they rarely led to proper stories. News desks were never interested in pretend manoeuvres. They wanted the real thing, and so did I. But the training exercise in Oman was timed to perfection. It gave the British troops the chance to carry out some dress rehearsals if they were to be involved in the ground war in Afghanistan. The scenario for the exercise, called Saif Sareea II, had been devised a year earlier, and the MoD denied that the arrival of 23,000 troops, tanks, armoured vehicles and fighter aircraft in Oman had anything to do with 9/11 or what George Bush was doing against al-Qaeda in Afghanistan.

However, all the reporters flying out to Oman had the same thought. The exercise was a timely event, and any story being filed back to London was going to mention the Twin Towers and the ongoing military action by the US.

The mood music was helped along significantly with the arrival in Oman of Geoff Hoon, the Labour Defence Secretary, who, when asked about what role British troops might have in any war in Afghanistan, informed us dramatically that they would take part in 'smoking out' al-Qaeda terrorists from their caves. I never knew whether he seriously believed what he said or whether he was just talking metaphorically. Either way, it made a great headline.

Unfortunately for Hoon, the Royal Marine commandos eventually sent to Afghanistan were called upon to do very little, let alone smoke terrorists out of their caves. The concept of terrorists living in caves was also a bit of wishful thinking. To the western mind, terrorists belonged in caves. However, it was more likely they housed themselves, like cuckoos, in other people's nests and never stayed longer than one night. Anyway, thanks to Hoon, the story from Oman acquired legs, as Fleet Street liked to say. The 'legs' jumped up and down when Hoon, having returned to London from Oman, announced to Parliament that the Royal Marines were ready to go to Afghanistan immediately.

I mentioned this to Rear Admiral James Burnell-Nugent, commander of the force being earmarked for Afghanistan. I interviewed him on board *HMS Illustrious*, the Royal Navy aircraft carrier that was steaming off Oman as part of the military exercise. He said it was too early to predict what role the Royal Marines would play and appeared somewhat dismissive of Hoon's projected timetable. While he was trying not to be controversial, the story that appeared in *The Times* the next day sat under a headline that read 'Hoon muddle over Marines', with a huge picture of the admiral standing on the flight deck of the aircraft carrier with a broad grin on his face and his arms folded. The mismatch between Hoon and the admiral was further underlined by the revelation in my story that about 240 of the Marines from 40 Commando Royal Marines, selected for potential duty in

Afghanistan, were due for ten days of rest and recreation at a beach resort somewhere in the region, starting on the 5th of November. Hoon apparently fumed at the admiral's perceived disrespect, but it really wasn't his fault. I was almost as mortified as he was at the unfortunate juxtaposition of the 'Hoon muddle' headline and the full-frontal grinning face of the admiral.

With so much excitement around, when the media party attending the military exercise was supposed to return home, I made a decision which brought me into immediate confrontation with our MoD minders. I decided to stay and hang out with the Royal Marines, who had encouraged me to stick around while they trained in the desert for an Afghanistan war scenario.

The plane carrying the rest of the reporters back to London took off without me. The only other journalist playing truant was Rupert Hamer, defence correspondent of the *Sunday Mirror,* a delightful reporter who was tragically killed by an improvised explosive device in Afghanistan in 2010. He and I ignored the fact that our Omani visa would expire the next day and went off in search of stories. But the British military machine was working at full tilt that day. As soon as the authorities realised that two reporters were missing, a particularly bumptious British Army public affairs officer tracked us down and informed us that we would be flown home the following day.

We were duly escorted – some might say frogmarched – to the airport and put on the first available flight back to London. Our ears were still stinging from the rebuke of the army officer who appeared to have taken it personally that his carefully-laid itinerary for the visiting group of reporters had been ignored by the man from *The Times* and his colleague from the *Sunday Mirror.*

The officer claimed that it was the Omani authorities who had insisted on us being booted out of the country and he was merely acting on their behalf. However, a week or so after being expelled from Oman, I received a phone call from the Omani embassy in London; the embassy official apologised profusely for the way the British Army had dealt with me and invited me to return to Oman at any time where I would be royally treated. The truth is, Rupert and I had broken the rules for the sake of the story we hoped to write. The action by the British Army was not that surprising, but the manner in which it was carried out was perhaps slightly more confrontational than was necessary.

CHAPTER 14
TALIBAN TOPPLED — SADDAM HUSSEIN NEXT

The post-9/11 war in Afghanistan was a spectacular success. The Taliban fell apart. The regime of the repressive, Sharia-obsessed political extremists was over. The most bizarre sight that perhaps summed up the tactics used to overthrow the Taliban was a CIA para-military officer with flowing hair and beard galloping across northern Afghanistan on a horse. It was an unconventional but highly effective rout. The tribal warlords of the Northern Alliance, the CIA, US Green Beret special operations troops, US Marines and the SAS/SBS carved their way to Kabul after the American bombing raids on the Afghan capital and Kandahar, assisted by Tomahawk cruise missile attacks from two Royal Navy nuclear-powered submarines. Afghanistan had been a burial ground for so many British, Russian and Afghan troops over the centuries that it seemed almost impossible to believe that outsiders could intervene and within two months claim victory. If only George Bush and Tony Blair had kept their focus on Afghanistan and not switched their attention to Iraq and Saddam Hussein, the future tragedy for the Afghan people might have been avoided.

We were all guilty of the same complacency. The defeat of the Taliban seemed so total, and with the installing of a CIA-approved leader in Kabul, there was a sense that the US-led mission had achieved all the objectives. It was good news for the population of Afghanistan. How little of the country's history had been remembered, how few lessons had been learnt. The Taliban had powerful friends and supporters in Pakistan. They would be back. All they had to do was rearm and wait and see what the incumbent in the White House proposed to do next.

President George W. Bush fancied Iraq and forgot about Afghanistan. Osama bin Laden, having been trapped at his hideout in the mountains at Tora Bora in northern Afghanistan, managed to escape with his bodyguards around him and survived American avengers for another ten years. So, victory was short-lived, even illusionary. Donald Rumsfeld, the hawkish US Defence Secretary with the looks of an ageing film star, turned up in Kabul with victory written all over his face and reminded assembled American troops, and the world, that the 'sole purpose' of the intervention had been to expel the terrorists from Afghanistan. Yet the formidable leader of al-Qaeda had been allowed to slip through the net to work his evil from the sanctuary of Pakistan, and in a few years the Taliban would be confronting the US and the West with the biggest war of modern times.

Several thousand US, British and other

coalition troops remained in Afghanistan in a peacekeeping and counter-terrorist role, and fighting continued. Britain's 45 Commando Royal Marines battle group was sent off to hunt down and kill an al-Qaeda/Taliban group, which had ambushed an Australian SAS patrol in south-eastern Afghanistan, but they were never required to open fire. Operation Condor, the mission that was expected to lead to the first clash between al-Qaeda and the Royal Marines, was wound up after a week when the enemy failed to materialise.

By early 2002, the momentum for action to topple Saddam Hussein from power in Iraq began generating such a head of political steam that British and American officials were briefing that intervention of some kind was inevitable by the end of the year. The continuing and rising threat posed by the Taliban was pushed lower down the Washington agenda. Initially, the argument from the Americans was that Saddam was linked to al-Qaeda, but when this was dismissed by British and other European intelligence services, the justification for war was switched to another topic: Saddam's accumulated weapons of mass destruction. The rest of 2002 was like watching a mammoth war game in which a large chunk of the world became more and more agitated by the power Saddam was thought to possess to wreak nuclear, chemical or biological havoc on the Gulf region and the rest of the planet.

The rhetoric and the fear factor became so extreme that on one occasion Geoff Hoon warned that dictators such as Saddam Hussein should be 'absolutely confident that in the right conditions we would be willing to use our nuclear weapons'. He told MPs on the Commons Defence Select Committee that Iraq was developing long-range ballistic missiles, and with nuclear warheads attached, Saddam could be in a position to attack Britain within a few years. It was scary stuff.

With Britain's combat troops pulled out of Afghanistan and no plans to replace the Royal Marine battle group with any future rotations, the fight against the Taliban was left to the Americans, assisted in some way by troops from Thailand, Canada, Romania and Australia. The MoD was insistent that the ending of Britain's role in Afghanistan was not 'Treasury-led'. No one believed that. Wars are an expensive business, and with Iraq now coming to the forefront it looked like the Treasury was going to have to fork up for yet another Bush-inspired military adventure.

Moreover, this time it wasn't going to be a few thousand mujahideen-style fighters, but a significant army of Western-equipped Iraqis. The Treasury had to start thinking of spending billions, not millions. But, of course, this was all behind the scenes. What had been discussed between Bush and Blair in early 2002 was not being formally promulgated as an approved strategy. Nothing was decided, although it was pretty clear to us defence correspondents that war with Saddam Hussein was being plotted and planned and that it would take place with or without a United Nations mandate.

By July, the MoD was already rebalancing its forces around the world to make sure that, if called upon to fight the Iraqi dictator alongside the Americans, the appropriate number of troops, tanks, warships and aircraft would be available and in the right place and preparing for combat. Despite heavy pressure on the defence budget and constant warnings from the Treasury that government finances could no longer justify keeping such large armed forces, 10 Downing Street was determined to provide a significant force for Iraq, to underline the perceived special status Britain enjoyed with its strongest ally. If the US was going to ship several divisions to topple Saddam, then Britain was not going to be slow in coming forward with a proportionate military package. This would enable Blair to boast that Britain was supplying the second biggest troop contribution for the noble cause of ridding the Middle East of a nuclear-armed dictator. I suspect Margaret Thatcher was proud of Tony Blair. She, too, would have been robustly behind America's invasion plans.

At the same time as Blair and Bush prepared for 'a big event next year', as one MoD military source put it, Iraqi defectors – and there were lots of them – hyped up the Doomsday scenario, warning that Saddam had made important advances in developing nuclear, chemical and biological weapons.

I countered this with a cautionary note in an article on the 11th of July 2002. I said the nuclear threat should not be exaggerated. Before the launch of the US-led offensive against Iraqi forces in Kuwait in 1991, Saddam might have been close to developing a bomb. Today, however, with most of his nuclear infrastructure destroyed, including uranium-enrichment plants, it seemed to me he was a long way from achieving his ambition to become a nuclear weapons power in the region.

I followed this up with another cautionary article on the 29th of August. This was less than two weeks before Blair published his famously controversial report on Iraq's weapons of mass destruction, drawn up by the intelligence services under the authorship of John Scarlett, chairman of the Cabinet Office Joint Intelligence Committee and subsequently promoted to Chief of the Secret Intelligence Service (MI6).

I pointed out that the only known store of nuclear material in Iraq sat in heavyweight sealed barrels at Tuwaitha research facility, south of Baghdad. It consisted of several tonnes of low-grade uranium and was monitored by the International Atomic Energy Agency.

The legitimacy of the Tuwaitha nuclear material contrasted sharply with what Western intelligence agencies believed was Saddam's clandestine programme to build a nuclear bomb and to develop other forms of weapons of mass destruction based on chemical and biological agents.

According to senior Whitehall sources, the dossier was not going to be revelatory but was intended to be an unclassified insight into

Iraq's progress in developing unconventional weapons since the United Nations inspections came to an abrupt halt in December 1998. Much of the detail of the Whitehall dossier had to come from Iraqi defectors because of the difficulty of acquiring primary-source intelligence from inside Iraq. So, from what I could gather, expectations from within Whitehall about the impact of the upcoming dossier were relatively muted. It would be a sensible document outlining everything that was known about Saddam's nuclear, chemical and biological dreams, based on historical facts. This would be mixed with an assortment of declassified material about the current and future status of a suspected clandestine programme whose credibility was dependent on the veracity of second-hand sources. These were the defectors allegedly in possession of intimate, albeit outdated, knowledge of Saddam's ambitions of becoming a Middle East nuclear warlord capable of dominating one of the most volatile regions on the globe.

In September, *HMS Ark Royal,* the Royal Navy aircraft carrier, left her Portsmouth home. She was kitted out for war, including a full complement of Harrier jump jets, a new helicopter called Merlin and a dark green 3.2 litre Jaguar XJ saloon. Only the British could contemplate taking a Jaguar to war. Actually, the carrier was setting off for a ten-week NATO amphibious exercise in the Mediterranean, and the Jaguar was to be available for officers' port visits in Gibraltar, Barcelona, Naples and Malta.

'It's not mine, it's the ship's,' Captain Alan Massey, the carrier's commanding officer, said.

But if the carrier's training mission was switched to potential warfighting mode against Iraq, the treasured Jaguar would have to be winched off. The families lining the harbour to say farewell to their loved ones, fearing that they might be caught up in a war, were probably reassured by the sight of the Jag.

The most obvious sign of approaching war was the much tougher retaliation against the Iraqis whenever American or British aircraft were fired on by Iraqi anti-aircraft weapons. The combat jets were engaged in UN-mandated patrols enforcing no-fly zones over southern and northern Iraq, set up after the 1991 Gulf war. On the 5th of September, after a burst of Iraqi ground fire aimed unsuccessfully at overflying aircraft, the US and Britain responded with a thunderous reminder of what the coalition had in store for Saddam. US Central Command, in charge of the combat air patrols, announced that twelve American and British bombers had dropped twenty-five bombs onto an Iraqi command and control centre at an airbase, 240 miles southwest of Baghdad. Was this over the top, in retaliation for a spray of anti-aircraft artillery? Under normal circumstances, perhaps. But with the likelihood of a 'big event' in 2003, it was all good politics and diplomacy, a punch of military aggression to send signals to Saddam that he should seriously start thinking of cooperating over the weapons of mass destruction impasse with the West if he wanted to avoid superpower bombing raids over Baghdad.

The psychology of the stepped-up retaliatory strikes clearly didn't wash with the Iraqi dictator. He totally failed to get the message, or if he did, he ignored it. Iraq had been identified as part of Bush's 'axis of evil' and Saddam was probably pleased to be selected for membership of such an exclusive club.

The Blair dossier was published on the 24th of September. I read it from beginning to end and although there were some interesting intelligence titbits, much of it was based on historical knowledge of Saddam's former capabilities and there was nothing in it which really made the heart leap in fear. Nothing to suggest that the Iraqi dictator was developing and plotting to use weapon systems that could be armed with nuclear, chemical or biological warheads. The bulk of the dossier was non-sensational. But there were two elements which raised eyebrows and worked well in the following day's newspaper headlines.

Blair himself, in a foreword, was fairly alarmist about the potential threat posed by Saddam, and a certain figure was highlighted which got newspapers, particularly the tabloids, extremely excited. The dossier explained that, based on 'reliable sources', Saddam could deploy chemical and biological weapons and that they would be ready to fire within 'forty-five minutes' of the order being given from Baghdad. Blair plucked out this number from the dossier and inserted it into his foreword.

This is where fact and fiction became somewhat merged. There was no suggestion in the dossier that Saddam would be able, within forty-five minutes, to launch a deadly non-conventional missile attack on Britain. The forty-five-minute timetable referred to the ability of Saddam's forces to launch an artillery strike with chemical shells or perhaps drop a bomb with a chemical warhead from an aircraft. But no one in his right mind held the view, based on intelligence, that Baghdad had the capability and will to launch a medium-range, or even long-range, ballistic missile, fitted with nuclear, chemical or biological warheads that could reach Britain or indeed, anywhere abroad where British soldiers were based.

But after a pointed question from the tabloids as to whether Saddam could attack, say, the British sovereign bases in Cyprus, in forty-five minutes, the nodding response from Geoff Hoon was enough to send the headline writers wild with excitement. Sure enough, 'our boys' are at threat from a chemical or biological attack within forty-five minutes was the story in *The Sun* the following day. The headline was: 'Brits 45mins from doom'.

I wrote a piece referring to the forty-five-minute launch timetable because it was spelt out in the dossier, but it seemed to me that if Saddam were to pick up the phone to the commander of his rocket forces and say, 'prepare for a chemical attack', it might well take about forty-five minutes to get things up and running. But that was a question of logistics and military training, and it was only relevant for battlefield weapons, not intercontinental ballistic missiles. It had nothing to do with any supposed plot by Saddam to be ready for a mother-of-all nuclear, chemical or biological attack within three-quarters of an hour of first thinking of it.

The dossier, in my view, was not 'sexed up', as the BBC Radio *Today* programme's Andrew Gilligan famously claimed in a highly controversial early morning report on the 29th of May 2003. But the loose talk, nods and winks and stretched interpretations offered by ministers and Whitehall officials on the day of the dossier's publication contributed to a Fleet Street maelstrom of imagination. Yet, I have no doubt it suited the British Government's cause. The headlines certainly helped to sway Parliament when confronted with Blair's request to go to war, and MPs voted in favour.

The dossier itself should have been couched in more cautionary language. Intelligence officers know full well that nothing is ever absolutely certain in their world, largely because they are relying on human sources, and even their best primary agents might still have ulterior motives for passing on supposedly secret information.

The Blair dossier was not a spin doctor's war pamphlet. However, as a document published at a time when Britain was edging its way towards a major military conflict, it was clearly intended to accelerate the momentum for a battle with Saddam. If it really had been deliberately and flagrantly 'sexed up' by Downing Street spin doctors, and if the intelligence had knowingly been blown up out of all proportion by Number 10 to give a false picture, then that would have been unforgiveable, and disastrous for the reputation of MI6 in general and John Scarlett in particular.

I knew from phone calls with Alastair Campbell that he was beside himself with fury over Gilligan's *Today* programme report and subsequent claims that he, as Blair's spin doctor, had been personally responsible, against the wishes of MI6, for inserting into the dossier the most controversial item of all: the forty-five-minute launch timetable. Campbell told me that was totally false. I had no reason to disbelieve him, but Gilligan had broadcast to the world that he had a secret source who had revealed everything to him. Whitehall, and in particular, Number 10 Downing Street, was in a frenzy. Who was this source?

But this was all to erupt later. In September 2002, the dossier was out; Parliament had done Blair's bidding and the vote went his way. In less than six months, Britain would be at war with Iraq.

By early October, the MoD was talking about sending a reinforced armoured brigade of about 15,000 troops to support the American war effort in Iraq. If the Gulf War of 1991 was anything to go by, the British Government appeared to be starting at a relatively modest and predictable scale of military contribution but had grander plans if required. And so it worked out. As the potential US invading force increased steadily in size and potency, the MoD applied a slide rule to the British battle plan and came up with a whole division, plus all the extras that go with an expeditionary force. About 45,000 British troops were involved in the Gulf War, and a similar total was to be sent to fight the Iraqis all over again in 2003.

No one in warfighting mood was impressed by anything coming out of Baghdad, least of all a 12,000-page report claiming to be the full and accurate historical account of Iraq's weapons of mass destruction programme, and its elimination by the UN. It was viewed by the US and Britain as a programme about past endeavours, not current inventories. American and British intelligence agencies dismissed the Saddam report as full of holes 'big enough to drive a tank through'. The countdown, as newspapers always loved to proclaim, had begun. With or without a UN mandate for war, the US, hand-in-hand with Britain, old allies together, were going to sort out Saddam once and for all.

My prediction was that the Americans had such overwhelmingly superior firepower and advanced technology that the war would be fast and furious and all over in a matter of ten days or so. The story was headlined, 'Why any war with Iraq may be over in a flash'; and there was a sub-heading contained within a large graphic which spelt out how the invasion could be prosecuted. It stated, '10 days to topple Saddam'.

While the prediction was a little optimistic – the fall of Baghdad actually took forty-two days – I foresaw that despite Saddam's pledge to counter-attack with 'the mother of all battles', and despite the fear that he might resort, out of desperation, to using chemical and biological weapons to stall an advance on the capital, it seemed inconceivable that the Americans with their trusty British ally would not prevail. The Americans, however, had decided that they would go it alone all the way to Baghdad. The British troops, once they had crossed the Kuwaiti border into Iraq, would occupy the southern part of the country, liberating Basra, the second largest city. Baghdad was to be America's prize. But to get there, the US Marines and armoured divisions would have to attack from the south, charging all the way through the country until they reached Saddam's seat of power. The original battle plan, to attack from the south and also from the north through Turkey was scuppered when the Turkish Government suddenly slammed shut the north route door and told the US it would not allow American troops to operate from its soil.

The logistics challenge for the US increased by a factor of ten. The decision by America's NATO ally also ruined my ten-days-to-topple-Saddam prediction because of the sheer time it would take to drive hundreds of tanks up from Kuwait, and have them refuelled along the way, never mind what level of opposition they would meet from the Iraqi forces as they progressed through the country.

A week before the invasion was due to be launched I flew out to the Gulf to interview all the senior British commanders. There was still at that stage a small but unlikely chance that Tony Blair would be prevented, politically, from authorising the involvement of British troops because MPs wanted a second UN resolution that would have specifically approved the use of force against Saddam. General Tommy Franks, the US coalition commander who, like the Gulf War maestro, General Stormin' Norman, was a big man, had to plan for the possibility of fighting without the British. There was talk of holding the British units back in Kuwait and only allowing them into Iraq once the US had defeated Saddam. The British would then take on a post-war peacekeeping role.

However, this prospect didn't go down well with the commanders I spoke to. The men and women under their command were waiting around in the intense heat to start a war, and if domestic politics was going to frustrate the military plans, it would seriously damage morale. When soldiers are ready for battle, they want to get on with it.

'I've talked to the 9,000 men and women under my command, and they recognise that, notwithstanding the political fallout, this job needs to be done,' said Rear Admiral David Snelson, commander of the maritime component of the 45,000-strong British force.

Speaking in Bahrain, the admiral admitted that it would be a shock for the US commanders if they had to start planning for a war without the British. In his Naval Task Force he had thirty Royal Navy warships and support vessels and two nuclear-powered submarines with Tomahawk land-attack cruise missiles.

'There's going to be a serious leadership challenge for military commanders if, having marched all our troops to the top of the hill, we have to march them down again,' one British military source said to me.

One man who seemed convinced that British troops would soon be crossing the Kuwaiti border into Iraq was Major-General Robin Brims, commander of the 1st (UK) Armoured Division, which, if given the go ahead, would have the responsibility of seizing Basra and covering the Americans' backs as they powered their way towards Baghdad. His division included 7th Armoured Brigade (the Desert Rats, once again), 16 Air Assault Brigade and 3 Commando Brigade Royal Marines. His Kuwaiti desert divisional headquarters was just north of the Mutla Ridge mountain range where so many Iraqi troops had died twelve years earlier.

General Brims was a thoughtful commander and he had no enthusiasm or sense of relish at the prospect of killing hundreds of Iraqi troops. He told me that even though, this time, the Iraqis would be defending their own territory, he hoped that the average regular Saddam soldier would surrender without a fight. He even raised the possibility that they could lay down their arms and actually join the US-led coalition. 'I wouldn't expect them to march north with us, but they could just go to their barracks and wait,' he said. He told his men that the objective was to disarm the Iraqis 'without undue attrition'. 'We have nothing against the Iraqi army,' he told me. Then he said something that sounded sensible at the time. 'After the war, Iraq will still need armed forces and they will have a role to play in securing their country's future,' he said.

If only those prescient words of a fifty-one-year-old British general had been heeded by Paul Bremer, the leather-booted US administrator who arrived in Baghdad after the fall of Saddam and started imposing rules on who could or could not serve the country. Saddam's army, after defeat, was disbanded, and any civil servant with membership of the Baathist party was sent home without a job. It was spring-cleaning on the grandest scale, aimed at ridding Iraq of anyone who had been a servant of Saddam Hussein. A week before the invasion of Iraq, General Brims had a different vision. 'Join us, British general tells Iraqi defenders' was the headline of my story published on the 12th of March 2003.

Before leaving for London, I met up with a host of Fleet Street correspondents who had been selected to go to war with the US-led coalition. They included Danny McGrory, my old friend from the *Daily Express,* who was to cover the war for *The Times* as one of the 'floaters' (an unembedded reporter who would not have to answer to the rules and regulations of an army or Marine unit commander).

Also there, waiting nervously in a hotel in Kuwait, was Chris Ayres, *The Times* Los Angeles correspondent who was to be embedded with the US Marines all the way to Baghdad. He had not covered a war and the prospect of being trapped inside a US Marine armoured vehicle as it thundered towards the Iraqi capital, with guns blazing, was not something he contemplated with any degree of pleasure or excitement, let alone anticipation of glory. I didn't know him, but when I bumped into him in the hotel lobby I tried to reassure him that he would be in good company, that the US Marines would look after him and that he would be all right. I realised at the time that my words probably sounded a little trite, but having placed my life in the hands of military types over many years, I hoped that my encouragement might help him to feel less nervous; I wanted him to view the assignment as a unique and extraordinary experience that could make his name as a war reporter.

But, as the paper's LA correspondent, there was no way he could have been prepared sufficiently for the sort of experience he was about to have. Halfway to Baghdad, after days of unbelievable battle clamour and personal terror, he asked to be allowed to leave his embed and return to the safety of Kuwait.

It took courage for him to admit he was too scared to complete his assignment. But he probably should never have been selected to embed with the US Marines. He duly left Iraq and subsequently wrote a book about his experience, admitting he wasn't cut out for war reporting. Meanwhile, McGrory calmly drove a rented car across the border and was confronted by Iraqi soldiers, who opened fire on him. Bullets flew everywhere, piercing the roof of the vehicle. He had to carry out a U-turn in order to save his life, and drove swiftly back across the border – but that was just a temporary hitch in his reporting mission. He had the car repaired and was back in Iraq before the foreign desk could think of reasons to bring him home. He was a true reporting warrior.

General Brims had told me that the intelligence he had seen made it clear that Saddam could resort to chemical weapon strikes. There was specific reference to chemical mines. But there was no physical evidence to back up the intelligence, no satellite pictures of Iraqi military units piling chemical mines onto trucks and laying them in the path of the invading troops. General Brims had little choice but to treat the intelligence warnings seriously, and all the frontline units had NBC suits to put on as soon as the alert sounded.

However, once the invasion began and for all the following weeks, there was no chemical attack, and the special forces assigned to hunt for weapons of mass destruction came up with nothing. All the sheds, warehouses, factories, mobile laboratories, back rooms, garages and other premises listed by Iraqi defectors as containing stocks of WMD produced not even a smell of chemicals. There was nothing to find, yet there remained a conviction even to the very end that Saddam had somehow buried his deadly arsenal of prohibited weapons in the desert. They would be found eventually, the most committed of the WMD specialists continued to predict, though with increasing perplexity and frustration. In London, Admiral Sir Alan West, head of the Royal Navy and a former chief of defence intelligence, told a press conference at the MoD, 'They will be found.' But he did acknowledge that it was unlikely Iraq possessed the huge stocks of WMD which had previously been suggested. The rowing back had begun.

Writing about the war back in London, it was part of my responsibilities to provide a regular assessment of the progress being made. This was not going to be a hundred-hour war to match the 1991 Gulf conflict, but the advance of the US forces up through the centre of Iraq continued at an extraordinary pace. The British troops had successfully taken Basra, partly due to a cunning piece of infiltration by some MI6 officers, backed by the SAS, who entered the city covertly and communicated back where the Iraqi commanders were located and what areas looked most vulnerable to attack.

I was asked on one occasion to attend the morning editorial conference to explain what the Americans were up to. I told them that they were engaged in a four-pronged attack leading towards Baghdad. I felt like Stormin' Norman giving his daily update. Graham Paterson, one of the most enthusiastic foreign desk executives I had ever dealt with, said everyone was impressed by my briefing. By April, about sixteen days into the war, there was a demand in *The Times* newsroom for action graphics to explain how Baghdad could be taken. Although there were pockets of serious resistance by the Iraqi forces, the fall of Baghdad seemed inevitable. Saddam must have realised the game was up because every time he turned on his TV he would see an American television reporter riding a tank or an armoured personnel carrier spelling out how close they were getting to the capital. It was brilliant propaganda. A total of 700 reporters were embedded with US brigades and divisions, and their daily dispatches were piling the psychological pressure onto the Iraqi dictator.

There was much talk in *The Times* office about what the Americans would do: would they mount a massive assault on Baghdad, risking casualties among civilians, or would they adopt the tactics used by the British in Basra that involved a number of lightning raids to undermine the Iraqi defenders. It took about nineteen days to liberate Basra; the Iraqis put up quite a fight, and the city's Baath party militia and Fedayeen fighters, a brutal force devoted to Saddam, put the fear of god into the citizens and dissuaded them from launching a popular uprising against them. I wrote that the British had finally achieved their objective with 'a combination of patience and aggression, kind words and heavy metal'. I couldn't see the Americans wanting to hold back, although wholesale street-fighting in a city with five million inhabitants was not a good prospect. I played it safe by saying there was a good chance the Americans might wait for reinforcements before entering Baghdad and that if the Iraqi Republican Guard troops were well dug in around and inside the city, it was going to be a significant battle.

However, the US had built up such a momentum that it might make little sense to stop the tanks and have them ticking over for a few weeks. But the message left with the editor and his team of executives was that the battle for Baghdad might be delayed.

In the end, however, there was no delay. Within, it seemed, a matter of hours, American armoured vehicles were spotted in the outskirts of Baghdad. 'So, they didn't wait,' one wise-guy news executive said to me. I smiled. You can't always predict it right, but the US decision to get into Baghdad as quickly as possible was a psychological blow of such proportions for those attempting to protect Saddam that the threat to fight the mother of all battles quickly dissipated.

No weapons of mass destruction had been found and there was no sign of Saddam himself. But in July, Uday and Qusay Hussein, his two sons who had been hiding in a mansion located north of Mosul, were dealt with in a huge explosion of firepower. Every American soldier went around with a picture of Saddam, hoping to be the one who would find him skulking in a palace cupboard or concealed in the boot of a departing limousine. No one imagined that Saddam would be discovered eventually hidden in a hole in the ground.

Two spectacular photographic moments

brought the Iraqi regime down and gave President George W. Bush the revenge he had been seeking for the Iraqi leader's plot to assassinate his father after the liberation of Kuwait: the pulling down of the huge Saddam statue in Baghdad in April, and, eight months later, in December, the emergence of the scared, bearded former regime monster being lifted out of his underground hideout by an American soldier.

Operation Iraqi Freedom was a classic war of fast manoeuvre. There had never been any doubt that the US, backed by British and other allies, would defeat the Iraqis. The Republican Guards were frequently referred to as Saddam's 'elite' troops, but they were facing a premier-division force with the most advanced weaponry in the history of warfare. There *was* a contest, but not much of one. The war was over. It took a blundering American civil administration, a total lack of foresight, poor intelligence and a determination to ignore the warning signs to unravel the victory and hurl the US and allies into what became the most dangerous internal uprising. It lasted so long that even when the Americans got tired of Iraq and left for good in December 2011, the civil and terrorist war was still raging, albeit at a lower level of violence. No one foresaw the emergence of a new extremist Islamic force that would prove to be so well-prepared and so well armed and financed that it would be able to seize control of at least a third of Iraq's territory and compel its millions of inhabitants to live life under a caliphate rule. ISIS was biding its time to burst onto the world scene. Little did the Americans know that, within a few years, they would be back in Iraq helping to fight a new enemy.

Not long after the war was officially declared over, I attended a drinks party in Whitehall, a select reception in which the heads of the security and intelligence services, the director of special forces and a bunch of senior military commanders and MoD civil servants clustered together with defence correspondents. It was an annual event hosted by the head of the D-Notice Committee, the advisory body available for journalists writing stories that might breach the Official Secrets Act. Towards the end of the evening, a senior army officer I knew well joined the group I was chatting to and then said, in a matter-of-fact voice, that he had to hurry away to investigate war crimes allegations against one of the most famous British commanders in the Iraq war.

It was said almost jokingly, as if he was about to look into something that was so ludicrous it wasn't that important. That's my only excuse. After hearing the words, my brain failed to click into scoop mode and I carried on talking to my companions as the senior officer left the room. I assumed, for some reason, that there was probably no story. The next day, instead of ringing the officer or just checking with the MoD press office, I got caught up with some other story, and it faded from my mind. No other defence correspondent had been standing with me when the officer uttered those words, and nothing appeared in any newspaper. It's still difficult to believe that my reporting antennae, normally switched on for the merest sniff of a story, had let me down.

A few days later, *The Sun* splashed the story that Lieutenant-Colonel Tim Collins, commanding officer of the Royal Irish Regiment, was under investigation after an accusation that he had struck an Iraqi civilian. The MoD confirmed that an alleged war crime could have been committed.

It was sensational enough on its own, but Colonel Collins had become a household name after making an extraordinary Henry V-type address to his men before going into battle. It began: 'We go to Iraq to liberate, not to conquer. We will not fly our flags in their country. We are entering Iraq to free a people and the only flag which will be flown in that ancient land is their own. Show respect for them. There are some who are alive at this moment who will not be alive shortly. Those who do not wish to go on that journey, we will not send. As for the others, I expect you to rock their world. Wipe them out if that is what they choose. But if you are ferocious in battle remember to be magnanimous in victory.'

A *Mail on Sunday* reporter was there when he made the speech in Kuwait on the eve of battle, and his magnificent words had been splashed all over the paper. The speech was so evocative that President George W. Bush hung a copy of it on the wall in the Oval Office. By all accounts,

Colonel Collins's address went straight over the heads of most of his men who may never have read a Shakespeare play, let alone *Henry V*. But back home, it made us all proud and patriotic. It was fine oratory, and summed up the supposedly noble cause behind the invasion. Now, here he was under investigation for an alleged war crime.

I was in southern Iraq when the story I should have written appeared as a world exclusive in *The Sun*. It was alleged that Colonel Collins had punched, kicked and threatened Iraqi prisoners of war and had pistol-whipped a prominent local civilian. I told no one that I had missed out on an exclusive of my own. I was mortified. But now the story was out, the foreign desk wanted me to investigate what it was all about, who was the prominent local official, and what really happened. I was in the right place and was under intense pressure to provide a story that would reveal even more than *The Sun's* front page exclusive.

The problem for me was that I was in Iraq as part of an MoD-organised trip. I was, therefore, subject to what was known as the Green Book, the list of rules that governed any visit planned by the ministry. I was under the MoD's protection, but also under its minders. Along with a few other reporters, I was being given a guided tour, as it were, of the battle for Basra, masterminded by the British, and had the chance to interview relevant commanders. The Green Book clearly stated that if any reporter stepped out of the closely protected environment of the

MoD-orchestrated trip, he would be on his own – and, what's more, would probably be kicked off the return RAF flight to the UK.

I met up with Matthew Hickley of the *Daily Mail* and Thomas Harding of the *Daily Telegraph* and we decided we had no choice but to opt out of the MoD programme and set off into the desert to hunt for the alleged victims of the Royal Irish Regiment commanding officer. Colonel Collins himself was not around to be interviewed, but his regiment had been based in Rumaila, site of the Iraqi oil fields in the south. That was the obvious place to start our investigation. All of us had had the same news desk orders.

The three of us got a lift out of the British base outside Basra and headed into town to find a taxi. I rang the foreign desk and explained that I was about to set off to see if I could find Colonel Collins's main alleged victim but I warned that I only had a day in which to do so because I was due to fly back with the MoD the following day. Alex Blair, on the desk, passed on a message she had been given by Ben Preston, now promoted to deputy editor, at the morning editorial conference.

'Ben Preston has told me to tell you that you are not to leave Iraq until you have found this person,' she said.

I could see myself spending fruitless days hunting for a man who, for all I knew, was a figment of someone's imagination. The accusation of a crime had apparently been made by a junior American reservist officer attached to the Royal Irish Regiment in a liaison role who had fallen out with Colonel Collins.

We set off, packed into the back of an ancient taxi. The driver brought a companion who sat in the front passenger seat. Neither spoke much English, and so it had been difficult to explain to them that we wanted to get to Rumaila, about thirty miles west of Basra. It was baking hot. After an hour of driving in the desert, with not a soul anywhere in sight, let alone a village called Rumaila, the taxi driver admitted he was lost and we came to a halt. The air was thick with dust. But we were in luck. A British Army Land Rover emerged through the dust and heat and stopped in front of us. The sight of a British Army officer when you are lost in the desert is better than any oasis I've ever come across in my travels.

The officer, a captain, said he was from the Duke of Wellington's Regiment and asked whether he could be of assistance. He knew where Rumaila was and offered to escort the taxi to the village, about half an hour's drive away.

The arrival of three Fleet Street reporters at a village in the middle of the desert caused quite a stir. We told the captain from the Duke of Wellington's Regiment what we were doing. We explained why we wanted to come to Rumaila. He had been such a lifesaver that it didn't seem right to lie to him. He offered to find the right people for us, and in no time at all he gathered all the elders of the village to the civic hall, including the village leader, Abu Mohaned. We all sat round the hall and I was invited to ask my questions. I told the village leader why we were there and asked if it would be possible to talk to the man who was supposed to have been pistol-whipped by Colonel Collins.

To our amazement, Mr Mohaned summoned the man to the civic hall. He turned out to be Ayoub Yousif Naser, a member of Saddam's Baath Party and, until recently, headmaster of al-Nukhaila primary school in Rumaila. It was all working out incredibly well. Mr Naser, a tall, quite imposing man, spoke quietly but convincingly and told us what happened when the Royal Irish Regiment arrived in the village. He claimed that during a night-time raid, Colonel Collins had pistol-whipped him, kicked him in the shins and ribs, and fired at his son's feet. He also alleged that the British commander subjected him to a mock execution. He accused the officer of putting him and his son up against a wall and ordering a soldier standing next to him to shoot them. They waited in fear of their lives but nothing happened. He presented his story in Arabic, and an interpreter translated for us. This was sensational stuff, but also alarming. The man sounded convincing but he was a hated Baathist, and local people admitted to us later that he was disliked. There were also no witnesses to the alleged mock execution and pistol-whipping. But when we showed Mr Naser a photograph of Colonel Collins, he told the interpreter, 'That's the man who hit me.'

The British soldiers had apparently arrived at the village at night and burst into Mr Naser's prefabricated house at about 10.30pm. He told us the door had been opened by his son, and Colonel Collins had demanded to know whether he was in the house. When he came down the stairs, having been woken up, the officer asked him whether he was a member of the Baath Party and whether he had any guns.

'I said "no" because I was tired. Suddenly, this officer took out his pistol and hit me on the back of the head. I was hit twice and I fell down. There was a lot of blood on my head. After he had hit me, I told him that I had guns. I had two Kalashnikov machine guns, one to guard the school and the other was held for the [Baath] party,' he told us.

After the guns were retrieved from the garden where they had been buried, he said he and his son were taken to the civic hall and told to face the wall. He heard the officer say, 'Kill them.' But then other soldiers arrived with bandages and started to tend to his bloodied head.

We asked Mr Naser to show us the head wound. He bent forward and pointed to the top of his skull. It looked like there was a small scar there, but nothing dramatic. His twenty-one-year-old son backed up his story. When he left to return to his home, we walked around the village asking people what they thought of the allegations. The majority of the villagers made it clear they despised the former headmaster. A student said most people felt he deserved what happened to him, and insisted the British soldiers had been friendly and polite.

Of course, it was important to remember that, under Saddam's regime, those who wanted a job in government, including teaching, had to be a member of the Baath party, but there was clearly no love lost for Mr Naser.

We thanked the village leaders for their help and I went off to make a phone call on my satellite phone. I got through to the foreign desk in a state of controlled excitement. The person who picked up the phone was Alex Blair.

I said, 'Alex, I have absolutely –.'

'Nothing?' she interrupted.

I went on, after an over-dramatic pause: 'I have absolutely everything.'

I even had a photograph of the former headmaster, and of his son, Nwafel. They were passport pictures because none of us had brought a photographer with us.

I was in a better position than my two colleagues from the *Daily Mail* and *Daily Telegraph.* Both those papers had praised Colonel Collins as a hero of the war and it was not in their interest to paint him as an alleged tainted hero. Whatever Mr Naser and his son said to us in Rumaila was not going to change the view of the editors of their newspapers. Colonel Collins, they had decided, was an iconic figure and needed to be protected from foul allegations.

I wrote my story straight and at length with every quote, and included the view of some of the villagers that Mr Naser was unpopular, even feared. The story appeared on the front page under the headline: 'The British officer took out his pistol and hit me on the head. There was a lot of blood.'

The foreign editor, Martin Fletcher, inserted the words, 'Tracked down by *The Times* to a small desert village in southern Iraq…' This was a little unfair to Matthew Hickley and Thomas Harding, who had also tracked down Mr Naser, largely thanks to the young officer from the Duke of Wellington's Regiment. But both the *Daily Mail* and *Daily Telegraph* treated the story very differently, downplaying the impact of Mr Naser's words and effectively reminding their readers that Colonel Collins was a hero, whatever some Baath Party headmaster claimed.

When *The Times* story broke on the 23rd of May 2003, every reporter from every foreign newspaper and broadcasting station working in Baghdad descended on Rumaila in their four-by-four vehicles and tried to re-interview everyone. By then I was back in Basra, satisfied that I had met the challenge presented to me by Ben Preston and had delivered the goods, providing *The Times* with a cracking story. I felt sorry for my two colleagues that their stories had been thrown away, largely because of their newspapers' political agendas.

Colonel Collins was never charged with war crimes.

CHAPTER 15
HOW GOVERNMENT SCIENTIST DAVID KELLY WAS EXPOSED

The infamous BBC *Today* programme report that accused the Government of deliberately 'sexing up' the intelligence dossier on Iraq's weapons of mass destruction programme was first broadcast before most people were awake on the 29th of May 2003. The story, produced by Andrew Gilligan, the radio programme's defence correspondent, was a bombshell. He claimed he had a source who was one of the senior figures in charge of drawing up the dossier. Later, he claimed that Alastair Campbell, Tony Blair's press secretary, had insisted on inserting the notorious 'forty-five-minute' phrase to underline the brief time it would take Saddam's forces to launch a chemical or biological attack. John Humphrys, the *Today* programme presenter, repeated the claim that the source behind the remarkable story was a senior official and at one point added that he was a member of the intelligence services.

But it was not until July that the identity of the source behind the story became a major issue. A battle had been going on between Geoff Hoon, the Defence Secretary, and the top hierarchy of the BBC. Hoon wrote to Gavyn Davies, the BBC chairman, demanding to know whether the corporation still stood by the Gilligan story. By now, Hoon suspected who the source was; an MoD official had come forward voluntarily and admitted to his superiors that he had met Gilligan a week before the broadcast and was concerned that he might be the one quoted anonymously as saying that Campbell was to blame for 'sexing up' the government dossier. The official told his bosses that this was not true. He denied raising Campbell's alleged involvement, and said it was Gilligan who had first referred to the Downing Street press chief, and that he had made no comment to the BBC reporter on this particular question. The story of the still-unnamed source admitting he had spoken to Gilligan appeared in *The Times* on the 9th of July.

Later that day, I rang the MoD press office and was informed that the name of the official who had admitted meeting Gilligan would not be revealed. However, I was told that if I came up with the right name, the press office had been authorised to confirm it. I had seldom experienced this sort of arrangement before; it seemed somewhat devious, and it was clear to me that someone inside the MoD, or perhaps, Number 10, wanted the name to be published. I think someone high up had decided that if the official was identified, it would provide better ammunition for Downing Street to take on the BBC.

The source had, therefore, become a pawn in the battle between the Government and the BBC over the issue of whether the Iraq WMD dossier was a truthful account of a genuine assessment of Saddam's secret weapons, based on authoritative intelligence, or whether it was a mish-mash of half-truths and over-egged assumptions wrapped up in alarmist language aimed at justifying the march to war. It was to be a witch hunt for Gilligan's source. It was not the most edifying of journalistic endeavours. Indeed, it was somewhat distasteful trying to uncover the source for a story written by a colleague. I certainly wouldn't like the Fleet Street pack to start delving into the sourcing of a story I had written. Sources are precious; their anonymity needs to be preserved if they are to remain a reliable and trustworthy fund of information. A source needs to know that their identity will not be revealed.

However, on this occasion, the source *was* the story. Every Fleet Street newspaper was dying to know who this man – or woman – was who had allegedly made some highly outspoken remarks about the British Government's integrity, or lack of it, in claiming to the public and to Parliament that Saddam Hussein, armed with weapons of mass destruction, posed a real and present danger to everyone's lives.

So, I started the hunt for the name. I trawled through the Civil Service List, which provides details of all the key officials in every government department, and also checked out names of MoD experts in nuclear, biological and chemical weapons. There was a mass of potential officials with the right sort of background. I drew up a list and rang the MoD press office. The conversation was bizarre. I gave a name and the answer was 'no'. I got through my list of about twenty-two names, and received a negative response in each case. So who was this person?

I had to go to the House of Commons for a different story and was sitting in the cramped *Times* office when the phone rang. A voice the other end, someone I knew well, said, 'It's Kelly.' My informant just had the surname. I had earlier been browsing through a list of MoD and Foreign Office officials who had attended a conference on chemical weapons and found a David Kelly. He was a specialist in chemical weapons. This must be Gilligan's source.

I rang the MoD and spoke to the same press officer I had been dealing with all day and asked, 'Is it David Kelly?'

The press officer replied, 'Bingo!'

I quickly asked a few more questions about David Kelly, what position he held in the MoD, his experience and where he had been overseas, and then rang the news desk. 'It's an MoD scientist called David Kelly – he was Gilligan's source.'

It was nearing first edition time, but this was going to be front-page news, so there was time to write the story. My colleagues Tom Baldwin, deputy political editor, who was close to Alastair Campbell, and Andrew Pierce, an esteemed inside-track reporter with good contacts in the BBC as well as Westminster, shared the bylines on the story. The only other newspaper to have the name David Kelly in its story about the Government/BBC battle was the *Financial Times.*

With the name out and confirmed by the MoD, mayhem followed. The Commons Foreign Affairs Select Committee, which had already investigated the BBC allegation about Alastair Campbell's alleged involvement in the Iraq dossier and cleared him with a majority verdict, now wanted to reopen their inquiry and summon Dr Kelly for questioning. Geoff Hoon agreed for him to attend, and Dr Kelly duly turned up in front of the cameras for what turned out to be a torrid affair. He was brutally questioned by unsympathetic and vengeful members of the select committee.

Dr Kelly, totally unused to such public confrontation and, clearly, insufficiently prepared for the kangaroo-court atmosphere, visibly wilted under the questioning and looked more and more unhappy. He spoke so quietly that at one point his words were drowned out by the sound of the electric fans working in the room. It was not a pleasant sight. It was parliament at its worst, playing before the gallery, and all on live television.

Three days later, Dr Kelly was found dead. He had walked out of his home in Abingdon, Oxfordshire, on Thursday evening (the 16th of July). His wife reported him missing and, after a wide police hunt, his body was found the next day at Harrowdown Hill, a local beauty spot about two miles from his house. His wrists had been cut, and all the signs indicated that he had committed suicide.

As someone who had been deeply involved in the whole Gilligan/Kelly affair, there was an unavoidable sense of guilt and regret, and overwhelming sadness that this dedicated government scientist, who had been thrown to the wolves for breaking Whitehall's rules about civil servants talking to the press, had come to the conclusion that he could no longer face up to a future in which his professional integrity had been damaged. That's how it seemed to me. The subsequent inquest recorded a verdict of suicide, although the conspiracy theorists accused the Government of arranging his death. Some medical experts claimed that if he had slashed his own wrists there would have been more evidence of blood. However, those who believed there was something more sinister behind his death ignored the overwhelming circumstantial evidence that demonstrated beyond much doubt that Dr Kelly took his own life after suffering a profound personal tragedy: the loss of his professional reputation.

He had only realised that he was probably Gilligan's source for the 29th of May BBC Radio broadcast after returning from a trip to Iraq. He was shown a transcript of Gilligan's report and recognised some of the technical detail as material that he had divulged during his lunch with him on the 22nd of May. However, much of the report he did not recognise as coming from the conversation he had had with Gilligan, which is why he told the Foreign Affairs Committee that he wasn't the reporter's prime source. Yet Gilligan had admitted the story was based on a single source. The full realisation of what he had done must have hit him so hard that he could no longer carry on.

After his death, there was a massive blame game. His local MP blamed the BBC; others blamed the Foreign Affairs Committee for being so aggressive. Questions were also raised about the MoD's handling of the whole affair. Who had authorised the press office to confirm David Kelly's name, and why wasn't he properly protected from the media firestorm?

I soon discovered that the press office strategy was initially discussed at a meeting in the Old War Office in Whitehall attended by Hoon, Sir Kevin Tebbit, the permanent secretary, and the minister's private office officials. There were various options considered, one of which was to make no comment. But the minister and assembled civil servants felt this would be unsustainable, believing that his name would emerge in due course. Another was to announce which official had come forward to admit he had met Gilligan for lunch, but this would look vengeful and would be unfair to a member of the MoD staff – even though he had transgressed. The third option was to tell the press office to deny that Dr Kelly was the BBC source, but lying was never going to be a sensible way forward. The 'Kelly naming strategy', however, wasn't approved until a later meeting at Downing Street, chaired by Tony Blair. He approved the strategy of confirming the name if guessed by enquiring reporters. The MoD concurred with that decision.

I was informed by the MoD that this was to be the process for uncovering the name of the chemical weapons scientist. So, for me, it was a process of elimination, throwing names at the press office until I struck lucky. But, having tried twenty-two names without luck, the telephonic nudge towards the surname, Kelly, provided a swift end to the search. I believe I would have got there eventually without the unexpected assistance, but the whispered name over the phone added spice and drama to what had been an undignified Fleet Street hullabaloo.

The Government set up an inquiry under Lord Hutton, a retired High Court judge and former Lord Chief Justice of Northern Ireland, to investigate the circumstances that led to Dr Kelly's death and to decide who, if anyone, was to be held responsible. Tom Baldwin and I were summoned to give evidence because of the role *The Times* played in exposing Dr Kelly as Gilligan's source for the 'sexed-up dossier' report broadcast by the BBC.

The inquiry was an eye-opener. The communications world had changed dramatically. So now, instead of dusty Whitehall files being produced, there was a demand for every email ever written about the dossier. If ever there was an occasion when journalists, press officers, ministers and civil servants wished they had never put their thoughts down in an email this was that moment. Emails are so totally different from formal memo-writing.

They are quick flashes of reaction, spontaneous bursts of emotion, and devastatingly revealing when exposed in the public domain. And they are so difficult to destroy. Deleting an email is easy, but so too is plucking it back from the ether when you know how. The emails of Alastair Campbell and the rest of his press office, including those of Tom Kelly, a senior member of Alastair's staff, were delivered to Lord Hutton.

I sat in the back of the inquiry room on the day of my appearance before Lord Hutton and listened to my colleague, Tom Baldwin, as he was questioned by the inquiry's leading barrister, James Dingemans QC. After one question, Tom replied, 'Mike Evans is the one you need to ask, he knows all about it.' Thanks, Tom. I duly took my place at the witness stand and faced the lawyer. He asked me to go through the process I had followed which ended up with the name David Kelly. I told him how, over the course of a day, I had phoned the MoD press office with twenty-two names until the right one came up. He seemed satisfied with that answer and did not follow it up with any cunning questions, such as, 'Did you receive any outside help in your quest for Dr Kelly's name?' or 'What was the response of the MoD press officer you spoke to when you produced the right name?' or 'Were you under the impression that the MoD was desperately keen to get the name out into the public domain?'

Several newspapers the next day recorded the evidence I had given about the twenty-two names. And that was it; I wasn't required to answer any further questions as the inquiry dragged on. Lord Hutton's report took some time to be published and was preceded by a separate publication delivered by the parliamentary Intelligence and Security Committee (ISC), which had carried out its own investigation. Its main judgment was that the Government was not guilty of 'sexing up' the Iraq dossier. Alastair Campbell was also cleared of any involvement. It looked like a bad day for Gilligan and the BBC.

Sir Richard Dearlove, MI6 Chief, had told the parliamentary committee, in private session, that the sourcing behind the intelligence material about the readiness of Iraqi troops to launch chemical or biological weapons within forty-five minutes was reliable. The ISC downplayed the significance of the forty-five-minute claim, saying it had added nothing particularly significant to the Iraqi military's known 'battlefield capabilities'.

One of the key points made by the ISC was lost in the general theme of the report, which was that Gilligan's accusation of a 'sexed-up' dossier was inaccurate. Buried in the conclusions was a paragraph that described the decision to delete a certain passage from Tony Blair's foreword to the dossier as 'unfortunate'. The passage read: 'The case I make is not that Saddam could launch a nuclear attack on London or another part of the UK (he could not)'.

Had these words been included as originally intended, the tabloids might have been dissuaded from running off with the idea that a nuclear bomb from Saddam was forty-five minutes away.

Lord Hutton's report came to the same conclusion as the ISC: the Government was not to blame for anything. The finger of accusation was pointed firmly at the BBC. Gilligan was axed, and Gavyn Davies, the BBC chairman, and Greg Dyke, BBC director-general, resigned. John Scarlett, chairman of the Cabinet Office Joint Intelligence Committee and overall author of the Iraq dossier, was also exonerated. Lord Hutton concluded that he had not been pressurised to 'sex up' the report, but added, bizarrely, that he may have been 'subconsciously influenced' to use stronger wording.

Fleet Street was divided. Some newspapers, including *The Guardian, Independent* and *Daily Mail,* denounced the Hutton report as a whitewash. It's always an easy response when an official report fails to come up with the conclusions a particular Fleet Street editor is expecting. But the 'subconsciously influenced' Scarlett (later appointed Chief of MI6) was a concept that was seized on as an illustration of how the eminent judge had pulled out all the stops to be as fair as possible to the Government.

Alastair Campbell had won his battle with Gilligan. The BBC reporter was out of a job and Alastair was still king of communications at Number 10. However, the previously stated optimism that Saddam's weapons of mass destruction would be found began to fade into oblivion. There were none to find, and the principal intelligence sources who were described by Sir Richard Dearlove as reliable turned out to be anything but trustworthy. It had all been a game played by Iraqi defectors who wanted to see the end of Saddam and his regime and thought, correctly, that an exaggerated, indeed untrue, picture of Iraq's WMD capabilities would help to persuade Bush, Blair and other leaders to march into their country to depose the dictator. Everyone, including Dr Kelly, believed there was a genuine WMD threat.

About five weeks before Lord Hutton delivered his conclusions on the 28th of January 2004, I flew to Kabul to report on how Afghanistan was surviving in the post-Taliban era and to spend time with NATO's International Security Assistance Force (ISAF), set up in 2001 to help the country get back on its feet after decades of war. Much of the focus then was on provincial reconstruction teams (PRTs), a mix of military and civilian. Their job was to assist the Afghan provincial governors and district elders to improve people's lives and generate new facilities, such as medical care centres and schools. I flew up to Mazar-e Sharif in northern Afghanistan where Colonel Dick Davies, a British officer, was running a PRT consisting of eighty-five soldiers and diplomats.

At the Mazar-e Sharif airport, I spotted someone in the distance, wearing an ankle-length green overcoat, stepping into the back of an RAF Hercules transport aircraft. It was General Abdul Dostum, the most powerful warlord in northern Afghanistan; he controlled his own army and had allegedly shot dead his first wife. He was also one of the heroes of the war against the Taliban, a key member of the Northern Alliance who brought his soldiers, tanks and artillery to join forces with the Americans. This tall, overbearing Uzbek slayer of the Taliban, a feared warrior figure, was being courted by the Afghan Government, the Americans and the British. If Afghanistan was to have a chance of forging a peaceful future, the warlords with their private fiefdoms had to be persuaded to play a positive role, even to become ministers in the Kabul administration. General Dostum's flight from Mazar-e Sharif to Kabul in an RAF Hercules summed up the delicate diplomatic moves being made to keep the warlord on side.

I subsequently sought to interview him, as well as his arch warlord rival, General Ustad Atta, both of whom had houses in Mazar-e Sharif. General Dostum agreed to give me a few minutes of his valuable time and I entered his house somewhat apprehensively. Outside, his bodyguards in huge four-by-fours watched me as I walked up the path. General Dostum shook my hand and indicated I should sit in the chair opposite him. He spoke not a word of English, and most of his answers to my questions, spoken to an interpreter, were short, unemotional and lacking in any reportable content. He had an awesomely confrontational face: solid, Mongolian features, a huge head and swept-back thick, grey hair that started halfway up his forehead. His eyes were those of a snake. When he spoke, only his lips moved; everything else, including his eyes, remained motionless. I scribbled down the meaningless utterances into my notebook, and then asked one more question. I had been told that President Karzai, the Afghan leader, wanted to offer General Dostum the job of minister of defence. So I asked him whether he wanted to be defence minister. He erupted, spouting what sounded like dark, deadly oaths at his interpreter, and even waved his arms in apparent protest.

I waited to hear what the warlord was shouting about. After two minutes of angry tirade, the interpreter turned to me and said, 'He said no.'

General Dostum promptly stood up and stormed out of the room. I asked the interpreter what had happened. He replied that I had insulted him. Of course he didn't want to be a puppet defence minister in Kabul; the city that is hated by everyone living outside the capital. General Dostum was the leader of men in his own empire. The interpreter said General Dostum had also asked who the hell I was and what was I doing asking such a stupid question. I reckon I was lucky to leave his headquarters alive! But it was an eye-opener into the political challenges ahead.

When I went to see General Atta, in an elegant room in a villa in the outskirts of Mazar-e Sharif, the atmosphere was very different. A Tajik, he was also tall and imposing but he was dressed in an expensive Saville Row striped, dark blue suit. He sat for the interview in an armchair, twirling worry beads in his hands, and answered my questions without once biting my head off. Everything he said underlined his continuing rivalry with Dostum, although in the new atmosphere of cooperation, both he and the deadly Uzbek were supposed to be handing over their heavy arms and behaving in more diplomatic fashion. After meeting the two men, I came away thinking both were as devious as each other, although General Atta was trying harder to sound and look the sophisticated man of peace.

Another man on a mission was the US Defence Secretary, Donald Rumsfeld. I was at the British Provincial Reconstruction Team headquarters in Mazar-e Sharif when I spotted away in the distance a large dust cloud filling the sky. In the middle, not yet visible, was Rumsfeld in a thirty-five-vehicle cavalcade that included two Humvees and a Chevy. He came with a warning to the defeated Taliban: if they so much as tried to get together again to threaten the Kabul Government, he promised they would be captured or killed. It was good Hollywood stuff, but empty words for the local Afghans who wanted to know how the toppling of the Taliban two years earlier had improved their lives.

One Afghan in his early twenties I got to know took me round the back streets and pointed downwards. 'Where are the roads we have all been promised?' he asked. While it was frustrating for the 'liberated' Afghans not to see dramatic changes transforming their country, it was a fact, though impolite to point it out, that Afghanistan was a country still in the fourteenth century. Even if America had ignored Iraq and focused all its immense capabilities and funds into redeveloping this nation ravaged by war for so many decades, it was never going to be an easy task. Much of the responsibility for pouring money and skills into Afghanistan lay with the American men and women who worked for USAID (US Agency for International Development), who were like inspired missionaries seeking ways of helping the Afghans and channelling money into local projects. Often they took personal risks and had to be protected when they ventured out of Kabul.

Meanwhile, the end of war in Afghanistan made no difference to the staggering levels of corruption that bled the economy and made vulnerable every international donation. Large villas with high surrounding walls started going up in Kabul. Visiting Afghanistan, as I did many times over the next eight or nine years, was always an experience of mixed emotions: amazement at the bravery and determination of the international military force wanting to play an historic role in converting Afghanistan into a better place for the Afghan people, and despair at the sheer scale of the challenge.

The first time I went to the ISAF headquarters in Kabul, I was taken to the inner sanctum area where the members of the mission were able to relax. It was a bizarre sight. Outside could be heard the cacophony of a city struggling against increasingly anarchic traffic jams, and here was a garden where the grass was thick and green and beautifully cultivated, and dotted around were the fattest rabbits I had ever seen, munching quietly and hopping around like they had found their personal nirvana. The surrounding walls were like a film set, created by Egyptians when they were serving at ISAF. I made a derogatory remark to a British official about the ridiculously thick grass and the rabbits but was given short shrift. These men and women were serving in a godforsaken country, away from their families, and deserved a place of peace and quiet amidst the hard toil of operating in Afghanistan, he said.

I bit my tongue. He had a point, of course. But the rabbits somehow seemed a little over the top. Also, how often did the ISAF staff leave the sanctuary of the headquarters and get their hands dirty in dangerous places where the Taliban still lurked? My Afghan friend – the one who had pointed to the dusty unmade-up track that ran alongside the area where he lived in Mazar-e Sharif – would probably have gladly served up one of the rabbits for his family dinner!

CHAPTER 16
WHAT THE BUTLER SAW

Everything comes round full circle. The Hutton report on Dr Kelly and the Iraq weapons of mass destruction dossier could not have been clearer. The Government was acquitted of misleading Parliament and the public with false claims of Saddam Hussein's deadly weapons. But, in July 2004, a second report was published. This time it was the turn of another peer of the realm, Lord Butler, former Cabinet Secretary, who had been asked to examine what went wrong with the intelligence evidence behind the dossier. It was a pretty devastating critique. MI6's sources proved to be of doubtful integrity. Sir Richard Dearlove, Chief of MI6, admitted to Lord Butler during the inquiry that his service had been required to 'ramp up' the intelligence coverage on Iraq.

In the context in which Sir Richard was talking, 'ramp up' did not mean 'sex up', but the whole issue of the BBC *Today* programme's allegation was revived. MI6 had begun to have serious doubts about their primary and secondary sources soon after the war in Iraq was declared to be over (declared somewhat prematurely by George W. Bush on the 1st of May 2003). With all his experience as a cabinet secretary, fully accustomed to reading top secret intelligence over many years, Robin Butler had no alternative but to conclude that MI6 'did not generally have agents with first-hand, inside knowledge of Iraq's nuclear, chemical, biological or ballistic missile programmes. As a result, intelligence reports were mainly inferential'.

Even more devastating was the judgment that the dossier had failed to include enough caveats, warning that the intelligence material was not one hundred percent proven and reliable. Lord Butler and his panel concluded that the dossier had been too definitive. The forty-five-minute claim should never have been included in the dossier, Lord Butler said, because the intelligence behind it appeared to be flawed. Some of the material that ended up in the dossier had arrived in the in-trays of intelligence chiefs by a series of Chinese whispers, with information hopping from one agent to another until it reached the ears of the Whitehall customers.

The notorious forty-five-minute assertion was based on 'uncharacteristically poor' intelligence. Dr Kelly had said as much over lunch with the BBC reporter. But Gilligan's accusation was that the intelligence had been deliberately spiced up by the public relations team at Downing Street to make the dossier 'sexier' and more dramatic, thereby encouraging Parliament and the public to believe that Saddam and his weapons of mass destruction posed an imminent threat. Lord Butler sided with Lord Hutton. Although his criticism of the Government's dossier was tough and illuminating, he did not accuse Downing Street of setting out to mislead everyone. Nor was there evidence, he said, of deliberate distortion of the intelligence. The fact is that Britain, the United States and most of Europe – and probably Russia and China as well – actually believed that Saddam Hussein had been secretly working on nuclear, chemical and biological weapon systems, in contravention of United Nations resolutions. It wasn't just Bush and Blair plotting to overthrow Saddam, with or without evidence of clandestine weapons programmes. The whole world was conned.

In the process of 'ramping up' coverage of intelligence in Iraq, MI6 became vulnerable to every whisper and nod from so-called agents and sub-agents in Baghdad. Gathering intelligence inside Iraq was always a near-impossible challenge. Saddam had developed a comprehensive spying network amongst the Iraqi population; and he sustained his regime with threats of such wholesale brutality for anyone who dared to consider disloyalty, that a foreign espionage agency such as MI6 or the CIA was forced to depend on agents whose veracity could not be wholly trusted. But Downing Street had promised that a dossier would be made public which would be based on secret intelligence. It was a risky move which caused heartache for intelligence chiefs, accustomed to total secrecy.

All those years earlier, in 1993, Sir Colin McColl, in his first and only press conference as MI6 Chief in the basement of the Foreign Office, had told reporters that he preferred to go back into the shadows because it was his solemn duty to protect the men and women who acted as his service's agents. Their names and their information had to be protected for ever. Publicity, he indicated, was anathema to a secret intelligence service. Yet Blair wanted Sir Richard Dearlove to open his files and fill the pages of a public dossier with clandestinely-acquired details of Saddam's weapons of mass destruction programme. Sir Colin would have been dismayed. It was Field Marshal Lord Peter Inge, a former chief of the defence staff and a member of Lord Butler's panel, who summed up the dilemma better than anyone. At a press conference after publication of the Butler Report, Lord Inge suggested, 'Intelligence and public relations should be kept separate.' With hindsight, I suspect most people in government, and certainly those in the intelligence services, agreed. All the mistakes, miscalculations, accusations of flawed intelligence and poor judgments highlighted by Lords Hutton and Butler were repeated on the 6th of July 2016, albeit in more forceful and comprehensive language, by Sir John Chilcot, former senior civil servant, in his near three million-word Iraq Inquiry report.

While the WMD issue finally had to be pushed to one side – thoughts of digging up the desert for buried components were soon forgotten – Iraq was coming back into the forefront in a serious way. The victory declared by Bush was going wrong. Violence and the stirrings of an ethnic Shia/Sunni war, as well as disillusionment with the US-led coalition, were forcing ministers to consider sending more troops back into the country. The key deadline was the first elections to be held in Iraq, set for early 2005. This would be a crucial milestone in the coalition's plans to transform Iraq from a dictatorship into a smoothly-run democracy. But it seemed the only way to safeguard the Iraqi electors' right to vote was to pour more and more troops into Iraq to protect them from violence and intimidation. Some democracy! A sign of the horrific eruption of violence to come was splashed all over the newspapers in November 2004. Three British soldiers from the Black Watch Regiment were killed in a suicide ambush attack. The regiment had been moved from Basra in the south closer to Baghdad on a temporary mission. It was the first time British soldiers had died from a suicide attack in Iraq.

I flew out to Basra at the end of January 2005 in order to be part of a Fleet Street pooled-reporting arrangement organised by the MoD for the period of the elections. The MoD was desperate for some good news. Apart from the deaths of the three Black Watch soldiers, there were other incidents which were highly controversial and had the potential for damaging the reputation of the British forces serving in Iraq. Notably, the murder of six members of the Royal Military Police during a routine visit to an Iraqi police station in the town of Majar al-Kabir in June 2003 during which they were targeted by hundreds of angry, armed protestors. There was no one near enough to rescue them. The most damaging incident involving British troops was the fatal beatings suffered by Baha Mousa, a twenty-six-year-old Iraqi hotel worker, while he was detained as a suspected insurgent by soldiers from The Queen's Lancashire Regiment at a holding facility in Basra.

There was quite a gathering of reporters for the elections, and the usual high-stakes competition to get the best front seats to watch the process. One reporter totally lost it when he was assigned to some minor location in southern Iraq with a logistics regiment. He shouted angrily at the poor young media officer delegated to draw names from the hat for the various positions. The reporter knew how difficult it was going to be for him to write a decent story. But, most of all, he wondered how to explain to his foreign desk why he had been embedded with a logistics regiment while other reporters were assigned to combat units who might be forced to open fire on insurgents trying to disrupt the election. It was the luck of the draw but he took it personally.

The day before we were due to go off with our assigned units, I was taken on a fast and rooftop-hugging helicopter ride over the city of Basra. I could feel the pressure of the sudden swerves and turns as the helicopter pilot sought to evade the danger of insurgents targeting us as we flew over the city. It was like a constant G-force sensation, and with the overwhelming noise of the rotor blades and engine, I felt my body being pulled one way and then another.

Later that evening, I was in the washrooms at the British military camp outside Basra when my right eye suddenly felt weird. I partially lost sight in the eye and peered into the mirror to see what could have happened. Right across the middle of the eye was what looked like a splash of black oil. I rinsed my eye with water, but the black splodgy mess stayed there. I wasn't alarmed; I thought something must have flown into my eye without me noticing. I went to see the military doctor and, after trying to wash out my eye with special fluid, he pronounced himself bewildered and concerned.

'Do you have glaucoma in your family?' he asked.

I told him my father had glaucoma and I had early signs of the eye disease. When I mentioned that I had had a particularly pressurised helicopter ride that afternoon, the doctor said he was worried that I may have had an acute glaucoma attack and that my sight might be at risk. I needed to go to a hospital immediately, he said.

He began making plans for me to be taken by armed escort across the border into Kuwait where the Americans had a large military hospital. Within half an hour, I was sitting in the back of an army Land Rover with two sergeants and four other specially-adapted Land Rovers filled with seventeen heavily-armed soldiers, and fitted with Browning heavy machine guns. I was in no pain, but my sight was still obscured.

I was being driven at speed by a small convoy of well-armed soldiers designated to get me safely down the road from Basra and into Kuwait. It was bizarre, unreal, confusing, scary but somehow strangely comforting.

I was in the hands of the British military and felt safe. What would happen at the American hospital, I had no idea. I just concentrated on the road ahead and felt a bit of a fraud. I wasn't injured, I had no blood seeping from a wound and nothing was broken. All I had was a black strip across my right eye that none of my escort soldiers could see. Before I left I had rung my foreign desk and warned them that I had had an accident which affected my sight. There was no mention either by me or by the desk that my 'accident' could mean me having to return home. I warned Kim Sengupta, a fellow defence correspondent on *The Independent,* that I was off to hospital in Kuwait but hoped to be back in time to cover the elections.

At the border, my armed escort waved me farewell and returned to camp. My Land Rover went on across the border and we arrived at a huge tented hospital around 1am. I waited for twenty minutes, and then a young doctor came to examine me.

He made up his mind very quickly: 'You've had a mini stroke which has blocked off a tiny vein in your eye. It's called a retinal occlusion. You're lucky it happened in your eye. It could have happened anywhere in your body, and it might happen again. My advice to you is to get home as quickly as possible and go to hospital.'

It was unbelievable. It wasn't an acute glaucoma attack after all – it was a stroke! I told the doctor I was in southern Iraq to cover the Iraqi elections.

He replied, 'Mr Evans, there will be other stories for you to write. This is your health, you should go home.'

I left the hospital in a state of confusion. Should I get a flight straight back to the UK or risk it? I had a story to cover, and no one else could take my place. I joined up with my two sergeants and at 2am set off back to the Kuwaiti border. I sat in the back while the two sergeants chatted away in the front. I kept silent for about half an hour and then I told them I had made a decision. I told them the doctor had warned me to get home as quickly as possible to have my eye checked out. But I was going to stay to cover the elections, an historic moment in the life of every adult Iraqi. I felt relieved. It was a gamble. If my eye deteriorated or I suffered another minor stroke, whether caused by a helicopter ride or not, my family would never forgive me. I was putting the job before my health – a crazy decision. But, despite the doctor's words, I felt fine; my overall sight was adequate, I was pretty fit and I didn't want to miss out on reporting on the important event about to take place across Iraq – although I knew that the main interest back in London would be on what happened in Baghdad, not Basra.

The capital was already suffering from rising violence, while Basra was relatively peaceful. But British troops were in Basra and if something went seriously wrong, they would be in the middle of it all, and that could be a major story. I thanked the two sergeants who had been amazingly reassuring company and went to catch a few hours' sleep in my tent before the early wake-up call, due at 7am.

The British troops in Basra included the Duke of Wellington's Regiment, who, like me, were back in Iraq for the elections. I looked out for the captain who had been so obliging when I was lost in the desert with my Fleet Street colleagues, hunting for the victims of the alleged British war crime, but I didn't spot him. One familiar face turned up, however. Paul Gibson, whom I had last seen in Kosovo when he was commanding officer of the 1st Battalion Parachute Regiment, was now a brigadier and commander of 4th Armoured Brigade, based in Basra. He was in charge of ensuring the safety of the 180 polling stations in Basra, although only as a standby force located in an outer security ring. The Iraqi police and army were responsible for guarding the polling stations and the voters.

The most dramatic sight on polling day were the queues of hundreds of women in their long black abaya garments. They put up with the embarrassment of having their bodies patted by strangers for hidden explosives, albeit inside a tent, and seemed generally in an excited mood. They chatted and laughed and even waved to us foreign journalists, watching as they trooped into their polling booths. There were a few mortar explosions and an improvised bomb was found close to one polling station, but there were no casualties.

One of the reasons for the successful security operation was that dozens of suspected insurgents and terrorists had been arrested. I was taken to a police station by an Iraqi officer and shown into a large cell holding about fifty prisoners. The prison guards all wore balaclavas over their faces. The prisoners were silent, and most of them were standing up. But two of the detainees were sitting cross-legged on the floor, and each of them stared at me with pure hatred in their eyes. The senior Iraqi police officer said they were al-Qaeda terrorists. They had been arrested while trying to blow up an oil terminal at al-Zubayr, south of Basra. It was the closest I ever came to a member of Osama bin Laden's terrorist organisation.

A voter at a polling station in one of the districts of Basra summed up the feeling of Iraqis on election day. Amer Hayyawi, a thirty-two-year-old household goods salesman, told me: 'The tyranny has gone, so this is a great blessing. This is the first time we have voted properly and I feel a zeal inside me. It's an exciting day.'

Then came one of the worst incidents for British troops since the Iraq campaign began. An RAF Hercules C130K transport aircraft was blown out of the sky en route from Baghdad to the huge American logistics base at Balad, southwest of the capital. The ten men on board, nine from the RAF and one from the army, were killed. Although I was in Iraq, it was difficult to discover what had happened. It looked like the plane had been targeted by ground fire, but in the hours after the aircraft had crashed no one knew for sure whether it had been shot down or had suffered a cataclysmic mechanical failure. The latter seemed highly unlikely, since the old workhorse Hercules was one of the most reliable of planes. If it had been hit by rocket-propelled grenades or machine gun fire, the Hercules must have been flying at an exceptionally low altitude. Confirmation that the aircraft had been struck by an arc of ground fire came much later, but the incident served as a warning to all of us that the dream of forging a democracy in Iraq and creating a peaceful country that would help to stabilise the region was an illusion. Ten British lives had been lost. Many more would be lost before Britain finally withdrew its troops from Iraq.

After my scary eye incident, I remained a little apprehensive throughout the rest of my trip to Basra, just in case another 'mini stroke' emerged. I avoided high-pressure helicopter rides. But, fortunately, although I only had partial vision in my right eye, it didn't prevent me from completing my assignment and I returned to London a week later. I made an appointment with Moorfields eye hospital in the City of London and was examined by a consultant called Plank. He confirmed the diagnosis made by the young American doctor in Kuwait and said there was nothing he could do to rectify the grey smudge across my right eye. However, he reassured me that over time it would improve, although there would always be some form of obstruction in my vision in that eye. He also said I should take a small Aspirin every day for the rest of my life. I never told the foreign desk what had happened, and they never asked. Life is busy and they had all probably forgotten that, at the start of my trip to Basra, I had rung in to warn them I needed to go to hospital. To them, I looked the same, but to me they looked a little blurred! I had ignored the advice of one doctor but accepted Mr Plank's.

Covering the British involvement in southern Iraq at that period in the campaign, there were already indications that the post-war planning back in Washington and London had been inadequate, if not downright negligent. A huge resentment was building up among the Iraqi people. Sometimes it was just the failure of the occupying forces to install air-conditioning units to provide relief from the intense, sweltering heat, or it was anger over the seeming inability of the foreigners to make their lives more pleasurable, more hopeful, or more secure. Bombings were occurring every day – not so much in Basra at that stage, but the country was awash with weapons, and resentful Iraqis tended to use them as a way of demonstrating their disgust at the lack of visible progress, following the downfall of Saddam. That was always the problem for the occupying forces. Despite the pledge of huge international donations, the American powerhouse in Baghdad thought that bigger was better, when in fact a myriad of smaller, less expensive projects could have made a difference in relatively quick time. The troops had to go around trying to keep the local population happy while constantly being on the look-out for hostile faces or men with guns on the rooftops.

No one had any notion that Iraq was going to erupt into one of the fiercest and most deadly civil wars. No one in London or Washington had the foresight to predict that the dismantling of the Sunni power apparatus, including the demobilisation of Saddam's army, would lead to a countrywide implosion that would subsequently create the perfect environment for the arrival of Islamic terrorists intent on exploiting the anarchy for their own ends. The evil stare of those two al-Qaeda detainees in the Basra police station cell set the marker for what became an apocalypse of violence and brutal terror for the next four years.

George Bush had claimed that Saddam himself was aligned to al-Qaeda, providing another reason for invading Iraq. European intelligence services, including MI6, disputed there was any link with Osama bin Laden's terror network. However, one of the last reports before the invasion written by Britain's Joint Intelligence Committee warned that military force against Saddam would inevitably motivate terrorist organisations to launch attacks against the West. The prediction was tragically accurate. The invasion was viewed as an attack on Muslims, and inspired Islamic militants around the world to join in the fight. Violence on an horrific scale broke out in Iraq, and all the good work that the US, Britain and many other nations had hoped would improve the lives of the Iraqi people had to be put to one side as the country's security once again became the primary role for the thousands of coalition troops.

Companies that were awarded lucrative contracts to rebuild power stations, manufacturing plants and oil facilities had to employ thousands of private security guards to protect workers from attack. In many places, it was just too dangerous to contemplate starting construction. Billions of dollars were fed into the system to rebuild Iraq, but much of it was wasted or lost in a black hole of corruption, or put on hold while the insurgency boiled over.

Covering the insurgency as a reporter was always a risk, but I never felt under as much threat as I did in Bosnia. In the Balkans there were no rules, no military to guarantee safe passage, because their humanitarian role didn't allow it. The media became targets for all factions, whether Serbs, Croats or Bosnian Muslims. In Iraq – at least, in the assignment I had – the British troops were my protectors, but if *they* were attacked, *I* was attacked. I went to Baghdad on a couple of occasions but didn't cover the war as a Baghdad correspondent. My role was principally down in Basra and surrounding areas where the British troops went on patrol. But one of my fondest memories in Baghdad was sitting in a garden in the company of General Sir Mike Jackson, now Chief of the General Staff, drinking cocktails before a pleasant dinner in his honour and listening to the bomb and mortar explosions outside the walls of the British residence. As an old Bosnia hand, I was well accustomed to the paradox of enjoying a social life amidst the sound and fury of warfare.

Meanwhile, the reputation of the British Army continued to take a battering. On top of the growing revelations about the brutal beating given to Baha Mousa before he died, seven members of the 3rd Battalion Parachute Regiment were charged with murdering an Iraqi civilian in southern Iraq, ten days after Bush had declared that the war was over. The military always say that in war soldiers have to make split decisions about whether to open fire or not. British soldiers are among the most professionally trained troops in the world, but in those split-second moments, in the heat of battle or when confronted by a potentially dangerous situation, they can take action that is either confirmed as justified and lifesaving or could send them before a judge in a court martial. There are legal firms waiting for these occasions to make public accusations and press for prosecution, which is why MoD lawyers have to go to war alongside soldiers whenever overseas campaigns are launched. The seven paratroopers were acquitted at their subsequent court martial.

In another case, Iraqi looters were reported to have been mistreated by members of the

1st Battalion Royal Regiment of Fusiliers after the fall of Saddam in 2003. The scale of the looting had taken every western government by surprise. When it started in Baghdad, Geoff Hoon was asked at a press conference whether it amounted to a serious breakdown in law and order. He made light of the looting, saying it was just a few people stealing gold taps and was not an unexpected consequence of the toppling of a dictator. But this was a serious underestimation of what was going on in Baghdad, and also in Basra and elsewhere in the country. There was mass looting, all in front of the world's television cameras.

One British Army lieutenant revealed in an internal military report: 'They stole everything imaginable, from grand pianos to air-conditioning units to front doors. By the end of the frenzy they were taking things simply because they were there.'

It was during this frenzy that looters in Basra were arrested and taken to a British military location called Camp Bread Basket, a giant warehouse. Four soldiers from the Royal Regiment of Fusiliers were charged with abusing them while in detention and photographing the prisoners' humiliation. Their conviction brought shame on their regiment but also raised questions about the standard of discipline amongst the troops facing one of the toughest and most hostile conditions since the worst days of the Northern Ireland conflict.

The growing revelations about the Baha Mousa case cast perhaps the worst light on the British Army's reputation in Iraq. Yet, at the same time, the vast majority of soldiers and Royal Marines who served in Iraq conducted themselves in accordance with the best professional standards, and there were some remarkable acts of courage and personal sacrifice.

The biggest news story of 2005 was not in Iraq but in London. The suicide bombing on the London Underground stations and a double-decker bus, which killed fifty-two people as well as the four home-grown British terrorists, came out of the blue. There had been no specific intelligence of such a plot, although it was later revealed that MI5 had had two of the bombers on its surveillance radar. They had been followed, but only as peripheral associates of other primary targets, and there was no follow-up on the two individuals after the terrorist plot that MI5 had been focusing on was foiled.

The British terrorists who plotted to kill as many people as possible in London's transport system were part of a new breed of Islamic extremists, skilled in counter-surveillance, trained in camps in Afghanistan, Pakistan or elsewhere, but not taking orders from al-Qaeda. They espoused the same violent ideology as Osama bin Laden's network, but were well-educated freelancers, knowledgeable about evading MI5's technical spying operations and proficient in making bombs.

On the 7th of July 2005, I had left for work and was travelling on a train to Waterloo. There had been reports before I left of a catastrophic power failure in central London that was causing chaos. I arrived at Waterloo to find people milling around in confusion. The Underground was closed. There were no buses. I walked as fast as I could across Hungerford Bridge to the Embankment the other side of the Thames, where the sense of bewilderment and also fear could be seen in everyone's faces. There was no more talk of a power failure. There had been bomb explosions. I had to get to the office quickly. There were no taxis, so I stuck my thumb out and a white van stopped. I explained I worked for *The Times*, and, in true British fashion, he invited me to hop in and drove me to *The Times* in Wapping, where the news desk confirmed that four bombs had detonated. Four suicide bombers carrying backpacks had killed themselves in the Tube and on the bus. More than 700 were injured as well as the fifty-two who died. It was a day of mayhem, and by the end of it, the big question was: how could MI5 and the police have remained in ignorance of such a devastating plot? The terrorist threat status had even been reduced by one level only a month previously because it had been assessed that while the likelihood of a terrorist attack was still relatively high, it was lower than it had been since the 11th of September 2001.

However, security chiefs for some time had warned that one day terrorists would succeed in setting off a bomb, despite all the vigilant procedures in place. The greatest worry was that it would be a dirty bomb, a device made up of a mixture of high explosive and some form of radioactive, chemical or biological material. The 7th of July bombers did not go down the dirty-bomb route but their great advantage over the police and MI5 was that they were prepared to die. Had they left their bombs and run off, with the devices timed to detonate an hour or so later, there would have been a reasonable chance of a member of the public spotting them and alerting the authorities. But the suicide bombers died with their bombs effectively strapped to their backs.

The 7th of July was a shock to everyone. Suicide bombings in London! There was an immediate alert for other devices. Fourteen days later, on the 21st of July, a second bomb plot by a different group of fanatics only failed because the detonating devices were faulty. On that day, I was attending a press conference in the media room at the MoD. John Reid, the new Labour defence secretary, was already talking to us when four security men burst into the room and grabbed him. They bundled him out so fast he could hardly get his legs to work. A touch melodramatic! After all, Dr Reid wasn't the US president, and there was absolutely no suggestion that this second terrorist plot in the same month was aimed at either him or the ministry where he worked. The MoD's security boys had clearly been watching too much television. The rest of us in the room wondered whether we should bundle ourselves out of the building, but there was no one from security to ask. By now they probably had Dr Reid hiding in a cupboard in the bowels of the ministry. We eventually left to discover that every policeman in London was hunting for four suicide bombers who were still very much alive and on the run.

CHAPTER 17
NO SHOTS TO BE FIRED IN AFGHANISTAN CAMPAIGN

It seemed there was to be no prospect of respite from covering wars. From 2005 onwards, Afghanistan, once again, was the big story.

I had been to Kabul and Mazar-e Sharif, but when the British Government announced that it would be sending a new batch of troops to serve in Helmand province in the south to coincide with NATO's expanded mandate, I knew that the focus of my reporting, both in London and in the field, was going to be Afghanistan.

A memorable moment came on Salisbury Plain in Wiltshire where the British Army's 16 Air Assault Brigade was training for the new mission. It was clearly going to be a potent force, prepared to take on the Taliban if the Taliban took on the British Army. However, nobody seemed to know whether there was going to be fighting or not. John Reid, the defence secretary, made what became a famous remark that he always complained was taken out of context and misquoted. But the fact is he did say he hoped that the troops being sent to Helmand would not have to fire a shot.

'We would be perfectly happy to leave in three years' time without firing a shot because our job is to protect reconstruction,' he said.

He went on to add a proviso that the brigade being deployed to Helmand would be sufficiently armed and equipped to respond robustly if attacked. Some of the newspaper reports neglected to add his cautionary remark, and when soldiers started dying, Reid's comment was thrown back at him.

His words were compounded by bizarre responses from the paratroopers serving with 16 Air Assault Brigade. When I asked a number of them during their training on Salisbury Plain what their mission was all about, each one replied with the same word which they repeated several times: 'Reconstruction'. They were going to Helmand province to reconstruct! This was what their political masters had told them to say, but it sounded somewhat false coming out of the mouths of muscled paratroopers who were trained to be shock troops. I don't think any of them had a clue about what they were going to reconstruct. But to help them get in the mood, the army had hired a bunch of Afghans living in Britain to add a touch of authenticity to the training.

With hindsight, it became tragically evident that the 3,300 troops sent off to Helmand were being dispatched on faulty or inadequate intelligence. Helmand had been relatively quiet, but this was because the only foreign troops in the province, before the British arrived, had been a handful of Americans running a provincial reconstruction team. The US troops had not adopted a proactive approach towards the Taliban. They rarely went out on foraging expeditions, seeking out Taliban fighters to kill. They stayed in Lashkar Gah, the provincial capital.

But there were plenty of signs of Taliban rearming and preparing for a fight. The southern provinces of Helmand and neighbouring Kandahar were the Taliban's strongholds and spiritual homes. The arrival of 3,300 British paratroopers in their midst was unquestionably going to be viewed by the insurgents as a deliberate provocation. It would clearly be a miracle if no shots were going to be fired.

Indeed, the Americans warned the British Government that it was sending an undermanned force to Helmand. When the Pentagon sent one of its most distinguished and experienced officials, Eric Edelman, to London to advise on deploying a bigger force to Helmand, his counterparts in the MoD did not react in the way he expected. Perhaps they had images of smiling bereted paratroopers walking around the streets chatting to the locals and saying 'boo' to the Taliban if they turned up in their black turbans. Some officials seemed to think that Helmand was just another Northern Ireland! But at the height of the struggle in Northern Ireland, the British Army had 22,000 troops confronting a few hundred terrorists, and although the troop numbers came down sharply, the battle with the Provisional IRA, the Loyalist terrorists and the various breakaway factions lasted more than thirty years.

By the time the 3,300 troops of 16 Air Assault

Brigade arrived in Helmand, there were about 5,700 British military personnel in Afghanistan, including 1,000 to help run the headquarters of NATO's International Security Assistance Force in Kabul. From the 1st of May 2006, ISAF was commanded by the alliance's Allied Rapid Reaction Corps, headed by Lieutenant-General David Richards, who had made such an impression as a brigadier in Sierra Leone in 2000. The British participation in Afghanistan was a small-scale deployment compared with the huge commitment in Iraq. There were still 8,500 troops in southern Iraq, and for the 2003 invasion there had been 45,000. But Iraq was a war, whereas Afghanistan was going to be about reconstruction!

Reid even declared that the brigade, based around the 3rd Battalion Parachute Regiment, would not be involved in chasing the Taliban or foreign terrorists. That was to be the preserve of the Americans. It all sounded like Britain was sending boy scouts to help spread good will and peace. Yet there was no doubt that one of the toughest brigades had been selected for the task, and at that time it was commanded by Brigadier Ed Butler, educated at Eton, with a wealth of operational experience behind him and a handsome devil to boot.

No one had imagined that this brigade would find itself under daily attack by the Taliban and that casualties would start to flow. From 'no shots to be fired' to an all too regular repatriation of dead soldiers in coffins was a dramatic, unexpected and shocking reversal of fortune for the British armed forces, and the fighting and casualty toll were to continue for more than six years. Somewhere there had been an appalling misjudgment, a fingers-crossed strategy which ended with the loss of more than 450 British lives and at least 2,600 injured, many hundreds suffering leg and arm amputations.

At the time of the British Government's announcement about the deployment of 3,300 troops to Helmand, military chiefs were adamant that running two operations at the same time – Iraq and Afghanistan – was perfectly doable. Yet within a matter of weeks, after continuous attacks by the Taliban on 16 Air Assault Brigade, there was a cry for more troops and more helicopters, and this placed unplanned pressure on the army. Fighting two wars was, after all, a bigger deal than the top brass had predicted. More troops were rushed off to Helmand, 900 to be exact, although only a third were combat soldiers; the rest were specialists in engineering, logistics and support services. Sadly, it looked like a panic move to make up for over-optimistic intelligence assessments about the security situation in the southern province. Six soldiers had been killed in three weeks, and it was clear to the MoD planners that, with the Taliban rising up against the British presence, there were serious gaps in military capability. It was another way of admitting that mistakes had been made.

In September 2006, Des Browne, the new defence secretary who was later, bizarrely, to be given a second portfolio as Scottish secretary, summed up the dilemma the military was facing. 'We do have to accept that it has been even harder than we expected. The Taliban's tenacity has been a surprise, absorbing more of our effort than we predicted it would and consequently slowing progress on reconstruction,' he said in a speech at the Royal United Services Institute in Whitehall. By the time of his speech, thirty-three British soldiers had been killed since their arrival in Afghanistan in June.

My first embed with the British troops in Helmand was in January 2007, by which time 3 Commando Brigade Royal Marines had already served for four months after rotating with 16 Air Assault Brigade. I spent several weeks with Chris Harris, a photographer working for *The Times*, travelling first to Lashkar Gah, where the British brigade commander had his headquarters, located in the middle of the town. It wasn't a heavily fortified bunker-building, but the headquarters staff and the civilian members of the provincial reconstruction team were protected by round-the-clock armed patrols and the now familiar perimeter walls made out of HESCO barriers. These were fabric-lined, wire-mesh containers stuffed with gravel and dirt, a British-designed fortification based on a simple but highly effective idea.

Lashkar Gah appeared relatively friendly, although the locals looked curiously at us whenever we ventured out of the camp. There was no sign of hostility, yet the camp seemed somewhat vulnerable, surrounded as it was by the Afghan residents going about their business. However, provided there were no Taliban hidden amongst them, life at the headquarters seemed safe enough. It wasn't like the Green Zone in Baghdad, the heavily secured centre of US-led coalition operations in Iraq that constantly came under mortar and suicide-bomb attacks.

But this was early days for the British in Helmand. Camp Bastion, the vast British logistics base in the middle of nowhere in Helmand's desert area, appeared to be even safer. Any Taliban approaching the camp with a view to launching an attack could be spotted a mile off – or so it was thought. The RAF Regiment had the task of guarding Camp Bastion and spent much of their time driving off in Land Rovers outside the perimeter fence to make sure there were no concealed Taliban mortar units setting up positions.

On my first day at Lashkar Gah, it was clear that, while the locals were not shooting at their British visitors, there was no evidence of appreciation of the efforts they were trying to make to improve their lives. Britain's campaign to win their hearts and minds, the classic counter-insurgency strategy, did not appear to be getting through to the Afghans. There was an ingrained resentment in their faces. It only needed one 'precision' bomb, dropped by a NATO aircraft, to fall in the wrong place and kill a member of their family in some other part of Afghanistan to undermine all the work carried out by the British provincial reconstruction team. Aid was fine, but what the Afghans wanted more than anything was security, so that they could carry on their lives without the fear of being attacked.

Just to remind everyone that the Taliban were ever-present, while I was there a suicide bomber detonated a device near the Helmand governor's house in the centre of town, killing himself and injuring several Afghan civilians.

My main plan was to go to Kajaki in northeast Helmand, which had a reputation for being one of the most dangerous places in the province. It was home for M Company 42 Commando Royal Marines, and it was coming under daily fire by the Taliban. The military agreed to take me and Chris Harris to Kajaki and we arrived by helicopter on the top of a hill overlooking a lake. We were driven down into their makeshift camp in Viking amphibious armoured vehicles. The camp was a disused former rural retreat that had also provided accommodation for workers employed at the Kajaki dam. The dam was now being earmarked for a major international development programme. The plan was to bring it fully back into service, with the addition of two more hydro-electric turbines.

The camp consisted of a number of small bungalows, painted, strangely, in light aubergine, and an open-air shower with a wooden surround to save our modesty.

Two weeks before I arrived, the Royal Marine commandos had fought for eight hours in what became known as the Battle of Nipple Hill, so called because of the shape of the topography where the Taliban were positioned. One Marine was killed in the ferocious fighting, but Nipple Hill, a strategic position that allowed a commanding view of the area, was cleared of the Taliban. But, as happened so often in the British military's experience in Afghanistan, there were not enough troops available to hold ground seized from the insurgents. M Company consisted of only about a hundred Marines. So, once the hill had been liberated, the Marines returned to camp.

Now, two weeks later, the Taliban were back on Nipple Hill. We came under rocket attack overnight, and at dawn the following morning sixteen insurgents carrying rifles and rocket-propelled grenade launchers could be seen scurrying from their firing positions. The Marines had a mortar position just outside the camp, and they fired more than forty rounds as well as machine gun fire in their direction. But they managed to escape. This was routine business for the Marines, and, after a time, we got used to the thunderous noise of mortar fire.

Looking out from the camp at the landscape ahead, it struck me that there was never going to be a situation in which the British troops could declare that Kajaki was safe from insurgent attack. The village in the distance was full of Taliban members. They could be watched and targeted, but unless someone was prepared to launch a full-scale ground manoeuvre and then post units permanently in and around the village, there were going to be endless battles of Nipple Hill. The Taliban were not going to go away.

To emphasise the seeming futility of war with the Taliban, I was given the chance to go on a nocturnal Taliban-hunting operation from the Kajaki camp. The previous night, suspected Taliban fighters had been spotted from a mountaintop observation post near the British camp known as Sparrow Hawk. Two armed sentries had been seen moving around in a building called Balcony House, set in a Taliban compound about two miles away. One of the Marines on Sparrow Hawk, armed with a Javelin anti-tank missile, fired one round, at a cost of £68,000. In the eight seconds it took to reach the sentries, both men had jumped down, but the heat-seeking Javelin missile did a quick switch and followed the human heat source, killing them as they reached a courtyard. An RAF Harrier jump jet fighter also dropped a 1,000lb bomb for good measure. Balcony House no longer had a balcony.

Yet the Marines on Sparrow Hawk, one of three mountaintop observation posts near the Kajaki camp, had seen other Taliban fighters in the same compound. A decision was taken to launch a night mission and to use snipers to pick off as many insurgents as possible.

I went to the operational briefing before we set off. Captain William Mackenzie-Green, the twenty-five-year-old commanding 10 Troop M Company 42 Commando, laid out a bizarre set of orders. When a target was sighted and identified as an armed Taliban insurgent and was judged by the sniper to be shootable, the code word would be 'vodka'. A second code word, 'lager', was for when a Taliban had been spotted but was not yet in the sniper's crosshairs, and 'Pepsi' was for when none of the requirements for action had been met. It sounded fun, but this was deadly stuff. The night mission was all about eliminating members of the Taliban insurgency by sniper fire.

I went off to join the full team of Marines selected for the operation and was given a large tin of thick black camouflage paste. 'Pile it on,' one of the Marines said. I took a hefty chunk and began slapping it all over my face and forehead until I looked like a member of the chorus line from the Black and White Minstrel Show. I turned to see what the Marines had done and saw them all grinning. They had applied the camouflage in delicate streaks across their faces. They looked like warriors, whereas I looked like someone in amateur dramatics. Chris Harris was there to record my embarrassment, although the picture never appeared in *The Times*.

We set off around 7.30pm, walking in a line. I was positioned close to Captain Mackenzie-Green. It was dark and quiet. The only sound, apart from the occasional bark of a dog, was the noise of forty pairs of combat boots striding along, the odd whispered oath and the heavy breathing of the Marine carrying the radio system on his back. We made our way slowly across open ground, slightly exposed by a beaming half-moon. The radio operator contacted base to say where we were.

We had just crossed a wadi (a dry riverbed), called M1 by the Marines, about a mile from the British camp. We were now in Taliban territory. The compound was visible as a dark form up ahead. Suddenly, shots were fired. Forty Marines and one journalist flung themselves to the ground as the bullets whizzed over our heads. Were we under attack by the Taliban? No, we were being shot at by the local police, who had a forward base outside Kajaki. One of the night staff had spotted a line of figures going past and several police officers had emerged and begun firing at shadows. The shots and ricocheting bullets set off a cacophony of dog barking, probably including the two flea-bitten dogs that had been adopted by the Marines back at camp.

A quick radio message with expletives was sent and the shooting stopped. The police had not been informed of the nocturnal mission for fear that they would tip off the Taliban. In Helmand province, and generally throughout Afghanistan, loyalties could be bought for less than ten dollars. No one could be trusted. The last thing Captain Mackenzie-Green wanted was to march his men into an ambush. Now we had been spotted, there was a risk that an Afghan policeman was on the phone to warn the Taliban in the compound that a British patrol was heading their way. But, despite the risk that we had been compromised by the trigger-happy Afghan police, Captain Mackenzie-Green decided to go ahead with the mission anyway. We waited on our bellies for another twenty minutes to make sure we were safe from further indiscriminate attacks, then staggered up from the ground and continued our progress towards what remained of Balcony House.

We reached a high wall, the perimeter of the compound, and split up into smaller units. We were now about 180 yards from the Taliban positions. There was no sound coming from the compound. One Marine unit moved to the eastern flank and another to the west, to provide firing points if the Taliban opened up. Three sniper teams climbed up to the top of a mound and settled down to wait for targets. An hour went by and the temperature dropped.

Three miles behind us, Marines from 42 Commando who were manning the observation posts on adjacent mountaintops – Sparrow Hawk, Normandy and Athens – watched every move we made through thermal imaging sights on high-powered optical equipment that could see for miles in the dark. Our body heat would have looked like glowing shadows. To make sure we avoided being targeted by friendly fighter jets flying overhead, each of us had infra-red sticks on our helmets, indicating we were not the Taliban.

At 10.30pm, Captain Mackenzie-Green leaned towards me and whispered: 'Team three and team two are 'vodkas', team one is 'Pepsi'. If the snipers shoot and the Taliban decide to react, which they always do, there could be some serious action.'

But nothing happened. The 'vodkas' were not quite as strong as required under the warfare rules of engagement. These stated that for a positive identification leading to a kill, the sniper must see the target carrying a rifle. It seemed the moment had passed. The Marines on Athens mountaintop fired several mortar illuminations to light up the night sky. There followed a rattle of machine gun fire as the mountaintop watchers opened up with rounds and tracers. But the Taliban refused to play, and it was time to move out.

The mission was not just about picking off individual Taliban fighters. The aim was to drive back the Taliban beyond an imaginary buffer zone about four miles from the hydro-electric dam at Kajaki. If workers were going to install two more turbines, they wanted to know they would be labouring within a safety exclusion zone. The Marines' job was to enforce the zone by pushing the Taliban further back. However, with so few troops to fulfil the task, the only option was to mount harassing raids on the Taliban compound. The sniper teams would have to return.

Life at the former mountain retreat was primitive. We slept on the floor in sleeping bags, and army rations formed the basis of our daily meals, cooked on a small camping-style gas stove. Sausages in a bag heated in hot water, with cold baked beans, provided the staple diet, although the Welsh stew was a favourite. The Marines we were with liked to add different sauces to spice up the food.

By the end of each day, Chris Harris and I were exhausted and generally slept well. We made several visits to the military observation posts on the three mountains which meant climbing the steep, stony slopes clad in flak jacket and helmet because of the risk of a long shot by the Taliban in their compound across the wadi. The observation posts were remote and living conditions were even more primitive than ours, but the Marines loved it. There were just a few of them and they bedded down in a bunker, out of harm's way, when it was their turn to relax from the boredom of staring through long-range binoculars for any movement of insurgents. The Taliban didn't exactly stand out. They fought in long, baggy pants and shirts, with flip-flops on their feet and turbans on their heads, similar in every way to the average Afghan male. Their favourite mode of transport was the motorbike – not the big, Hell's Angel style bikes, but ones with basic engines. However, they had total knowledge of the terrain, and the Kajaki Royal Marine unit too often found the 'enemy' racing away down a side track and disappearing.

I later spent a few days in Kabul for a session of briefings that always seemed to be overly optimistic about progress being made. But the men and women of ISAF had to believe they were making progress to improve the lives of the Afghan people, otherwise the sacrifices being made would have been to no avail. General Richards was convinced that the classic method of creating 'ink spots' of stability would work.

The idea was for the ink spots to spread slowly out into whole districts and regions, driving out the Taliban in the process and filling the areas with development programmes and promises of protection. He felt this would keep the insurgency under control while persuading the locals to put their trust in their ISAF-supported government.

With the Taliban never far away, and their intimidation always present in the rural communities, it seemed a tall order for the Afghan people. They had endured generations of war and, despite the well-meaning efforts by ISAF and donor nations, they didn't trust foreigners. Many of the Afghans preferred the strict laws and Sharia justice meted out by the Taliban if it meant they could harvest their opium-producing poppy fields without fear of outsiders attempting to change their lifestyles.

Tony Blair had said that he wanted British troops in Afghanistan because ninety percent of the heroin on the streets of Britain emanated from Afghan poppy fields. However, the soldiers and Marines sent to Afghanistan had very little to do with the annual poppy harvest that continued to flourish; they couldn't try to stop the drug traffickers from scooping up all the brown paste that oozed out of the poppy heads for transiting to the heroin laboratories. MI6 officers had a go at persuading Afghan farmers to switch from poppies to wheat crops, and handed out huge sums of cash in the process. The farmers were very grateful and took the money, but carried on growing poppies, knowing that if they stopped, they'd get a visit from the local Taliban commander who raked off a percentage of the drug profits to buy arms.

Back in London, I was soon to have a shocking piece of news. On the 20th of February 2007, I was attending a lunch in the boardroom at *The Times* in Wapping. Robert Thomson, the editor, Ben Preston, the deputy editor, Roland Watson, the foreign editor and I, among others, were there to host a special guest, a senior official from the Foreign Office. When the main course arrived, my mobile phone rang. I apologised and left the room to take the call. It was Dave Williams from the *Daily Mail*.

'Mike, Danny has been found dead,' he said.

Danny McGrory, our mutual friend and colleague, had just returned from a trip to Pakistan, researching material connected to the terrorist production line that seemed to run from that country to Britain. Dave said a cleaning lady had gone to Danny's flat in north London and had discovered him slumped in an armchair with a computer on his lap. He was fifty-four, living alone, having broken up from his wife, and now dead. This was an unbelievable tragedy, and I had to tell the editor immediately. I returned to the boardroom and informed the editor and Roland Watson that I needed to talk to them urgently.

Making our apologies to our guest, we left the room and I broke the news. At first they didn't register what I was saying. They looked totally shocked and bewildered but couldn't quite grasp what it meant. Had Danny been killed on a story or what? I told them about the discovery by the cleaning lady. Dave Williams used the same cleaner and she had phoned him. He had then rung me immediately.

Thomson contacted David Chappell, the managing editor, and told him to get hold of the family and make all the arrangements. We returned to the lunch, but the poor guest was understandably concerned about what was going on. Ben Preston, still in ignorance of what had happened, looked troubled, too. The editor explained that an emergency had happened and he needed to leave. The lunch ended soon after.

The guest was incredibly understanding and I escorted her out of the building to her car. I told her briefly that a colleague had died. The news of Danny's death remained a secret from the rest of the staff on the newspaper. At that stage, the most important thing was to contact Danny's family. Danny and his wife were separated but not divorced, and he was very close to his children. I had a busy afternoon ahead of me, writing a big foreign story, but when the office was finally told about Danny I had a phone call from the editor of the obituaries department. He asked whether I could help by providing some personal anecdotes about Danny for the obituary, which was to appear in the paper the next day. I said I would like to write the obituary myself. He admitted he had hoped I would offer. I was given the name of an uncle living in Ireland who was happy to talk to me. I needed basic biographical material about his school days and early career. The rest was in my head.

It was the hardest and easiest piece I had ever had to write. Hard, because this was my friend and I was writing the obituary of a man who a few days earlier had been sitting in his swivel chair next to me, joking and moaning at the same time about this story or that, or making gloomy comments about his lifestyle. And easy, because I knew what I wanted to say about Danny. Despite all his skills and talents as a journalist, he never boasted about his exploits; he always reported what he witnessed and discovered in dangerous parts of the world without ever introducing the personal pronoun 'I' into his copy. Unlike so many reporters who, when faced with danger, told the readers what they had had to endure under fire, Danny remained the true observer, reporting what was happening around him without interposing his personal experience.

'I dived into the ditch as bullets flew around me,' was the standard favourite of reporters wanting their desks and their readers to know what trials and tribulations they were having to suffer in order to write their stories.

I wrote the obituary in about an hour and sent it upstairs. It appeared the next day, and everyone seemed to like it, including Dave Williams, who had been close to Danny as a friend and fellow war reporter for many years.

Danny's funeral was an extraordinary event. At least 300 people, a large percentage of them reporters, turned up at the church. Anyone who had shared a reporting experience with Danny wanted to be there to pay their respects to a great Fleet Street man. He was buried at the Highgate cemetery, in North London, famous for being the burial spot for Karl Marx. The most sought-after cemetery in London, it was a fitting location for Danny McGrory, who died far too young. It was later disclosed that he had an enlarged heart. It was also a fact that he had been under huge professional and personal stress for some time. I believe that some alarming incident in Saudi Arabia, where he had been in some considerable danger, had been lingering in his mind. But, typical of him, he had not talked about it; he simply bore the stress inside him. Stress may well have played a part in his death.

CHAPTER 18
WANKERS IN A MONET LANDSCAPE

In February 2007, I met General David Petraeus for the first time. He was already a legendary figure, one of America's counter-insurgency experts. He was in London en route to Baghdad to take over as US commander of the coalition forces in Iraq. A highly influential and delightful intermediary, Devon Cross, an American who knew everyone of importance in Washington, had fixed for a few journalists to meet General Petraeus in a hotel. It was to be strictly off the record. There were about eight of us assembled when Petraeus walked in. He was smaller than I had imagined, slightly bowed and dressed in a lightweight suit. He spoke to us for about an hour about his ambitions for his new job. He spoke quietly and intently. It was a brilliant session. One of the things he revealed to us was that he planned to set up several gated communities to provide security for Sunni and Shia communities, similar to the one that had been established at Fallujah in Anbar province.

It was a good story and I asked Devon, who served on a defence advisory board at the Pentagon, whether I could write a story without quoting Petraeus. She approved, and we ran a piece the following day. Petraeus, I was told, was pleased.

I was to meet Petraeus on a number of other occasions, both in Baghdad and subsequently in Kabul when he took over as commander of ISAF at relatively short notice after the enforced resignation of General Stanley McChrystal. General McChrystal, a dedicated warrior who had spent much of his career serving in covert missions as a special operations commander, was the victim of a classic misjudgment on his part. He invited a journalist, Michael Hastings of *Rolling Stone* magazine, to join his personal circle to write an inside piece for his journal. The general should have been less trusting, or at least should have made it clear that not every word spoken by him and his close assistants could be included in the article. But the off-the-record rule was clearly not established beforehand. The result was a torrid tale of dismissive comments from McChrystal's staff about senior figures in Washington, including Vice-President Joe Biden. In addition, McChrystal was supposed to have indicated his disappointment about his commander-in-chief, President Obama. He was summoned back to Washington and his distinguished career came to an abrupt halt.

Who could have predicted that General Petraeus's career, even more illustrious than McChrystal's, would also, years later, be severed by misjudgment of a different kind? By then I was *The Times* Pentagon Correspondent based in Washington and became immersed in one of the biggest political shocks for a decade.

The career demise of another military figure took place in 2007. Lieutenant-Colonel

Jorge Mendonca, commanding officer of the 1st Battalion Queen's Lancashire Regiment, had been charged along with four soldiers from his unit and two members of the Intelligence Corps with offences connected to the death in British custody of Baha Mousa. The Iraqi hotel receptionist who died of asphyxiation in a detention centre in Basra had suffered ninety-three separate injuries. Colonel Mendonca, holder of the Distinguished Service Order, was charged with negligently performing his duty, which was to ensure that Mousa and other Iraqi detainees were not mistreated.

At the long-running court martial in Bulford, Wiltshire, he was acquitted. Three other members of his regiment were also acquitted, as were the two defendants from the Intelligence Corps. Only one of the seven defendants was convicted. Corporal Donald Payne of the Queen's Lancashire Regiment (QLR) had pleaded guilty at the start of the court martial to a charge of inhumane treatment of a prisoner.

I attended many of the hearings during the trial. It was an extraordinary story, British soldiers accused of a war crime. When all but one were acquitted, there was a huge outcry, with claims, particularly from the QLR, that the soldiers had been unjustly pilloried. Colonel Mendonca made a statement about how privileged he had been commanding the regiment in Basra, and was later promoted to full colonel and entered for a senior army staff college course which could have pushed him further up the ladder to brigadier.

In early May, I spoke to the MoD about possible further investigations into the treatment of Baha Mousa. I was informed that an internal MoD investigation was underway which could lead to dismissals from the army. Army sources confirmed that Colonel Mendonca would also be included in the inquiry. I wrote a story which was headlined, 'Acquitted soldiers face army inquiry into prisoner abuse'.

The day the story appeared my phone rang. It was an irate Colonel Mendonca. He accused me of deliberately stirring things up against him and said my story had added to the personal stress suffered by his wife. I tried to explain that the story was faithfully based on what the MoD had told me, and that it was true there was an internal inquiry underway. He was so angry and appeared to be accusing me of making up the story. There was nothing I could say that would console him, and he slammed the phone down. The conversation left me shaking. Colonel Mendonca subsequently resigned his commission, indicating his disgust at the way he had been treated by the army.

Early the following year, Brigadier Robert Aitken, selected to carry out an investigation into allegations of prisoner abuses in southern Iraq by British soldiers, including the fatal treatment of Baha Mousa, concluded in his report that some soldiers had behaved disgracefully. He said Iraqi detainees had been treated 'in a deliberate and callous manner'. But he concluded there was no evidence of systemic maltreatment of prisoners.

After publication of the report, General Sir Richard Dannatt, Chief of the General Staff, declared, in reference to the Mousa case, 'This case is not closed and I am not satisfied or comfortable that there are people potentially who have done wrong things [and] that they think they have got away with it. I am afraid that is not the case.'

No one could accuse the British Army of running amok in Iraq in the summer of 2003, a time when violence on a scale never foreseen erupted against the occupying forces. There were, however, a number of disturbing incidents in which Iraqi civilians were mistreated. The history of warfare is peppered with ignoble acts as well as deeds of extraordinary valour and sacrifice. It is the unwelcome price that has to be paid for training young men to go into battle to fight and kill the enemy.

The killing of Baha Mousa, in particular, was an act of such gross wickedness that, as Brigadier Aitken acknowledged, it besmirched the fine reputation of the whole of the British Army. However remiss the pre-deployment training, however forgetful commanders may have been about what was acceptable under the Geneva Conventions, the soldiers who inflicted the injuries on Baha Mousa must have known that what they were doing was wrong.

The family of Baha Mousa was compensated financially for his death in British custody, but to this day only Corporal Payne has been convicted for the attacks on the Iraqi prisoner. He was sentenced to twelve months in prison, reduced to the ranks and dismissed from the army.

Iraq remained in the news after a debacle over the British troop presence in Basra. Ever since the occupation began following the US-led invasion in 2003, there was a general feeling that, while Baghdad would continue to be a dangerous and violent city, there was hope for Basra. This was because the same tribal extremes were not so evident. Basra was dominated by Shia communities. Although there were large numbers of extremists in the region, all loyal to the anti-American, anti-foreigner, hugely powerful and volatile cleric, Muqtada al-Sadr, the British commanders felt it was possible to do a deal under which the troops would exit Basra itself, leaving security to the locals. The British presence would hold fort at the barracks outside the city and be available for security requests when required.

However, the eventual departure of the last remaining unit based at Saddam Hussein's old Basra palace was carried out under highly controversial circumstances which were to cause one of the most embarrassing moments for Britain, and particularly for the British Army.

I had slept on the roof of the Basra palace, staring up at the stars and chuckling at the thought that the Iraqi dictator had once dined and slept down in the cavernous rooms below. Not that he used the palace very often; he was hated by the Shia and preferred to bed down in his palace in Baghdad, where he could be surrounded by his Sunni devotees. For me at that time, the palace seemed a safe refuge, filled as it was with troops and guarded by armoured vehicles. But as more and more British troops took up residence in the barracks at the airport outside the city, one unit was left to carry out city patrols, 500 soldiers of the 4th Battalion The Rifles. The palace became a focal point for daily mortar and small arms attacks by Shia extremists.

Nine soldiers of the regiment were killed in the summer of 2007. It was an Iraqi version of Rorke's Drift, the famous nineteenth-century Anglo-Zulu battle in Natal province, South Africa, when a unit of British soldiers guarding a British mission was surrounded by thousands of attacking Zulu warriors. But unlike the Rorke's Drift drama, the Basra palace siege was regarded as unsustainable, and secret negotiations got underway between British officers and local Shia leaders for the soldiers to be withdrawn to safety, with assurances that they would not come under attack. In terms of saving lives, it was undoubtedly a prudent and practical arrangement. Nevertheless, it seemed humiliating for British troops to be pulled out under such circumstances. The deal was dependent not only on the Shia extremists behaving themselves during the withdrawal but also on the ability of the Iraqi troops in town to maintain peace and security in the future without their British mentors in tow. It was a deal fraught with risk, and it was to prove disastrous.

The 500 soldiers duly left the city under the cover of darkness on the night of the 2nd of September 2007. The convoy of troops and armoured vehicles was not attacked. Within a matter of hours, there were no British troops left in southern Iraq's capital city, and the 5,500 soldiers still serving in the south were all based at the airport stronghold.

The withdrawal took place before Basra had been granted 'Provincial Iraqi Control' status, conferred when coalition commanders and the Iraqi Government agreed that Iraqi troops were ready to take over responsibility for an area. British officers admitted that it would be some time before the resident Iraqi force, the 10th Division, would be in a fit state to hold its own against the Shia extremists and keep Basra safe.

The MoD persistently denied there had been any deal involving the release of a number of Shia extremist leaders held by the British, but there remained suspicions that the secret negotiations had included a prisoner release. In any event, the announcement of a limited ceasefire by al-Sadr, leader of the Mahdi Army that had been attacking the British, provided reassurance that the Rifles would be allowed to leave Basra palace without being shot at. The British thinking was that since about ninety percent of the shootings and bombings in Basra had been aimed at the troops based at Basra palace, their withdrawal would lead to a dramatic drop in violence in the city. But that didn't take into account the fact that there would now be a security vacuum in which the extremist militias would battle for supremacy against a weak Iraqi force. The residents of

Basra expressed dismay at the departure of the British. Their fears proved justified: a power battle ensued and Basra became a city of terror.

Six months later, in March 2008, Nouri al-Maliki, the Iraqi prime minister, launched an offensive to retake Basra from the militias, flying to the city to take personal control of 30,000 Iraqi troops who swept down from Baghdad. The Shia militias still refused to disarm, and fighting broke out. A Shia civil war looked likely and there were concerns that British troops at the airport would have to return to the city to join with the Iraqi troops to try and restore order in Basra. The September 2007 withdrawal of 500 members of the 4th Rifles now seemed a black mark on Britain's record in keeping the peace in southern Iraq.

However, when the real story broke about Operation Charge of the Knights, Maliki's offensive against the militias in Basra, the humiliation for Britain appeared infinitely worse. Deborah Haynes, our Baghdad correspondent, and I provided a new insight into the developments that led to the Maliki-inspired offensive, and, on the 10th of April, *The Times* ran a big story headlined: 'Baghdad snubbed British troops and called US into Basra battle'.

Maliki was reported to be so angry at the way the British had left Basra in the hands of al-Sadr's Shia militia that he turned to the Americans for help. About 550 US troops, including some from the 82nd Airborne Division, along with attack helicopters, were sent to Basra to assist the Iraqi forces. Baghdad made no request in the early stages for British military assistance. I rang the MoD to find out what had happened and was told a remarkable story. Brigadier Julian Free, commander of 4 Mechanised Brigade and Britain's most senior officer in Basra, had flown to Baghdad two days after Operation Charge of the Knights had started to try and see Maliki to ask him what was going on. Maliki refused to see him. The brigadier had flown to Baghdad with Lieutenant-General Lloyd Austin, one of the top American commanders in Iraq. Maliki chose to speak to General Austin, leaving Brigadier Free waiting outside the room. MoD sources admitted Maliki seemed to have it in for the British because of the deal reached with the Shia militants six months earlier.

Although British firepower was brought in eventually, the abiding impression was that the UK force had been snubbed. Only the Americans, it seemed, could be trusted to sort out the Shia militants in Basra. The Americans basically took over the job the British were supposed to be doing. No wonder the mood among the British soldiers at the Basra airport camp was said to be 'miserable'. To make matters worse, the whole operation appeared to have been conceived almost overnight. None of the US generals in Baghdad knew what Maliki was plotting until the last moment, so all the planning had to be done in a rush. It was ill-conceived, and initially the Iraqi troops failed to make any real headway. However, with US firepower on tap and Americans providing advice and support, the Shia militants were finally forced into submission.

The end result was that British troops had to return to patrolling in Basra, albeit only about 150 of them, from the 1st Battalion Royal Regiment of Scotland. It was an admission that the troop withdrawal from the city the previous September had been premature. General Petraeus, commanding the US and multinational forces in Iraq, was quoted as saying that he had been satisfied with the pull-out, leaving Basra to the Iraqi army. But he was being diplomatic. There were other senior American commanders in Baghdad who were bewildered by the British move.

A month after the article appeared, I flew off to Afghanistan with Richard Pohle, a *Times* photographer, for a three-week assignment embedded with British troops in Helmand province. A new commander, Brigadier Mark Carleton-Smith, was in charge of 16 Air Assault Brigade back in Helmand. The difference in the size and potency of the brigade was remarkable. In 2006, with the wishful thinking of 'no shots to be fired', the brigade was 3,300 strong. Units sent to some of the most isolated outposts, such as Musa Qala, Sangin and Nowzad, found themselves under siege. In Musa Qala in the summer of 2006, a platoon of about thirty soldiers was camped in the district office, holding off a swarm of Taliban fighters. The concept of deploying mere platoons to these remote locations proved disastrous, and fatal. Soldiers were dying every single day.

Musa Qala was eventually abandoned under a deal with the local elders, under which they agreed to keep the Taliban out. However, the Taliban was not interested in committing to such arrangements and soon occupied the town. They were only driven out after a huge operation led by Afghan forces, with British help, a few months later.

Now Brigadier Carleton-Smith had 7,800 soldiers under his command, and Musa Qala, in April 2008, was occupied by a battle group of about 700 British soldiers, supporting a battalion of 600 soldiers of the Afghan National Army and 350 members of the Afghan National Police. Lessons had been learnt.

Meanwhile, Afghan soldiers were being persuaded to cast aside their beloved Kalashnikov AK47s and train to fire the American M16. A visit to Camp Tombstone in the middle of Helmand province, where the Afghans were being taught how to fire the American assault rifle, reminded me of an occasion when a British defence secretary, Malcolm Rifkind, was invited to pick up a mortar round and insert it into the launcher. He put it in the wrong way up. The Afghan soldiers looked as if they didn't know what to do with the M16. They were bewildered, confused and angry. The Kalashnikov had been their fighting weapon for so long it was clearly anathema to them not only to hold a foreign rifle in their hands but also to be told to fight in a different way. The traditional method, honed after decades of war, was to advance against the enemy firing from the hip, spraying bullets in all directions on automatic mode until the magazine was empty. But the American and British trainers were trying to instil some discipline into the soldiers. They encouraged them to believe that it was better to fire only when a target was spotted, and to do so with accuracy rather than deluge the enemy with a wall of bullets, most of which missed.

The American and British trainers explained that the M16 should be fired from the shoulder, not from the hip. This caused much anguish among the Afghans. I sympathised with them. The Kalashnikov is the most famous rifle in the world; it is beautifully designed and built to withstand the most ferocious weather conditions. A soldier armed with a Kalashnikov can leap into a river, swim across and know for sure that the rifle will still work when he reaches the opposite bank.

One of the British officers involved in training the Afghans admitted, 'There's no question the Kalashnikov is a good rifle. You can bury it in the sand for ten years, dig it out and it'll fire first time.'

Cleaning the AK47 is also easy. You just cover it in diesel and it sparkles. Now the Afghan soldiers at Camp Tombstone were being told that the AK was yesterday's weapon, and the M16 was the future. It was no surprise when one of the soldiers, looking in disgust at the American rifle, blurted out, 'This is made of plastic – it'll break.'

But the M16 is lighter and more accurate, and

the instructors were hopeful that the Afghans would come round eventually. It seemed they had no choice. They would keep their AKs at home, as part of their cultural tradition, but in future they had to fight the Taliban with an infidel weapon.

Richard Pohle and I were in Helmand during the opium season when the poppies were at their most magnificent, forming a sea of reds and pinks and purples. In a piece I wrote for *The Times* I compared the splashes of colour with a picture by Claude Monet, the French impressionist painter. It was a breathtaking sight. Helmand province is largely desert, but down the middle on each side of the Helmand River is an extraordinarily fertile green belt in which the poppy flourishes.

On one occasion, I was on patrol with a platoon of soldiers from the 2nd Battalion Parachute Regiment, walking along a dry, muddied track and gazing at the field of poppies running alongside when there was a crackle of voices from the radio held by the Afghan interpreter. The radio was tuned into the frequency used by the Taliban. The interpreter told the platoon leader that there were Taliban fighters nearby. They had spotted us and spoke excitedly of ambushing the British.

Suddenly, the Monet landscape took on a different hue. There were several farmers across the other side of the field, one of them wearing a black turban. It didn't mean he was a Taliban – black turbans were not unusual – but he was running off, and we didn't think it was for a lunch break. The 2 PARA platoon commander decided to stay put, ordering all of us to lie down in the irrigation ditch beside the poppies. The rest of the farmers carried on with their work, scraping off the resin from the poppy heads as it oozed from slits made with razors. There was no Taliban ambush, probably because the opium trade was as important for them as it was for the heroin barons. They didn't want the British with their heavy boots trampling down the poppies in hot pursuit. So the crackling voices on the radio were just trying to scare the British troops.

It takes twenty days to harvest the poppy crop. All the resin is put into saddlebags, and the farmers then wait for the arrival of a mysterious individual known only as 'The Businessman' who turns up at the same time each year to buy the poppy resin. To my untrained eye, it looked like a bumper crop. So much for Tony Blair's dream of destroying the heroin trade in Afghanistan.

I stayed with 2 PARA for several days. One morning, during another patrol, I came across two young Afghan boys standing side by side. They must have been about eight or nine years old. They weren't smiling but they looked friendly. As I walked past them in my flak jacket and helmet, I said, 'Salaam', the everyday Arabic greeting.

'Salaam, wanker,' one of the boys replied.

Nice to know that British soldiers had taught the Afghans a little bit of western lingo!

When I got back to the office in London,

Roland Watson, the foreign editor, came up to me and said, 'There was a memorable word you wrote in all your stuff from Helmand: Monet.'

CHAPTER 19
DATELINES

Datelines on stories are treasured by reporters on foreign assignments. Travelling to Afghanistan opened up many possibilities. Having already achieved Kabul, Lashkar Gah, Sangin, Kajaki, Musa Qala, Jalalabad and Mazar-e Sharif, for my latest trip I added one more: Garmsir. This is a town in the southern end of Helmand where the British were in charge but were soon to hand over to the US Marines, who planned to fill the area with a massed presence of troops.

The problem with Garmsir, as with Kajaki and so many other places where the British held sway, was that there were not enough troops available to take ground from the Taliban and hold it. So the 2nd Battalion Mercian Regiment in Garmsir had made many ventures further south to hunt for the Taliban, but invariably, after a day-long patrol, they had to return to camp. The US Marines, with their full composite of weaponry, including their own aviation assets, helicopters and Harriers, were determined to push out from Garmsir and drive the Taliban away.

I went to Garmsir, again with Richard Pohle, the photographer, during the final weeks of the Mercian Regiment's tour in the area before the surge of US Marines arrived. For the first big piece I wrote, my intro reflected the mood in Garmsir: 'From the Taliban to Afghan families, and British soldiers sweltering in the heat, everyone in this part of Helmand is waiting for the Americans'.

It was May 2009. Conditions were tough, sleeping accommodation was primitive and malarial mosquitoes were rampant. Intense heat and swirling dust made each day a challenge to remain cheerful, but the British soldiers never seemed to mind. In between daily patrolling and cleaning their rifles, they always had food to look forward to. The British Army eats three big meals a day, even if the food has to come out of plastic bags.

The Taliban had already had a taste of American firepower in Garmsir. The previous year, after the British had come under withering attack from the Taliban, 3,000 US Marines from the 24th Marine Expeditionary Unit mounted a large-scale offensive against the insurgents in the area. They killed an estimated 400 Taliban fighters and destroyed Jugroom Fort, a Taliban stronghold eight miles south of Garmsir district centre. The Taliban were forced to move further south. Only a few months earlier, British troops had attempted to do the same to Jugroom Fort but failed. In the process, they participated in an extraordinarily courageous rescue mission to pick up a soldier who had been fatally wounded and left behind. British servicemen volunteered to be strapped to the side of an Apache attack helicopter to be ready to jump to the ground and retrieve the body of their fallen comrade. The body was duly rescued.

However, once the Americans had left Garmsir, the British troops could do little else but try and contain the Taliban. Garmsir is not far from the Pakistan border and Taliban reinforcements were able to cross into Helmand with relative impunity. Richard and I shared a tent with about eight soldiers, two of them American bomb-disposal specialists who could only be described as 'cool dudes'. Their daily routine was to get up and have breakfast, then return to the tent and lie on their beds watching videos or listening to music until they were called out. We would all go out early on Taliban-watch patrol, but they would be reclined on their beds as if they had not a care in the world.

One morning, four Taliban insurgents had been spotted moving onto a bridge on Route Cowboys, which ran north to south past a line of small patrol outposts six miles from Garmsir. The insurgents started to dig and were clearly intending to bury an improvised explosive device (IED) on the bridge, hoping to catch a passing convoy. Two Belgian Air Force F16s were summoned to blast the Taliban to the next world, but as we watched from the ramparts of the camp at Garmsir, there was a sudden warning shout on the radio. 'Stop, hold fire, there's a boy with goats approaching.'

A young Afghan with a few goats around him was approaching the bridge. Everyone in operations rooms within sight of the bridge and even back at Camp Bastion, the main British base in Helmand, was watching on their computer screens as the goatherd slowly approached the bridge. The Taliban carried on burying their device. One of them could be seen walking backwards holding a wire and disappeared from view. Another one left the scene on a motorbike, leaving two Taliban insurgents on the bridge. At last the goatherd was clear of the bridge, and the two F16 pilots were ordered to target the remaining two insurgents, not with bombs but with cannon fire to strafe the area. Both insurgents were killed, and the bridge remained intact. The two other Taliban bomb-layers escaped.

At 4.30am the next day, I joined one hundred soldiers to walk to Bridge Three, as it was called, on Route Cowboys in a mission to make safe the IED. My tent companions, the two US Marine bomb-disposal guys, were with us. One of them, a Texan with a thick moustache who had hardly spoken, turned to me and said: 'Don't use my name, Sir, just say I'm from USMCEOD (US Marine Corps Explosive Ordnance Demolition).'

We approached the bridge. The comforting sound of a small Hermes surveillance drone, buzzing above our heads, monitored our progress and watched out for anything suspicious in the bushes or behind the trees. Before we got there, we all had to walk along a terrifyingly narrow sluice gate wall over a deep irrigation canal, and then leap across a gap of about two feet and land, balanced, on a wall beyond to reach the other side. It was challenging enough for me in a heavy flak jacket and helmet, but for soldiers weighed down with 100lb bergens on their backs and a rifle in their hands, it was a truly gargantuan task to complete the tightrope walk and leap without falling into the water. One soldier bottled it and toppled into the water with a huge splash. One of his comrades had to jump in and grab him, and his rifle.

The journey from the camp to Bridge Three took five hours, partly because our walk took us past a compound where the Taliban were suspected of having a presence. The patrol was ordered to check it out. It was still early when the search took place. Sleepy and scared-looking Afghans stood around, as if expecting to be shot at any moment. No Taliban were found. When we reached the bridge, the one hundred soldiers spread out, convinced that the Taliban were watching from somewhere.

The first tentative moves towards the buried IEDs were made by a young lieutenant only two years out of Sandhurst. Twenty-five-year-old Lieutenant Ed Hattersley, of B Company 2nd Battalion Mercian Regiment, lay on the ground and began scratching at the earth, removing the loose soil with a paintbrush. The rest of us watched and waited. The lieutenant found enough evidence to indicate there were several devices buried, and my two tent comrades were summoned to perform their skilful duty. They uncovered four mortar shells stuffed with explosives and linked together. It was known as a 'daisy chain' device. With nothing more than body armour and helmets to protect them, the two US Marines picked up the mortar shells and carried them away from the bridge. At a safe distance, they packed their own explosives around the devices and moved away to safety. One of them turned to us and said, 'Sixty seconds – heads down.'

We all counted under our breath, stuck our fingers into our ears and shoved our chins into our chests, bracing for the explosion. The bombs were destroyed. The IEDs had been planted at about 5pm the previous day. It was now 11.30am the day after, and one hundred men were exhausted from the strains of a seven-hour mission.

Thursday nights in Helmand were unlike any other nights in the province. There was a certain ritual which the Afghan soldiers enjoyed, much to the amazement of their British military trainers. However, like all good British soldiers who have been instructed to respect local cultures, they turned the other way, and eventually became accustomed to it. Thursday night was when the younger Afghan soldiers liked to dress up and put make-up on – especially the better looking ones. During the day, these soldiers went on patrol with rifles and backpacks and tried to emulate their British mentors. By night (on Thursdays), the same soldiers returned to camp attired in dresses, with their faces coated in rouge, their eyes heavy with mascara and their lips ruby red with lipstick. Dropping all attempts to look like soldiers, the young Afghans became coquettish and flirty, and often held hands with their senior officers.

Why this happened every Thursday night I was never too sure, but the ritual, if that's the right word to describe it, was clearly enjoyed by the Afghan men. The following morning, the lipstick had been removed and the military uniform was back on, but there were often late arrivals for patrols. Some British defence minister or other had once stated that the long-term plan for Helmand was not to try and turn it into Hampshire or Kent but to improve the lives of the local Afghans within their own culture. I doubt he had in mind at the time the culture of the Thursday night ritual!

Every time I went to Afghanistan, I became more and more convinced that the Taliban would never be defeated. They were not just Taliban; they were Afghans. They would always be there, and for as long as foreign troops stayed propping up the government in Kabul, the insurgents would have a cause.

When President Obama announced he was sending 33,000 more troops in a surge deployment, most of them to Helmand, it might have seemed to the outside world that the sheer force and presence of so many extra American troops would drive the Taliban away and convert the southern province, so crucial to the insurgents, into a conflict-free region where farmers could grow wheat and cereal and take their produce to market in safety.

However, superior numbers do not guarantee victory – just ask the Russians. In traditional military parlance, battle commanders like to have a two-to-one or three-to-one troop advantage over the enemy, but that's in general warfare. In counter-insurgency, it doesn't work like that. The Taliban can plant an IED and disappear on a motorbike back into the community. A suicide bomber can approach a checkpoint wearing the traditional garb of a farmer and carrying a shovel in his hands, hiding beneath his flowing knee-length white shirt a vest stuffed with explosives. It's what the military like to call asymmetric warfare, and no matter how many US Marines are poured in as reinforcements, the insurgent always has the edge.

The Americans and their allies bring the most advanced weapons and surveillance systems in the world to fight the enemy, but the enemy fails to play ball. The Taliban don't need night-vision goggles and drones that can monitor the movement of troops from 15,000ft. It's their territory and they know how to exploit their local knowledge.

In 2010, I was to be given the best dateline of all, in terms of journalistic prestige. James Harding, who had been editor of *The Times* since 2007, had been on a trip to Washington and during talks with senior administration officials, including General Jim Jones, the national security adviser, he had been asked why his newspaper failed to have a correspondent based at the Pentagon. James Harding returned to London with an idea in his head. Soon after, I was summoned to see Keith Blackmore, the deputy editor, who told me the editor was thinking of sending me to Washington to be their first Pentagon Correspondent. He suggested it would be for a year or two. I reacted with excitement, although I knew that a posting overseas at this stage in my career might not be welcomed in the same way by my family. But it was a great opportunity.

It would be the first time that *The Times* would have its own dedicated correspondent based at the Pentagon. One former Washington correspondent, Ian Brodie, had made good contacts at the Pentagon and wrote authoritatively about defence matters. But staff at the DC bureau generally concentrated their efforts on the White House and the mass of general news stories, such as school shootings and tornados, which had to be reported on in the limited time available because of the five-hour time difference with London. I told my family about the Washington offer and, although there were some reservations, it was just too good a proposal to turn down. Washington was to be my dateline for the next three years.

It was not only journalism that had taken me to some of the most exciting datelines around the world. For fifteen years, I ran *The Times* cricket club, and got to know other cricket-loving journalists. As a result, in 1995, I was invited by Mihir Bose, who had just joined the *Daily Telegraph* from the *Sunday Times* as a specialist sports writer, to go on a three-week cricket tour of India. It was a sumptuous and well-organised tour, with Mihir in charge like a splendid maharajah.

When Harvey Elliott, a long-time friend

and former defence correspondent on the *Daily Mail,* decided to form a touring cricket side, I leapt at the chance to join up. Thus was born the Fleet Street Exiles. Harvey, along with Dave Williams of the *Daily Mail,* recruited a wonderful assortment of characters who loved cricket but were not necessarily the finest performers on the field. On tours that took us to Australia, Kenya, the Caribbean, Sri Lanka, Oman, and elsewhere, there were some historic moments: Mike Bealing, a photographer then working for the *Daily Telegraph,* getting six wickets at the Galle Test Match stadium in Sri Lanka; a large Australian player smacking all of our bowlers over the boundary in Adelaide; a retired policeman doing the same in Bermuda, scoring a century without wearing gloves; and me out first ball trying to hit a six to win the match in Mombasa after I had come in as the eleventh batsman with only one run required to move from a tie to a victory. Above all, it was the camaraderie – and in the Caribbean, the piña coladas on the beach – that made the Fleet Street Exiles so special.

CHAPTER 20
THE TIMES MAN AT THE PENTAGON

For the first three months of my new life in Washington DC, I had to be escorted every time I went into the Pentagon. It took that long for the security boys to check me out, to make sure I was *bona fide* and that I had a right to be in the United States of America. Being escorted is a pain because it requires queuing up to go through an initial stage of checks in an outside security office before entering the front doors of the massive building and waiting for the media centre assistant to turn up. Then one has to queue for a second time to get a visitor's pass.

The foyer is awash with heavily armed security guards. You go up the escalator, past a Marine sentry point to the right, and then onwards down the endless corridors to reach the press centre room where all the information officers, some in uniform, some who were civilians, sit with phones stuck to their ears. I had to log in to prove that I was there in the world's largest office building, before being taken into the Pentagon press corps working area, a space so small that often there's standing room only.

It's sectioned off to provide desk tops for computers and phones for all the resident correspondents, including representatives from the three big news agencies, AP, AFP and Reuters, as well as the Pentagon reporters from the *New York Times, Washington Post, Wall Street Journal, Los Angeles Times, Christian Science Monitor* and the other major newspapers. Mixed in with them are the reporters writing for the military newspapers, such as *Stars and Stripes, Army Times* and *Marine Corps Times*. The television correspondents are down the hall, each with their separate, tiny offices.

For an interloper like me, representing a newspaper that they had at least heard of but had probably never read, it was like walking into a foreign commune. I was a Brit claiming to be a correspondent there at the Pentagon, for heaven's sake. Most of the reporters were immediately welcoming. Others were curious.

The first event of the day was the gaggle: the gathering of Pentagon correspondents in the press secretary's office for a session of fairly meaningless questions and answers. Meaningless because the questions, however cunningly phrased, were generally met with non-committal answers, such as, 'we never talk about intelligence', 'I can't go beyond what I have already said', 'I have no knowledge of that', or, if you are lucky, 'I'll get back to you on that'. Geoff Morrell was the press secretary to the defence secretary, Bob Gates. Morrell was a belligerent character who put up with us – but only just. He often let others handle the gaggles but would always front up the occasions when the gaggle was elevated to a press conference in the media theatre.

It was fun – the give-and-take, the banter, the comments of exasperation by Morrell, and the daily reminder, for me, that this was the Pentagon, the heart of America's military superpowerdom. Compared to the MoD in London, and NATO headquarters in Brussels, this was the real deal. When I was granted my Pentagon pass, I had the freedom to walk anywhere I wanted in the vast building, going along the different rings of corridors. I was like an excited schoolboy. But I was also an experienced defence and security correspondent, and it wasn't long before I became part of the Pentagon Press Corps family, an accepted Brit, even though *The Times* man's accent was a source of constant amazement and comedy. I once made the mistake of leaving the press room with the words, 'See you all anon.'

Kevin Baron of *Stars and Stripes,* one of the cheeriest of the bunch, responded, 'Pip, jolly good show.'

The first time I swiped my Pentagon pass through the security system, just like all the other inhabitants of the building, including generals, admirals and spooks, I felt a sense of exhilaration, like I was a member of a vast secretive family. Of course, having a pass did not mean I could expect to be handed sensational stories just by entering the building. But being a pass-carrier gave me a sense of belonging.

I soon settled into a routine: travelling each morning the five stops to the Pentagon on the subway was one and fixing to see officials to make contacts and set up interviews was another.

As *The Times* first Pentagon Correspondent, there was a lot of meeting and greeting to do; it was a lot of work just to embed myself into the huge empire and to make people realise there was a Brit walking the corridors. Everything was different about the Pentagon. When I had spent a few hours there, I would head off to *The Times* office at the National Press Building and join my colleagues. In the three years I was in Washington, I had some of the best *Times* correspondents working in the DC bureau: Giles Whittell, master intro-writer and former Moscow correspondent; Tim Reid, ace reporter; Alex Frean, later to become US business editor in New York; Catherine Philp, who had reported courageously from Baghdad and other hotspots around the world; David Taylor, former head of news in London; and Nico Hines, only in his twenties but proving to be a highly talented story-getter. He was later succeeded by Devika Bhat from the foreign desk. Matt Spence – not a trained journalist but an invaluable member of the bureau as office manager and mother hen to us all – was younger than any of us. He was a smart American with experience of working on the staff of political heavyweights in Congress and had an encyclopaedic memory.

More important than anything for a foreign correspondent is the support of the foreign desk back in London. Richard Beeston who had foreign corresponding in his blood, Suzy Jagger, who became deputy foreign editor, and Roland Watson, who was twice foreign editor, were among the best. They always enthused over stories. The smell of a scoop would transform their day, and also make their lives easier at the morning editorial conference. Jim McLean, David Byers and Imre Karacs (the night foreign editor) were also enthusiastic grabbers of stories.

One of the great privileges as a resident correspondent at the Pentagon is to be invited to join the secretary of defence on one of his many trips. It's not cheap, and Richard Beeston needed some convincing when I rang to say that I had been asked to go on a trip to Iraq and Afghanistan with Robert Gates in August 2010. It struck me that it would be a golden opportunity to get to know the man. Beeston agreed. There are normally about seventeen or eighteen journalists on these trips, not all Pentagon correspondents. Sometimes, columnists are invited from the most prestigious papers. It's a bit like a royal tour, where the royalty are the esteemed opinion writers of the Washington circuit.

The deal is that on the journey the secretary of defence will emerge from his lair, which is well away from the media, and have an attributable chat with the journalists who have to gather round as best they can in the limited space. Much of the chat is about the secretary's itinerary, his hopes for this or that, and always underlining the importance of being briefed in the field by senior military commanders. Not particularly newsworthy, but Gates, while never indiscreet, was generally more forthcoming than his successors, Leon Panetta and then Chuck Hagel. The best part was the opportunity it provided for asking questions about the running news story, whatever it was.

For the 2010 trip, Gates had his own plane, Air Force Three, for the main part of the journey from Andrews Air Force base to Iraq. Then we switched to a C-17 Globemaster super transporter for flying into and within Iraq, and on to Afghanistan. The C-17 was decked out to carry VIPs and hangers-on (seventeen American newshounds and I were hangers-on in this case). Gates spent the whole of the C-17 flights concealed inside a steel box that looked like a large garden shed. It was at the front end of the plane, no doubt with hot and cold running water, a Queen-size bed and a phone to speak to the US president.

For his travelling delegation, it was all about pecking order. One relatively senior Pentagon official was forced to sit in the second row of a line of seats in the middle of the plane. The front row, with a scattering of generals, had plenty of leg room, but the second row was so jammed up against the front row that the official spent the journey with his legs and feet twisted and contorted while he tried to read the endless verbiage in the special, top-secret file given to all the officials to consume before they landed.

The mass of officials and journalists, exhausted and overfed, landed at 11pm at a remote Iraqi airbase. But the time difference meant it was 6.30am the next day, so it was straight to work, on to helicopters and down to Ramadi in western Iraq to speak to troops and get exceedingly hot. It was 130 degrees and rising. Gates had a different baseball cap for each occasion. Then it was back on the C17 to fly to Baghdad for an official ceremony in which America's combat operation was swapped for an 'advise and assist' mission. The speeches, including one from Joe Biden, the vice-president who turned up as Obama's representative, became progressively long.

Gates looked pretty cool throughout the trip. His tradition when visiting US troops in war zones was to shake the hands of about 1,000 of them by the time he had completed the trip and give them each a coin denoting their service. The poor officials, still clutching their top-secret files and sweating in their suits, flak jackets and helmets, looked like versions of Quasimodo by the time they climbed on board the plane for the next part of the trip.

The same sort of itinerary was followed in Afghanistan, with trips to locations where the US troops were based, and briefings with senior military types. No time for relaxing, just a non-stop journeying machine, and comparatively little to write about. But I noticed that whatever Gates said, however boring, duly appeared in the *New York Times* and *Washington Post* the following day, with intros such as: 'Robert Gates, the secretary of defence, arrived in Kabul yesterday to hold a full range of talks with senior officials, as President Karzai' etc., etc. If I had written that for *The Times,* I would have rightly been asked, 'What's the story?'

Being in Washington and going to the

Pentagon every day provided a totally different viewpoint of the world and, sadly, a more realistic insight into the way the US approached the so-called special relationship with Britain. There was, unquestionably, a degree of disillusion over the way the British military performed in both Iraq and Afghanistan, and there was growing amazement at the wholesale cutbacks in Britain's defence capabilities.

There was astonishment when the Conservative Government in London decided to reduce the size of the regular army to a mere 82,000 soldiers. There was also bewilderment over the bizarre proposal to build two aircraft carriers, yet have one of them mothballed or sold, and to have a gap of several years in which the Royal Navy would have no carriers at all. David Cameron reversed the decision to have only one operational carrier, but there were officials in the Pentagon who doubted whether Britain could any longer be relied on as a proper military partner.

Certainly, in both Iraq and Afghanistan, the US was taking a huge share of the burden, and one crucial aspect of that commitment was the sheer scale of the American casualties. In August 2010, when researching a piece on the Afghanistan war, I discovered that more than 1,000 American servicemen had lost limbs, and I asked the Pentagon if I could go to a military hospital to see some of the wounded and talk to someone who was trying to survive without legs or arms. The Walter Reed Army Medical Centre in Washington was the obvious place to visit, and it was arranged for me to interview a soldier who had lost both legs. I arrived at the hospital and met up with the public relations guy who gave me bad news. The First Lady, Michelle Obama, had arrived before me, and the soldier I was to interview was in a section of the centre that was cordoned off for security reasons. I could interview the main doctor involved in the prosthetic work for the disabled servicemen, but that was it.

I had promised the foreign desk in London to come up with an emotive interview with an Iraq or Afghanistan war veteran who was struggling with his new life. I sat with the doctor and chatted, and after about ten minutes, this guy walked past with one leg and one arm. The doctor hailed him: 'Hey, Sergeant, come and meet this reporter from *The Times* of London.'

The soldier's name was Sergeant Keith Maul. He had a prosthetic right leg and an empty sleeve on his right side. He was friendly, cheery and happy to sit down and talk to me. His story was extraordinary. He had been in Iraq for only a week and a half. An event changed his life forever on the 9th of February 2009, when he was nineteen and recently married to a local girl from a small town in Pennsylvania. He was a combat engineer attached to 856 Engineers of the Pennsylvania National Guard. Before he left home, his father had warned him to prepare for the worst. One morning, he left the comparative safety of his base at Taji, twenty miles north of Baghdad, to carry out a routine road-clearance operation with a number of heavy vehicles. 'I was aware of a crowd of people, and then suddenly a guy came out and threw four Russian RKG-3 grenades at us. Two of them exploded on my vehicle,' he said.

He was hurled back but didn't realise he had been seriously injured. 'Then I saw my right leg lying on the ground, and the only thing holding my right arm up was my uniform. That's when the pain set in,' he told me.

Sergeant Maul had been a Walmart supermarket employee before he'd joined the National Guard, and that had been his first experience of war. He had already spent eighteen months in and out of hospital and was waiting to receive a special powered knee to help him climb stairs. He thought he was lucky. 'At least I'm alive and breathing and, fortunately, I didn't suffer infection, so my wounds were clean.'

He appeared to bear no grudges. Indeed, he was so philosophical it was humbling to listen to him. 'When I woke up in hospital, I looked down and realised that my arm and leg had gone. It wasn't a big surprise for me, but when my family came to see me for the first time it was much worse for them. But when I started to joke about it, they felt a bit better.'

Iraq was never a popular war, but Sergeant Maul, with an eight-month-old son, disclosed that every time he went home to Johnstown in Pennsylvania he was greeted wherever he went by locals who wanted to shake his hand. 'But when I go out in Washington, I just get stares,' he said.

For combat veterans like Sergeant Maul,

the future will depend on the promise made to him by the staff at Walter Reed that he will be looked after for the rest of his life.

CHAPTER 21
FIVE NATIONS IN SIX DAYS WITH BEAR ESSENTIALS

In early 2011, there was another chance to travel with Bob Gates – only this time in some style. We flew in his Air Force Three plane, with comfy seats, attentive staff and good food on proper plates. There was even wine if requested. The trip this time was more exotic; neither Iraq nor Afghanistan were on the itinerary. Instead, we were heading to Russia, Egypt, Israel, Palestine and Jordan – all in six days.

Libya was the story. The NATO decision to bomb Colonel Muammar Gaddafi's forces which were engaged in a civil war in Libya had been taken, and airstrikes involving Britain, France, the US and Canada had been underway for a month. There was every expectation among the group of journalists approved for the trip that Gates would give us juicy morsels each day about the bombing campaign which would enable us to send home authoritative stories about progress or setbacks.

The reality is that defence secretaries rarely know the detail of daily events unfolding in some far-off war zone. Gates was fine on policy and strategy but he was never in a position to give us a General Stormin' Norman-type rundown of bombs dropped, bullets fired and casualties suffered. Nevertheless, apart from a brief flutter of different news in Israel – rockets landing from Gaza not far from Tel Aviv where we were visiting – I spent the trip writing about Libya.

It turned out to be a very expensive way to get information. My bill for the six days was extortionate, largely due to our charming hotel hosts in St Petersburg and Moscow charging for two nights at each place although we only stayed for one.

'Why?' I asked.

'Because, Mr Eevans, you arrived urrly and we gave you yourr rrooms strraightaway, so we charge you for two nights,' said the receptionist in the first hotel.

'But –'

'No buts, Mr Eevans. You'rre in Rrussia, and this is the way we do beesness.'

As a relief to the frantic rushing around, going from one meeting and briefing to another, the personalities on the trip helped to provide some comic moments. At the start of the trip, standing at Andrews Air Force base in Washington, waiting for the rest of the journalist clan to turn up, a chap I hadn't met before approached me.

'Hi, I'm from the *Wall Street Journal*,' he said.

I asked him why Adam wasn't coming. Adam Entous was the paper's Pentagon correspondent, a nice guy, and I had thought he was listed to come on the trip.

'Well,' he replied, 'Adam is a reporter; I'm a columnist.'

Bret Stephens, the columnist, turned out to be a highly amusing travelling companion, although he worried excessively about the article he planned to write at the end of the trip. In St Petersburg, our first port of call, we went our various separate ways to eat out and then gathered in the hotel for a late-evening briefing from one of Gates' senior advisers.

I had eaten at the gloriously named National Vodka Museum with about eight others, including David Ignatius, a prestigious columnist on the *Washington Post* and an inveterate thriller writer. On the plane, the guy from Fox News, a brilliant mimic and cartoonist, dashed off a cartoon of Ignatius and got it just right: distinguished, serious, very important, quite posh, impeccably courteous but also one of the lads, happy to join in the fun.

At the National Vodka Museum, we drank vodka and ate delicious blinis with salmon caviar and cream, and flattened, pan-roasted chicken. Later, at the hotel, I recounted the meal we had had to my fellow travellers who had ventured elsewhere.

A voice from an armchair said, 'I had bear.' It was the columnist from the *Wall Street Journal* who had eaten in another restaurant.

After the briefing, which elicited nothing sensational for the columns of *The Times* of London, I asked Bret Stephens why he had eaten bear and what it was like.

'Well,' he said. 'It was a choice between duck

or bear. I asked the waitress what the bear was like. She replied, "Feeefty-feeefty." I asked her what that meant. She replied, "Feeefty times eez goood and feeefty times eez not so goood."'

I guffawed. 'So then what happened?' I asked.

'The waitress asked, "So you will have zee duck?" I said no, I would have the bear.'

I had to ask Bret: 'So was it goood or was it not so goood?'

'It was disgusting,' he replied.

For the rest of the trip, we ate out and briefed out on that wonderful line from the waitress.

'So what did you think of the briefing from the Russian Defence Minister?'

'I thought it was feeefty-feeefty; OK in parts, otherwise rubbish.'

Despite his culinary adventure, the columnist suffered no after-effects.

Throughout the trip, the favoured columnist was David Ignatius. Such a serious dude; he always engaged in very quiet, very earnest discussions, and always had his arms folded and his head tilted to one side, often wearing very elegant sunglasses. I never heard him once speak above sotto voce. Everything was turned inwards to go with the arms-folded persona. The bear columnist continued to have a nice line in humour and didn't even blow his top when, after interviewing Gates on the last leg of the trip, from Jordan to Washington, he took too long to write his piece. When he went to file it from his laptop using the one internet connection that would work on the plane, the line had gone down and he missed his deadline. He was hopeful his paper would use it on Monday, the following week. I didn't like to point out that a reporter would never be allowed to miss his deadline. He was right though. The *Wall Street Journal* did use it on Monday. It was a good piece. No mention of bear, however.

Most of the trip was a blur, with too many briefings from people who had little to say and not enough time to see anywhere. But even brief glimpses of a country are better than looking at an atlas. Treasured moments included a photo occasion beside the frozen river in St Petersburg (the famous Hermitage museum was closed for decorating!), an evening walk in the streets of Cairo to admire the fading but stylish architecture, a meal with assembled Pentagon correspondents overlooking the sea in Tel Aviv and a ride through Ramallah in Palestine with views of nothing but depressing, dilapidated buildings.

Wherever we went, I was part of the 'travelling-with-the-secretary' party, which meant that I was treated with a degree of respect unfamiliar to a British journalist accustomed to more robust antipathy from officialdom. Israel was the exception. Security always comes first in Israel, no matter how many impressive passes a journalist may have hanging around his neck. I made it into the press conference with Bob Gates and Ehud Barak, the Israeli defence minister, but by the time the two men had finished being nice to each other and saying how wonderful relations were between the US and Israel, there wasn't much time for a decent question and answer session.

The last port of call was Jordan, but that turned out to be an occasion for Gates to meet with VIPs on his own while we journalists sat around in the airport lounge with nothing to do or write. All in all, a great trip for good company, but somewhat unproductive. One of the most illuminating moments occurred in a hotel bar in Moscow. Gates came down to join us for a strictly off-the-record social occasion and mused wistfully about his time as director of the CIA, which he had clearly enjoyed more than his job at the Pentagon.

It's not difficult to see why. The Pentagon is too big, too bureaucratic and has too much money to waste. When it wants to do something on a grand scale, it has to get approval from the big guns of the administration, including the secretary of state, and, of course, the president and commander-in-chief. Obama made it clear from the beginning he didn't want wars to be part of his legacy unless he had been responsible for bringing them to an end. Even when he agreed, under pressure, to send 33,000 surge-troops to Afghanistan in 2010, he attached a condition. He wanted all US combat troops out of Afghanistan by the end of 2014. So two steps forward and one step firmly back. The hierarchy at the Pentagon was not best pleased, because it gave the Taliban a timeline, and an incentive to stay the course and wait for the US combat troops to leave.

But the Pentagon is still an immensely powerful part of the Washington Government machine. Apart from having all the paraphernalia available for waging war, it's in charge of the biggest intelligence agency in the US, the National Security Agency. The signals intelligence super-agency comes under the defence secretary's wing, is housed at Fort Meade in Maryland, also home of a vast US Army set-up, and is always headed by a senior military figure.

I once took a taxi to Fort Meade for a US Army event, and was driven in error to the wrong side of the huge barracks, and found myself confronted by dozens of gun-toting policemen. I was at the entrance for the National Security Agency, which resides inside a building that looks like a super-structured container ship. 'This is a highly restricted area,' one police officer helpfully said, his head sticking through the window. 'You may come in to do a U-turn, but then please leave immediately.' It was the closest I ever got to visiting the NSA.

So, with the NSA and the might of the US military behind it, whenever the Pentagon speaks, it has a lot of hutzpah. It has an empire of capabilities available for the president. The five-sided Defence Department employs 23,000 people and occupies nearly four million square feet of office space. It's a thunderstorm of activity involving uniformed and civilian brains who are in charge of different sections of the world. There are people who do nothing else but draw up contingency plans to strike at potential enemies or react to scenarios not even imagined by the average ordinary human being. Someone once added up the number of phone calls made on an average day at the Pentagon, and it was 200,000, running along 100,000 miles of telephone cable.

You enter this scheming complex for the first time like a man lost in a desert. There's the A ring and D ring and E ring etc., etc., and there are 17.5 miles of corridors. But the designer of this mighty concrete beast thought of a way of ensuring that whichever colonel in whatever room you wished to visit, you would take no more than seven minutes to get from one place to another, wherever it is in the building. As a newcomer, it's possible to go round and round the concentric rings and not know where the hell you are. It can certainly take longer than seven minutes to track down the particular colonel you've agreed to meet. For a start, there are 131 different stairs and nineteen escalators. Get on the wrong one and you're in D ring instead of B ring.

On the night of the 2nd of May 2011, we were told that President Obama would be making a statement from the White House late that evening. Something big was about to be announced. There were instant rumours that it was about Osama bin Laden. Everyone was glued to the television screen. Obama, as cool as ever, not even a glimmer of a smile or look of triumph, told the nation that America's Number One enemy, Osama bin Laden, had been killed by US Navy Seals after the leader of al-Qaeda had been traced to a compound in Pakistan. It couldn't have been more dramatic if the words had been delivered by Clint Eastwood.

The Times Washington bureau went into overdrive. There was one thing I was desperate to find out: the codename for the operation. This was such an historic event that there had to be a good codename, and I knew it would look great on the front page of *The Times*. I've always loved codenames for operations, except for British military ones; because instead of selecting an appropriate word or phrase, the MoD just chooses from a list of meaningless names, such as Operation Herrick in Afghanistan, Telic in Iraq and Ellamy in Libya.

I rang a contact at the CIA. The mission to find bin Laden was a CIA operation. It had been running for ten years. The Langley, Virginia agency would surely have a Hollywood-style name for the biggest mission of the lot? I got nowhere. The official name of the operation was not being released. I pushed and pushed. The contact was the nicest and quietest of CIA careerists and was his usual patient self. When I asked once more for anything that would stand out as a meaningful code of any sort to highlight what had happened shortly after midnight Pakistan time on the 2nd of May, I got the answer that sent my heart beating like a wild African drum.

'Geronimo,' the CIA contact replied. 'That's not the code for the operation, but was the word used to let the White House know that bin Laden had been found and killed.'

I thanked him profusely, dialled the foreign desk and literally shouted down the phone. 'Here's your headline! The code for killing bin Laden was "Geronimo"!'

The next day, *The Times* splashed the story with the headline: 'Geronimo: the moment US killed bin Laden.'

The next three days were a blur of activity, fighting to discover everything about the Navy Seal operation and how bin Laden could have hidden away for so long in the compound in Abbottabad – at least five years – without being detected. Was there Pakistan collusion? The ISI, Pakistan's intelligence service, was famous for being the most duplicitous, cunning and dangerous agency in that part of the world and was perfectly capable of secretly harbouring the leader of al-Qaeda for its own nefarious purposes. The ISI and the Pakistani Government denied any knowledge of bin Laden's whereabouts, even though he was living outside a town which contained a garrison bristling with Pakistani Army troops.

The most exciting prospect for the Americans and for Western intelligence services in general was that the Seals brought away with them bundles of discs, hard drives and letters which had the potential of exposing bin Laden's command structure, his network of trusted lieutenants and any future terrorist plots.

On Saturday, the 7th of May, I was summoned to the Pentagon media briefing room for an off-the-record press conference about what had been found at bin Laden's compound and other details of the Seal mission. Saturday was the worst day of the week for me because there was no paper the next day, but the online version would be running as usual. I rang the online news desk to warn them that there would be a cracking story coming later in the day. I arrived at the Pentagon twenty minutes before the briefing to find the place absolutely packed. There was one empty chair at the back. Every reporter in the room was trying to look cool and relaxed, but the truth was, we were all brimming over with excitement.

Our briefer was going to be a CIA officer. Ten more minutes to wait, then in he walked, accompanied by a cluster of other CIA and Pentagon officials. The CIA man – a tall, slim, academic-looking man in his early forties – explained that he was to be referred to only as 'a senior US intelligence official'. He said a video had been found that showed bin Laden sitting in an armchair in his compound watching himself on the television. The CIA man nodded and the video sprung to life on a screen to his left. It was an amazing sight. The most feared terrorist leader on the planet was an old, sad, somewhat bored-looking, middle-aged non-entity, slouched in a cheap armchair with a blanket wrapped round him. He had a remote control in his hand and was flicking from one channel to another. All previous descriptions of bin Laden had highlighted how tall he was – about 6ft 4in – but in the video he looked hunched up, as if he was sitting in a cold room.

The CIA briefer spent forty minutes

going through the discoveries made after bin Laden had been found. It had been a military operation, so it wasn't the CIA man's job to give us all the operational details. Enough had come out already from excited White House officials spilling the beans – much of it wrong. It was a classic adventure story. It could all have gone so wrong. Some things did go wrong, such as the crash-landing of one of the super stealthy Black Hawk helicopters that ferried the Seal Team 6 commandos to the compound.

However, the tall individual who had been spotted walking inside the compound each day, like a prisoner doing his daily exercise routine, fortunately turned out to be the man every CIA director for ten years had been yearning to find. Even the calm CIA briefer must have been affected by all the excitement. He took endless questions, including one from me at the back of the room. After an hour, we all had one of the best possible stories to write. I ran from the Pentagon down to the Metro for the five stations to King's St, and then a taxi to my house in Old Town, Alexandria. It took me no time at all to write the intro, and the rest of the story flowed. By the time I had finished I had written 1,200 words and the piece was filed by lunchtime – 6pm in London.

It was a USA glory week, and the White House, Pentagon, State Department and CIA milked it to death – not surprising after a wait of ten years. US special forces had had bin Laden trapped inside his Tora Bora mountain stronghold in Afghanistan in 2001, yet he managed to escape. Months later, he had been spotted elsewhere in Afghanistan, or at least a tall man looking like him. But by the time authority back in Washington was given to drop a bomb, he had gone, never to be seen again, except on al-Qaeda propaganda videos. That is, until the 2nd of May 2011 when US Navy Seals climbed the stairs to his bedroom at the Abbottabad compound and confronted him with lethal force. So, there was plenty to shout about, and the full drama of Operation Neptune Spear, the official codename for the mission, could have come straight from a Hollywood blockbuster.

CHAPTER 22
GENERAL DAVID PETRAEUS AND THE MIDNIGHT CALL

General David Petraeus, master counter-insurgency strategist, America's military hero and Obama's saviour, was seemingly untouchable. He was a four-star general with five-star prospects who may even have contemplated, despite frequent denials, a future political career in the White House. It was no surprise that, when General Stanley McChrystal, the US commander in Kabul, was sacked after he and his private staff were quoted being indiscreet and dismissive of the Washington administration in the *Rolling Stone* magazine, Obama sent for Petraeus to replace him. There was no one else with such glitter and such impeccable command experience. He arrived for his new job in July 2010, and everyone, from Obama to the whole of NATO, breathed a sigh of relief.

So, it was an extraordinary surprise when the foreign desk in London and I spotted, in a throwaway paragraph buried in a long piece in the *Washington Post* in February 2011 about likely changes in the US military top command, that General Petraeus was expected to leave the

Kabul posting. He'd only arrived eight months earlier. Even if he remained in post until the summer, it was nowhere near the length of time everyone in NATO had expected him to serve. The Petraeus magic was surely required in Kabul for longer than twelve months. General McChrystal only served for a year in Kabul, but he was fired.

The Washington bureau chief, Giles Whittell, and I began to make enquiries. I spoke at length to Geoff Morrell, the Pentagon press secretary. Although he didn't confirm that Petraeus would soon be leaving Kabul, he was remarkably forthcoming about the strains and stresses the four-star general had been facing. He said he couldn't stay in Kabul for ever. His exact words were: 'General Petraeus is doing a brilliant job but he's been going virtually non-stop since 9/11 [and] he can't do it for ever.'

He went on to tell me that President Obama and Bob Gates 'are already thinking about that'. Morrell said no final decision had been taken about when Petraeus would hand over command in Kabul but that when his departure was announced it would be a natural development given the strain of running the war. 'This is a heck of a demanding job. He's superhuman, and if anyone can do it at such breakneck pace, he can, but he will have to be rotated at some point,' Morrell went on.

When I heard him say that, I thought it sounded bizarre. Petraeus had agreed to take on Kabul even though, technically, it was a demotion because his previous job had been commander of Central Command, responsible for American security interests in twenty countries, including Afghanistan. He agreed because the president of the United States appealed to him, one more time, to help run a war. There was never a suggestion that after eight months the White House and Pentagon would start looking to replace him. As for the line that poor Petraeus was suffering from stresses and strains, well of course he was, but he was a top-notch four-star superhero. Stresses and strains came with the job.

The only thing that came into my mind as Morrell was speaking was that Gates did have an obligation to think about where Petraeus might serve next. In other words, top jobs in the military become available when other four-star generals retire, and the defence secretary has to consider who would be best to succeed them. Was such a job becoming vacant, and was Petraeus's name at the top of the shortlist?

Two top jobs *were* becoming available later in the year: chairman and vice-chairman of the Joint Chiefs of Staff, the number one and number two appointments in the US military hierarchy. I suggested in the story I wrote for *The Times* that Petraeus was the obvious candidate to replace Admiral Mike Mullen, the incumbent chairman of the Joint Chiefs, even though the hero of Iraq and Afghanistan had not served in the role of chief of staff of the Army. This would have been the more normal career move to be a candidate for the top appointment as the president's chief military adviser.

As it happened, I was back in the UK at the time because my mother had died at the age of ninety-eight and I had returned in haste for her funeral. She was the sweetest and gentlest person. Although she had reached a great age, her death was traumatic for me, especially because I was across the other side of the Atlantic when I got the phone call from my brother and sister. My father, who had been such an influence in my life, had died at the age of ninety-six in 2004. I contacted the foreign desk in London and told them I was flying back immediately. Despite the sad loss of my mother, I was determined to be involved in the story about Petraeus. Throughout my career, I never wanted to miss out on a good story, whatever my personal circumstances. Some would say that was selfish but it's the way I always approached my job as a reporter. I thought the Petraeus story was a strong one. Morrell had clearly indicated that Petraeus was not going to remain in Kabul for a long period of time and that consideration was already being given at the highest level in the Pentagon to finding a replacement. The impact of this development had to be placed in the context of the extraordinary status Petraeus enjoyed in the military firmament. He was not just a four-star general. He was on a pedestal all by himself. The only possible reason for replacing him so quickly, relatively speaking, was that Obama and Gates were thinking of giving him the sort of promotion worthy of his talents and experience. I wrote my contribution to the story and sent it off to Giles in Washington. He told me he had also eventually spoken to Morrell and got a similar series of responses to the questions about Petraeus's future.

The foreign desk loved the story and planned to use it on the front page, although not the splash. I went to bed that night thinking how so often in my career I had had to write stories when I was supposed to be off, either on holiday or on compassionate leave for family reasons. I once helped write a splash about Israel using white phosphorus chemical munitions in attacks on Gaza while I was on holiday in Spain.

At midnight, the phone next to my bed started to ring. I picked it up and sleepily said, 'Hello?'

'What the fuck is going on?! What the fuck have you done?! Your fucking story! You've got to get it changed. I want it changed now and I want you to ring me back to let me know you've changed it. I can't tell you how fucking angry I am.'

It was Geoff Morrell. He was obviously beside himself with fury. My heart was thumping. I had no idea what he was talking about. Giles and I had written the story carefully but, based largely on what Morrell had told us, it was all about Petraeus leaving Kabul, which we anticipated would be a shock to NATO.

I failed to calm Morrell but I discovered what was making him so angry. The headline on the front page of *The Times* was: 'Petraeus to quit Afghan job'. Now I could understand why

Morrell had rung me. That four-letter word, 'quit', didn't justify his tirade of four-letter swear words, but the headline made it seem as if Petraeus was so fed up with running the war in Afghanistan, he was quitting. I knew why the backbench of night editors had selected the word, 'quit' – it was shorter and snappier than 'leave' – but it changed the impact of the story. Anyone just reading the headline – probably Morrell – would have thought that for once in his life Petraeus had become a quitter. The story itself was fine. It had all the quotes from Morrell, explaining why the great man would not be staying in Kabul for too long. But, for Morrell, it looked like he had revealed to *The Times* that Obama's personal appointee for the Kabul job had decided to give up.

I expostulated that the headline had nothing to do with me, but Morrell would have none of it. It was my responsibility, he said, to get the headline changed, and immediately. I said I would try. I rang the foreign desk and spoke to Imre Karacs, the night foreign editor, and explained the situation. He said he had had a similar conversation with Giles Whittell, who had also received an irate phone call from Morrell. He said he would talk to the backbench and see what could be done. I insisted that the word, 'quit', had to be replaced with something less explosive.

I rang Morrell to say the headline would be changed. He had calmed down slightly. I was tempted to tell him that his midnight expletives the day after I had attended my mother's funeral were unacceptable, but, wisely, I put the phone down without further comment. The backbench agonised over the headline on the story, not wanting to soften the impact so much that it turned the story into a minor event. It was still a big story and would be followed up by every other newspaper, on both sides of the Atlantic. They settled for 'Search on for General Petraeus successor'. Not a good headline, and when the deputy editor, Keith Blackmore, spotted it in the morning he was not happy. He had left the previous evening with a story about Petraeus quitting and came into the office the following morning with a front page piece about a search for someone to replace the great man. I was told he was angry with everyone, including Giles and me, for changing the headline without consulting him.

Morrell had won; his swearing had pushed us to meet his demands. It was a salutary experience. The story was one hundred percent accurate. The original headline was ambiguous and somewhat confrontational, but the second choice was too boring. A better headline, and acceptable in my view, never mind Morrell, would have been 'Petraeus in shock exit from Kabul'. Would that have provoked Morrell to grab the phone and shout at me? Possibly, but I would have been able to argue on safer ground, and the headline would have survived the night. As it was, when Gates came under questioning in Congress over our story about Petraeus quitting Kabul, he informed them it was untrue. The impression given was that

Petraeus was staying in Kabul. Morrell and I knew that was not the case.

Within less than two months, the Petraeus story moved on just as we had predicted. There were strong rumours in Washington in early April that Obama had offered Petraeus a non-military appointment as director of the CIA. This was duly confirmed at the end of April. It was also announced that he would hand over his command in Kabul in July, after just twelve months in the post.

Close associates of the general told me off the record that it was a stunning blow that Obama had bypassed Petraeus for the top job of chairman of the Joint Chiefs of Staff. The president had someone else in mind, a military man described as Obama's favourite general: General James Cartwright of the Marine Corps who was then the vice chairman of the Joint Chiefs. He had a close relationship with the president, but he had no combat experience.

Petraeus's associates complained to me. 'How could the president choose Cartwright instead of Petraeus?' they asked. There was no question that Petraeus himself had wanted the top post, and only considered the CIA appointment after realising he wasn't going to succeed Admiral Mike Mullen. As one of Petraeus's associates told me, 'It appears they don't want him as chairman of the Joint Chiefs because he's too well known, too celebrated, and would have influence beyond his position. It's tragic.'

The appointment of Petraeus to the CIA

was part of a reshuffle of Obama's top security team. Gates at the Pentagon was retiring and Leon Panetta, director of the CIA, was slated to be his successor as defence secretary. However, when all the nominations for these jobs were announced by the White House there was one name and one appointment missing from the list. There was no mention of the next chairman of the Joint Chiefs of Staff, and no reference to General Cartwright.

Something had upset Obama's plans. I soon picked up whispering against General Cartwright. There were basically three issues which made it difficult for Obama to persist with his nomination: General Cartwright didn't get on well with Admiral Mullen, and the incumbent chairman normally had a role in recommending his successor. His leadership style and lack of combat experience in Iraq and Afghanistan were also sore points; and there was a lingering personal hiccup which was potentially embarrassing for a military man who was favoured to take command of America's fighting forces. An anonymous accuser had claimed that, on a visit to Tbilisi in Georgia in 2009, General Cartwright had had an improper relationship with a young female military aide, a captain in the Marines.

The allegation had been fully investigated by the Pentagon's inspector general's department and he had been cleared of the suggestion that he had had an improper relationship with the aide. But the inspector general concluded that General Cartwright had mishandled the incident in which the aide, drunk and upset, visited his hotel room alone late in the evening and either passed out or fell asleep on a bench at the foot of the bed. The general, who was then sixty-one, and married, denied he had done anything wrong, but the inspector general said he was at fault for not having the aide removed from his room, and he was accused of being over-familiar with her.

General Cartwright appealed against the findings and, as a result, Ray Mabus, the US Navy secretary, the most senior civilian appointee in the naval service, dismissed the inspector general's conclusions. Obama was aware of the case but had chosen to push ahead with his nomination. He was, however, persuaded to change his mind, perhaps fearful that Congress would give the general a hard time when his nomination came up for debate in the Senate. Obama told his favourite general his name was being removed from the shortlist. So much for the grand plan.

It was too late for Petraeus because he had already accepted nomination for the CIA job, and it was clear Obama, and possibly Gates, wanted anyone but Petraeus to succeed Admiral Mullen, who had been a stalwart and fairly outspoken chairman but never a threat to the White House. Petraeus might have posed a threat in the minds of the Obama clan. So, with General Cartwright out of the running, the Pentagon had to look elsewhere, and turned to a man who had only just been promoted to be chief of staff of the US Army. General Martin

'Marty' Dempsey had taken over as leader of the US Army in April, and must have received the shock of his life when he was informed Obama planned to nominate him to succeed Admiral Mullen in the autumn.

General Dempsey, a likeable chap with a good singing voice and an abundance of combat command experience in Iraq, had hardly had time to get to grips with heading the army before he was whisked off to the highest leadership post in the military. So in a matter of weeks, the most famous general in America's modern military history had been forced to leave the army he loved and had become a civilian to serve as the boss of the CIA; Obama's favoured general for the most illustrious military appointment in the land was effectively told his career was over; and a third general was plucked from relative obscurity from a job he'd had no time to digest to be the right hand man of the commander-in-chief.

CHAPTER 23
THE WORLD'S MOST CONTROVERSIAL PRISON

I made my first of many trips to the US terrorist detention camp at Guantanamo Bay, Cuba in November 2011. The procedure for getting there was fairly straightforward. When a trial hearing or pre-trial legal session is due, the Pentagon puts out an email, offering a limited number of seats on the chartered aircraft flying to the US Naval base on the southeast corner of Cuba. For the run-of-the-mill cases, there's a good chance of getting one of the seats, partly because Guantanamo has become a passé story, but mostly because the one trial that everyone in the world is waiting for, that of Khalid Sheikh Mohammed and four other terrorist suspects accused of planning, financing and masterminding the attacks on the 11th of September 2001, is still some way off.

Meanwhile, there are innumerable pre-trial tribunal hearings, mostly on esoteric legal issues that wouldn't normally attract a reporter, but they provide an opportunity for the media to observe what the US likes to call the most dangerous terrorist suspects on the planet.

Journalists fly there in a comfortable chartered civilian aircraft from Andrews Air

Force base. The trip takes three hours and costs $400 for a round trip – not a bad price for staying in a Caribbean island, albeit lacking in the usual luxury offerings, such as sunbeds and piña coladas that one would expect on other islands in the region.

When we all arrive at the naval station, we go through the same process as the hundreds of 'enemy combatants' who were brought to Guantanamo from Afghanistan, Pakistan and the secret 'black' prisons of the CIA dotted around Europe, north Africa, Asia and elsewhere. We climb into a coach, which is then driven onto a ferry that takes twenty-five minutes to cross the water to the windward side of Guantanamo.

We journalists could climb out of the coach and let the strong sea breeze waft through our hair as we approached what used to be called Camp X-Ray but is now known as Camp Delta. The terrorist suspects, including Khalid Sheikh Mohammed, didn't have the comfort of seats on the coach. They were chained to the floor, dressed in the infamous orange jumpsuits.

When my American colleagues and I arrived, we were greeted by Rear Admiral David Woods, commander of Joint Task Force Guantanamo, the boss of the detention camp. He was a typical toothbrush-haired American commander. He was smiling but clearly had absolutely no intention of telling us anything of interest.

We had come for a tribunal hearing for Abd al-Rahim al-Nashiri, the alleged architect of the suicide boat bomb attack on the US guided-missile destroyer, *USS Cole,* in Aden in 2000 that killed seventeen American sailors. The first thing a journalist does on arrival at the huge former hangar where the media centre is set up is to grab a seat and internet connection.

Once set up in the 'office', we all trooped off to find our accommodation, a row of tents containing up to eight camp beds. It was dormitory life, back to my schooldays. Wherever you stand in this part of Guantanamo, which is well away from the actual detention facilities, you can't avoid the imposing courtroom, a purpose-built structure surrounded by a high steel-mesh fence and an array of cameras. It cost ten million dollars to build and is proudly described by the authorities there as the most technologically sophisticated courtroom in the US (well, this bit of Guantanamo is leased to America – leased by the Cubans to the US in a treaty decades before Fidel Castro took power). The microphones are so sensitive inside the courtroom they can scoop up confidential whisperings between defendants and their lawyers, which, when disclosed by chance, led to scenes of outrage by counsel. The courtroom dominates the whole area. In the sunset, it takes on a formidably eerie appearance, with the fencing and overlooking cameras silhouetted menacingly.

Before leaving for Gitmo, as it is known worldwide, I had been warned to bring extra clothing. The weather was always temperate, but at night the tents are blasted with ice-cold air conditioning, principally, so we were told, to dissuade the fearsome indigenous banana rats from entering the tents and biting your ankles. The first night was so cold I slept in a sweater and my anorak and long thick socks, but still woke up at 3am with my teeth rattling and my whole body shivering. In my tent we made a quick decision. Never mind the banana rats, the air conditioning gets turned off – or at least down to an acceptable temperature.

To eat a decent breakfast at Gitmo, you have to be up early to catch the minibus to travel about three miles further inland to enjoy the same menu savoured every day by the military and civilian employees. It's the usual cooked food spread you can find anywhere in the world where American servicemen and women are based; unless it's an outpost in Afghanistan, where fried eggs and bacon are never guaranteed. After breakfast, I joined the select ten journalists who had won the lottery to attend the court hearing, starting at 10am. The lottery was carried out on board the chartered plane en route to Gitmo, with names in a hat – no more sophisticated than that. My name had actually failed to come up, but on the first day one of the reporters backed out, worried he might miss a deadline by being stuck in the courtroom, and preferring to watch the proceedings on the screen in the media centre. I took his place.

The problem with the screen option is that while you can type away on your laptop, the CCTV inside the courtroom has a tendency to focus on the judge or the prosecutor and rarely swings round to have a look at the defendant or defendants. So much can be missed. To catch every twist and turn, every shake of the head, every gesture from the terrorist suspects, you have to be in the public viewing section at the back of the courtroom, which is located behind a thick glass partition. There's only room for ten journalists, including a court artist. The rest of the chairs are taken up by representatives of human rights organisations attending as official observers, and a curtained-off area where families of terrorist attack victims sit to watch the men accused of killing their loved ones.

On the first morning, after successfully getting though two separate layers of security checks, we reporters and the court artist were ready to catch our first glimpse of al-Nashiri. We soon discovered there was a routine that had to be completed before anything serious started. The head of the guard force in charge of everyone in the public gallery liked to crack a few jokes. He must have thought it was the best way to cheer us up, in particular the victims' families. They seemed to love it. The jokes were unbelievably awful. He had his own version of 'why did the chicken cross the road?' The families lapped it up, and when he asked if they wanted more jokes, they all nodded their heads. We were cocooned from the activities in the courtroom and were being forced to listen to a bit of military vaudeville.

Each of us had had to conform to a very strict set of rules: no pens, no notebooks with metal ring binding, no phones, no laptops, no tape recorders. Just pencils and paper. The ban on pens followed a cunning move by a television reporter who brought in a miniature tape recording device disguised as a pen. He was caught. Pens were subsequently banned.

The guard force handed out small pencils and sheets of paper to all reporters who had forgotten or ignored the regulations. When the court hearing began, it was instantly Alice in Wonderland. The security specialists in the world's most sophisticated courtroom had built in a forty-second delay for the audio to reach our ears in the public gallery. This ensured that if anyone uttered something top secret, by mistake or deliberately, the court security officer could press a button and a red flashing light would come on. The audio flow would also be smothered by white sound. Absolutely any mention of the CIA and its interrogation methods, especially the infamous waterboarding technique, caused the light to flash.

Being forty seconds behind everyone on the other side of the glass partition meant we were prevented from hearing anything classified. But at least we had the drama of the flashing red light. Back in the media centre, the only indication of a security hiccup was a blank screen.

The first alleged senior al-Qaeda terrorist to appear in a capital case at a Guantanamo Bay military tribunal since President Obama came to power walked into the courtroom unshackled. Al-Nashiri had already spent nine years in detention. Before proceedings began, the forty-six-year-old Saudi Arabian, flanked by two guards wearing light blue surgical gloves, turned and waved towards the back of the court, roughly in our direction. He wore no handcuffs or restraints because his defence team had asked for him to be unfettered throughout the hearing, and the military judge, Colonel James Pohl, agreed.

For most people in the world, Gitmo is for ever symbolised by the stark pictures of detainees arriving in 2002, hooded, shackled and in orange. Some newspapers still refer to Gitmo as the torture camp, even though the so-called 'enhanced interrogation techniques', including waterboarding, stopped in 2003 and were banned by Obama in 2009.

Colonel Pohl tended to lean favourably towards the defence counsel's demands for their clients, to prove to the world that his courtroom was a civilised place. But there were shackles on the floor underneath the chairs where defendants sat, ready to be clipped around the ankles in emergencies.

Al-Nashiri was one of three terrorist suspects who had been given the waterboarding treatment while being held by the CIA in a secret prison, prior to his transfer to Gitmo. He had also been threatened with a power drill to his head, scrubbed by a tough wire brush and told his family would be harmed. But here he was, 5ft 5in tall and looking fit and clean-shaven. He was dressed in prison garb, a loose white top and pantaloons with black trainers. When the judge asked him if he spoke English, he replied in perfect English: 'I do not speak English.' He relied on the Arabic interpretation fed through earphones.

Among other offences, he was charged with perfidy, murder in violation of the law of war, terrorism and hijacking. Sitting at the back, watching everything forty seconds late, it was unreal and sometimes quite comical. When the judge waved his arms and said something important we were listening to the chief prosecutor focusing on some legal technicality. When the chief prosecutor, the elegant, straight-backed, very slim, very tall uniformed Brigadier-General Mark Martins, sat down and was replaced by a pudgy lawyer from the Justice Department, we had to listen to the general's remarks for another forty seconds. When the brain becomes accustomed to the delayed-action system, it's relatively straightforward, but there were always light moments, like when the judge entered the courtroom, we all stood up because everyone in the court in front of us was standing, but when we sat down, the delayed audio told us: 'All rise'.

Al-Nashiri's future seemed to be set in concrete. Richard Kammen, his civilian defence lawyer, asked the judge whether his client, if acquitted, would remain indefinitely in Guantanamo. The judge had to acknowledge that the case before him was somewhat unique. In a federal court, he said, an acquitted defendant 'leaves the court, goes out into the street and goes home'. Al-Nashiri would not be doing any of that, whatever the conclusions of the military panel of jurors selected for his eventual trial.

Al-Nashiri, along with fourteen other so-called high-value detainees, are held at Camp 7, a detention facility so secret that no one in authority ever talks about it, or even acknowledges its existence. Khalid Sheikh Mohammed (KSM to the guards) is also in Camp 7. How they live, what they do each day, where their detention camp is located, are all classified bits of information. One defence lawyer did manage a brief visit to see his client at Camp 7 but had to travel there blindfolded. Normally, counsel see their clients in a special camp facility which requires a ride in an armoured vehicle and shackles for the detainees. The other two main camps, 5 and 6, the latter where the vast majority of the inmates are held, can be visited by outsiders like me.

I've done the tour of both camps. I've been to prisons before, when I was home affairs correspondent for the *Daily Express,* and I always left with an impression of an overpowering smell, noise, and clanking of metal on metal. But Camps 5 and 6 are different. Camp 6, home for at least 120 detainees when I first visited, was quiet and ghostly, the inmates wandering around in communal pods, a closed-in twilight world where their every move is watched by armed guards standing in a semi-circular corridor that runs around their barred community living space. There is seldom any physical or verbal contact between guard and detainee. In fact, it's discouraged by their superiors. All the detainees get their three meals a day, cooked Arabic-style and delivered as takeaway meals – except they have nowhere to go to take it away. They can watch television, read books, and attend education courses. But for the safety of the teacher, the 'students' are chained to the floor. They all wear the same clothes, the floppy white shirt and pantaloons, and seem oblivious to the possibility that strange visitors are gazing at them like monkeys in a zoo.

The only time you hear voices is when the detainees enjoy some rest and recreation outside their communal prisons. There's the odd shout in Arabic. Twenty minutes inside Camp 6 and then it's off to the facility next door, Camp 5. This is where detainees who refuse to adhere to acceptable disciplinary standards are housed, each in an individual cell. The orange jumpsuit comes out of the wardrobe for all of them, to underline the fact that they have misbehaved. Among the three dozen or so in Camp 5, many of them will have at some time mixed together a revolting cocktail of urine, spit and faeces to throw at the guards when they come to open the letterbox-style opening slit in the cell door. They stay in Camp 5 until the detention authorities decide they have learned their lesson. Both Camps 5 and 6 are supposed to be not much different from the traditional maximum security prisons in the United States in terms of environment, regulation and way of life. But the Gitmo detainees are all judged by the Pentagon to be so threatening to the security of the US and its citizens that they need to remain locked up even though most of them have never been charged with a terrorist offence. Lawyers in the federal system back in the US would never have stood for it.

The most notorious inmate of Gitmo is Khalid Sheikh Mohammed, who allegedly admitted to his CIA interrogators that he had masterminded the attacks on 9/11.

When I saw him for the first time at the Gitmo courtroom, he was brought in by two guards wearing the usual blue surgical gloves. There had been only two photographs ever printed of Khalid Sheikh Mohammed, one soon after he was arrested in Karachi, when he looked sullen, unshaven and quite plump, and the second one at some unknown time with a long beard and looking much thinner in the face. Now, here he was, sauntering into Courtroom 2, smaller in size than one had imagined, no more than 5ft 6in, with a large, bushy beard coloured red with henna, and wearing a black vest over his white robes and a turban around his head. The vest had been reluctantly approved by the judge after KSM said he wanted to wear a combat jacket to denote his warrior status. That was denied, although in subsequent legal arguments he was eventually allowed to stroll into court with a camouflaged jacket. But that was for a later hearing.

It's a bizarre experience to see an individual just a few yards away, albeit separated by our glass partition, who has been charged with the murder of 2,976 people. There were no histrionics, no angry glares at the prosecution or at us, no waving of his arms; he just sat down quietly in the front row of desks and chairs to wait for the judge. His four co-defendants took another twenty minutes to get settled into their seats, one behind the other, the last one the smallest of all, Mustafa Ahmed al-Hawsawi, sitting on a chair in the fifth row with a white cap on his head.

KSM, who grew up in Kuwait but went to college in North Carolina, seemed relaxed. He swivelled round to smile at his associates, all detained in Camp 7, built to house those suspected of having the most comprehensive knowledge of the workings of al-Qaeda. His henna-red beard was so bushy it seemed to cover his whole chest. Throughout most of the hearing, he kept his head bowed, which pushed the beard even further down his body. He focused on the court documents, seemingly interested in following the procedures. He may have been waterboarded 183 times before telling his CIA interrogators what they wanted to know, but now he looked fit and healthy and relaxed. According to CIA documents, he had confessed to planning 9/11 'from A to Z', and to involvement in at least thirty other terrorist plots. Allegedly, he also admitted to beheading Daniel Pearl, a reporter with the *Wall Street Journal* who was kidnapped by al-Qaeda in Karachi in January 2002.

Observing from the public gallery and trying to write everything down forty seconds after the words had been spoken, it became clear that the defendants were going to try to put as much pressure as possible on the judge to meet their various demands. KSM had already won his right to wear a black vest, and was two days away from winning his argument to don a camouflage jacket. But, first, their defence counsel asked the judge to let the five defendants decide whether to appear in court or not. General Martins said he wanted the five men to be present at all hearings. Colonel Pohl, ever the flexible judge and not wishing to be countermanded by some future appeal court, agreed a formula which he hoped would suit everyone. He ruled that, for this week of hearings, the defendants could opt not to be present. However, each morning they would be obliged to sign a piece of paper informing him that they planned to remain in their cells.

Thus followed a bizarre ritual which began about 5am each morning, starting with KSM. A designated security guard – sometimes a woman, despite complaints from the detainees that this was an insult to Islam – was required to go to his cell and the cells of the other four individuals and ask them through the prison bars whether they intended to appear in court, and to sign a document if the answer was in the negative. He or she then had to appear in the witness box and answer a series of incredibly dull but legally significant questions put to them by a member of the prosecuting team, such as: 'Was the document in English or Arabic?' 'Did the detainees answer in English or Arabic?'

'What time were they woken up?'

The system devised by Colonel Pohl was laborious but seemed to work to the court's satisfaction, until KSM thought up a ruse to upset the smooth running of the tribunal. On the first day, following the ruling, he said 'yes', but then said 'no' when he got to the court and had to be detained in a holding cell within the courtroom complex. The next day he said 'yes', then 'no', but after half an hour in his holding cell he summoned his guard and told her he would like to join the proceedings after all, during the morning break. The judge acquiesced. This was when KSM entered the court for the first time wearing a camouflage jacket. KSM was not a man for outbursts, but was clearly a master of the theatrical gesture.

At this stage in the week, KSM had only spoken once when the judge addressed him. He seized the opportunity to say there was 'no justice' in the court. He spoke in Arabic in soft tones.

But now, to the astonishment of those in the public gallery, and probably to the prosecution, when KSM's civilian counsel, David Nevin, a dapper lawyer from Idaho, told the judge his client would like to say something, Colonel Pohl agreed. But he added, on the condition that he was not planning to breach any classification rules. This assurance was given with a smile from the accused, who then proceeded quietly to denounce the US for killing 'thousands of millions' of people. Everyone in court had to listen to his 'statement', uninterrupted. It was definitely round one to KSM. Too late, Colonel Pohl said he would not allow this to happen again.

Guantanamo Bay trips were mostly about the hearings and, when allowed, visits to Camps 5 and 6. But, gradually, the Pentagon agreed to relax the rigid regulations covering journalists. Instead of having to be escorted everywhere, especially outside the area of the media centre and accommodation tents, we could explore unaccompanied, although, of course, searching for Camp 7 was prohibited. Several reporters hired bikes or went sailing. Some of us trooped off to the beach and swam in the warm sea. There was something extra special about swimming in the sea and relaxing on the beach a relatively short drive away from the three detention camps holding America's most feared captives.

CHAPTER 24
HONOUR, GALLANTRY AND THE TRAUMA OF WAR

Having covered six wars for *The Times* over a period of twenty years, the one memory I shall always retain is the sense of personal sacrifice made voluntarily by so many thousands of men and women. When a war has lasted for more than a year, the return of body bags on military transport planes, tragically, becomes a ritual, and there is almost a feeling of inevitable complacency about the whole process. Soldiers, Marines, sailors and airmen go to war and many of them die. It's an accepted reality. While the return of bodies is always a sombre occasion, the nation as a whole rarely becomes angry or rebellious or driven to overturn the government that has allowed young men and women to go to battle in a country thousands of miles away. The anger and suffering is left to the families of the dead who have to find ways of living the rest of their lives with one key member – or, in some cases, several members – of that family absent forever.

Newspapers are fickle. They start off a war with huge news spreads, covering every aspect of the war, and when the first soldier is killed in action words of grief and agony pour out of the reporter's computer, and pictures of the victim and his loved ones appear under emotional headlines. After a time, the outpourings are reduced, in size and quality. The constant announcements of more deaths from the MoD, or from the Pentagon in Washington, are greeted with less and less interest. But there are exceptional circumstances: for example, when a helicopter is brought down by 'friendly fire', or if there's an ambush in which many soldiers are killed, or whenever anyone from the SAS or the SBS – or the equivalent in the US – dies in an exceptionally gallant mission.

When a war drags on into years, the huge double-page spreads are replaced by one-paragraph stories slotted into a column of similarly short tales that require no photograph and minimum detail. They are called 'nibs'.

The war is given a lift once a year when the MoD announces the latest list of gallantry awards, and amazingly young men and women in uniform stand up in the main briefing centre in the ministry headquarters in Whitehall and answer questions about the action they had taken which their superiors judged to be worthy of a Military Cross or Conspicuous Gallantry Cross, or, on the rarest of occasions, the Victoria Cross.

Veteran reporters like me gaze at these men and women, most of them in their twenties, with a sense of awe and also bewilderment. Why did they act the way they did? Why were they prepared to face the hatred and violence of the enemy without any apparent concern for their own safety? Too often, they would reply that this was what they were trained for, and they rejected the notion that they were braver than anyone else. To a degree this is true; in the fury of battle, men trained to kill are also instinctively guided by an urge to protect their comrades, and that is when the greatest acts of bravery are performed. There must be hundreds of occasions in war where individuals in the face of grave danger make a split-second decision that saves lives. But not all of them end up in the MoD for a gallantry awards ceremony, because there are rules about medals. The action on the battlefield has to be witnessed and then corroborated, and the officer in charge has to recommend a bravery award. Gallantry is not always spotted, and is certainly not always acknowledged. There is a bureaucracy that has to be satisfied.

Nevertheless, every year there is a long list of men, and also women, who make the grade and are duly awarded what is assessed to be the appropriate level of honour. It's not like the civil service in the UK where a public official who rises to a certain rank will automatically receive an MBE or OBE or CBE or even a knighthood. In the field of battle, a bravery award is given, not for loyalty or long service, but because of extraordinary courage. Over the years, many individuals honoured for bravery have stuck in my mind, but the two most outstanding examples – perhaps because they were so young and still alive – were Private Johnson Beharry and Trooper Christopher Finney.

Private Beharry and Trooper Finney were both younger than Lieutenant-Colonel H. Jones and Sergeant Ian McKay, the Falklands War VC winners, when they were selected for the highest award after their deaths in combat.

Private Beharry, born in the Caribbean island of Grenada, was just twenty-four when, on two occasions, in May and June 2004, he found himself in an ambush while driving his Warrior armoured fighting vehicle, and fought to save the other men with him, including his wounded commander. In the second incident, he himself received a near-fatal head wound but carried on regardless until losing consciousness. For mere mortals like Fleet Street reporters, including the bravest of war correspondents, this sort of gallantry and battlefield bravado is almost impossible to understand. The MoD tries to re-enact the scene of the battlefield by reading out the stirring citation for the VC. But when the soldier himself stands before us, he is just an ordinary bloke in a smart uniform. Nothing he says can quite relive for us reporters the experience he went through.

Private Beharry, a modest soul, was still receiving hospital treatment for his brain injury when he was presented to us – another indication of the extraordinary qualities of this humble soldier.

Although Britain had been involved in numerous wars over two decades, the vast majority of the VCs had been awarded in the two world wars. VCs were rarer in the modern era, not because the level of gallantry was any less special but because wars had changed in character and substance. The 1991 Gulf War was a non-stop, all-action, brief campaign in which the enemy was driven back so swiftly and so overwhelmingly that there was hardly time or requirement for individual acts of bravery. The 2003 invasion of Iraq was, likewise, a thunder-and-lightning occasion in which America's shock-and-awe battle strategy was an all-embracing mighty sweep of firepower which smothered the enemy with violence. Even in mass manoeuvre warfare, however, there are moments when individual actions make all the difference.

Private Beharry was an ordinary soldier who displayed qualities that could never be taught in a classroom or in a training exercise. His two acts of selfless gallantry sat perfectly and appropriately alongside the citations for bravery written for all the other members of the VC club.

Trooper Christopher Finney was even younger than Private Beharry when he won his medal, and I was struck by his quiet composure when he was presented to the press. There was nothing macho about him. He seemed almost embarrassed by being shoved into the limelight. His case was different. To be awarded a VC, he needed to have demonstrated exceptional bravery 'under enemy fire'. But he had saved the lives of his comrades while under so-called friendly fire. He was only eighteen at the time when two US Air Force A10 Thunderbolts, devastatingly effective ground-attack aircraft, opened fire on his Scimitar armoured vehicle. The American pilots mistook the British Army light tank for an Iraqi one.

Under fire from an Iraqi MiG or attack helicopter, he would have won a VC. But under the rules, he had to be given a George Cross. Both medals enjoy the same prestige, but so often a George Cross is associated with acts of bravery by civilians; for example, police bomb disposal officers called upon to risk their lives to defuse an explosive device in a public place. But Trooper Finney, nineteen when he received the George Cross, was, like Private Beharry, a soldier with an instinct for boldness without which several of his comrades would have died. Trooper Finney was also the youngest member of the armed services to win the George Cross.

In my career as a defence specialist for *The Times*, I was privileged to listen to the accounts of these brave young people, and thought of my father. He had leapt off his torpedoed ship into the freezing water in the English Channel, leading his men to safety. It was an act which was to remain part of his life for the rest of his days.

For nations engaged in wars, the victories and defeats are matters of public record. For individuals, the memories, most of them harsh and painful, are locked away but never forgotten. We of the post-World War generation cannot truly comprehend the suffering of our parents. But I know that what my father achieved in his life after the end of the Second World War – becoming a brilliant teacher –

will have been moulded by his experiences in France and Germany in the '39-'45 war. Meeting young soldiers who fought so bravely in the modern wars helped me to understand at least something of what my father must have endured.

When I returned from my first assignment in the Bosnian War, my father, whose sight was then failing fast, wrote me a letter in which he praised me for my courage and told me how proud he was of his younger son. The words were scattered across the page in topsy-turvy fashion, so determined was he to put his thoughts on paper even though he could scarcely see what he was writing. But the message came through clear enough and I have kept the letter. But was I courageous for doing my job as a defence correspondent in a war zone? And would I have been a coward if I had refused to cover the wars? I knew when I was taking risks, but I never once thought to myself that I was engaging in an act of bravery. What I do know is that my first experience of covering a war did not put me off. I went back again and again to Bosnia, always apprehensive but also excited. I felt the same when I went to Kosovo, Iraq, Afghanistan, Sierra Leone and the Former Yugoslav Republic of Macedonia.

However, certain incidents and experiences can linger in the mind. *The Times* and *Sunday Times* decided jointly on one occasion to bring in a stress counsellor for a private session with those of us who had reported from war zones. The unprecedented event was arranged by Gill Ross, *The Times* foreign desk manager who was devoted to the paper's network of foreign correspondents. We gathered somewhat sceptically in a room in the main News International building at Fortress Wapping: Jon Swain, legendary *Sunday Times* correspondent who reported from Vietnam and in every war since; his foreign correspondent colleague, Christina Lamb; Catherine Philp, who proved her courage in Baghdad and elsewhere; Pete Nicholls, a great *Times* war photographer; and three or four others. After an embarrassed silence, a few of us began to open up. It was strangely cathartic. One of them referred to the 'dark tunnels' he had suffered in his mind.

I was lucky; I was shot at, mortared and driven in armoured vehicles where there was a high risk of buried explosive devices, but I was never injured. I had friends who were not so lucky, like Rupert Hamer of the *Sunday Mirr*or, who died in an explosion in Afghanistan, and Marie Colvin of the *Sunday Times*, deliberately targeted by artillery fire in Syria.

Luck plays a significant part in the survival business. Journalism can be a dangerous profession. Every time a colleague is injured, kidnapped or killed while trying to do their job, it reminds me that, in a war zone, there is always the risk that there could be a hidden danger – an ambush by Kalashnikov-armed insurgents, a buried landmine, or a sniper concealed in the trees.

A reporter with a notebook is as vulnerable to the next bullet as a soldier armed with a rifle or machine gun.

INDEX

A

B

C

D

E

F

G

H

I

J

K

L

M

N

O

P

R

S

T

V

W

Michael Evans, author

Publisher Information

Rowanvale Books

Rowanvale Books provides publishing services to independent authors, writers and poets all over the globe. We deliver a personal, honest and efficient service that allows authors to see their work published, while remaining in control of the process and retaining their creativity. By making publishing services available to authors in a cost-effective and ethical way, we at Rowanvale Books hope to ensure that the local, national and international community benefits from a steady stream of good quality literature.

For more information about us, our authors or our publications, please get in touch.

www.rowanvalebooks.com
info@rowanvalebooks.com

Lightning Source UK Ltd.
Milton Keynes UK
UKOW07f0310051216
289180UK00010B/37/P

9 781911 240983